RENEWALS 458-4574
DATE DUE

**WITHDRAWN
UTSA LIBRARIES**

Also by Philip Arestis

THE POLITICAL ECONOMY OF ECONOMIC POLICIES (*co-editor with Malcolm Sawyer*)
MONEY AND BANKING: Issues for the Twenty-First Century (*editor*)
MONEY, PRICING, DISTRIBUTION AND ECONOMIC INTEGRATION
RELEVANCE OF KEYNESIAN ECONOMIC POLICIES TODAY (*co-editor with Malcolm Sawyer*)
WHAT GLOBAL ECONOMIC CRISIS? (*co-editor with Michelle Baddeley and John McCombie*)
POST-BUBBLE US ECONOMY: Implications for Financial Markets and the Economy (*with Elias Karakitsos*)
FINANCIAL DEVELOPMENTS IN NATIONAL AND INTERNATIONAL MARKETS (*co-editor with Jesús Ferreiro and Felipe Serrano*)
ADVANCES IN MONETARY POLICY AND MACROECONOMICS (*co-editor with Gennaro Zezza*)
ASPECTS OF MODERN MONETARY AND MACROECONOMIC POLICIES (*co-editor with Eckhard Hein and Edwin Le Heron*)
ON MONEY, METHOD AND KEYNES: Selected Essays by Victoria Chick (*co-editor with Sheila Dow*)
IS THERE A NEW CONSENSUS IN MACROECONOMICS? (*editor*)
POLITICAL ECONOMY OF BRAZIL (*co-editor with Alfredo Saad-Filho*)
FINANCIAL LIBERALIZATION AND ECONOMIC PERFORMANCE IN EMERGING COUNTRIES (*co-editor with Luiz Fernando de Paula*)
ISSUES IN FINANCE AND INDUSTRY: Essays in Honour of Ajit Singh (*co-editor with John Eatwell*)

Also by John McCombie

ECONOMIC GROWTH AND THE BALANCE-OF-PAYMENTS CONSTRAINT (*co-author with A.P. Thirlwall*)
WHAT GLOBAL ECONOMIC CRISIS? (*co-editor with Philip Arestis and Michelle Baddeley*)
PRODUCTIVITY GROWTH AND ECONOMIC PERFORMANCE: Essays on Verdoorn's Law (*co-editor with Maurizio Pugno and Bruno Soro*)
GLOBALISATION, REGIONALISM AND ECONOMIC ACTIVITY (*co-editor with Philip Arestis and Michelle Baddeley*)
ESSAYS ON BALANCE OF PAYMENTS CONSTRAINED GROWTH: Theory and Evidence (*co-editor with A.P. Thirlwall*)
THE NEW MONETARY POLICY: Implications and Relevance (*co-editor with Philip Arestis and Michelle Baddeley*)
GROWTH AND ECONOMIC DEVELOPMENT: Essays in Honour of A.P. Thirlwall (*co-editor with Philip Arestis and Roger Vickerman*)
ISSUES IN FINANCE AND MONETARY POLICY (*co-editor with Carlos Rodríguez González*)
THE EUROPEAN UNION: Current Problems and Prospects (*co-editor with Carlos Rodríguez González*)
ECONOMIC GROWTH: New Directions in Theory and Policy (*co-editor with Philip Arestis and Michelle Baddeley*)

Unemployment: Past and Present

Edited by

Philip Arestis

and

John McCombie

Selection and editorial matter © Philip Arestis and John McCombie 2009
Individual chapters © contributors 2009

All rights reserved. No reproduction, copy or transmission of this
publication may be made without written permission.

No portion of this publication may be reproduced, copied or transmitted
save with written permission or in accordance with the provisions of the
Copyright, Designs and Patents Act 1988, or under the terms of any licence
permitting limited copying issued by the Copyright Licensing Agency,
Saffron House, 6-10 Kirby Street, London EC1N 8TS.

Any person who does any unauthorized act in relation to this publication
may be liable to criminal prosecution and civil claims for damages.

The authors have asserted their rights to be identified as the authors of
this work in accordance with the Copyright, Designs and Patents Act 1988.

First published 2009 by
PALGRAVE MACMILLAN

Palgrave Macmillan in the UK is an imprint of Macmillan Publishers Limited,
registered in England, company number 785998, of Houndmills, Basingstoke,
Hampshire RG21 6XS

Palgrave Macmillan in the US is a division of St Martin's Press LLC,
175 Fifth Avenue, New York, NY 10010.

Palgrave Macmillan is the global academic imprint of the above companies
and has companies and representatives throughout the world.

Palgrave® and Macmillan® are registered trademarks in the United States,
the United Kingdom, Europe and other countries.

ISBN-13: 978–0–230–20244–3
ISBN-10: 0–230–20244–6

This book is printed on paper suitable for recycling and made from fully
managed and sustained forest sources. Logging, pulping and manufacturing
processes are expected to conform to the environmental regulations of the
country of origin.

A catalogue record for this book is available from the British Library.

A catalog record for this book is available from the Library of Congress.

10 9 8 7 6 5 4 3 2 1
18 17 16 15 14 13 12 11 10 09

Printed and bound in Great Britain by
CPI Antony Rowe, Chippenham and Eastbourne

Library
University of Texas
at San Antonio

Contents

List of Tables and Figures	vii
Acknowledgements	x
Notes on the Contributors	xi

1. Introduction   1
   Philip Arestis and John McCombie

2. Kalecki on the Causes of Unemployment and Policies to Achieve Full Employment   7
   Malcolm Sawyer

3. The Relevance of Keynes Today with Particular Reference to Unemployment in Rich and Poor Countries   29
   A. P. Thirlwall

4. Aggregate Supply in the New Consensus   57
   James Trevithick

5. Growth and Unemployment in an Extended Kaldorian Model   83
   Mark Roberts

6. A Post Keynesian Macroeconomic Policy Mix as an Alternative to the New Consensus Approach   104
   Eckhard Hein and Engelbert Stockhammer

7. The 'Unemployment Bias' of the New Consensus View of Macroeconomics   131
   Giuseppe Fontana

8. Unemployment and the Natural Interest Rate in a Neo-Wicksellian Model   149
   Philip Arestis and Elias Karakitsos

9 Is Inflation Targeting Inimical to Employment? 181
   Mark Setterfield

10 Labour Market Search and Monetary Shocks: A Theoretical
   Consideration 202
   Jagjit S. Chadha and Qi Sun

Index 225

List of Tables and Figures

Tables

2.1	Unemployment rate and output gap for various countries, 2005	23
3.1	Average levels of unemployment and consumer price inflation before and after 1992 (%)	42
8.1	Numerical model	167
10.1	Calibration of key labour market parameters	210
10.2	Key variables	211
10.3	Other key calibration parameters	212

Figures

2.1	Relationship between p-curve and w-curve involving insufficient capacity	19
2.2	Range of w-curves and effects on unemployment	20
2.3	Time series on unemployment and output gap for OECD area	24
2.4	Time series on unemployment and output gap for UK	25
2.5	Time series on unemployment and output gap for Greece	25
3.1	Keynesian involuntary employment	39
3.2	The relationship between the change in unemployment and the change in the inflation rate, 1980–91 to 1992–2006	43
3.3	The relationship between inflation and unemployment across countries, 1992–2006	44
3.4	Reconciling the natural and warranted growth rates	49
4.1	The textbook version of the Keynesian fix-price model	58
4.2	The initial *General Theory* assumption of fixed money wages	59
4.3	Aggregate supply in the long-run	60
4.4	The level of employment when the target real wage exceeds the market-clearing real wage	63
4.5	Testing for the presence of involuntary unemployment	65
4.6	Aggregate supply at less than full employment	68
4.7	Aggregate supply at two different money wage rates	68

4.8	Aggregate supply, aggregate demand, and the determination of the absolute price level	69
4.9	Balanced deflation	70
4.10	An increase in aggregate demand reduces the real wage	71
4.11	Real wage stickiness	74
4.12	The Keynes effect, the Pigou effect, and the downward slope of the aggregate demand schedule	78
5.1	Phase diagram for the extended Kaldorian model	89
5.2	Absence of a long-run growth–unemployment trade-off $(-\gamma\eta + \phi > 1)$	94
5.3	Existence of a long-run growth–unemployment trade-off $(-\gamma\eta + \phi < 1)$	94
5.4	Absence of a growth–unemployment trade-off, even in the short run $(\rho = 1)$	95
6.1	Conflicting claims, inflation and distribution	110
6.2	The NAIRU as a non-attractor	115
6.3	The NAIRU as an attractor	116
6.4	An inflation targeting central bank stabilizing the NAIRU	119
6.5	Persistent change in the *ex ante* real rate of interest and the NAIRU	121
6.6	A Post Keynesian policy mix	125
7.1	The transmission mechanism of monetary policy in the New Consensus view	133
7.2	The zone of discretion of the 'opportunistic' strategy	142
8.1(a)	Steady state	164
8.1(b)	Derivation of the *YG* curve	164
8.2	Unstable model $(A > 0, B < 0)$: interest rate, inflation and natural interest rate	166
8.3(a)	The dynamic adjustment of the interest rate, inflation and the natural interest rate to a temporary drop in demand	168
8.3(b)	Dynamic adjustment of output to a transient drop in demand	168
8.3(c)	Wage inflation, *ULC* and unemployment response to a transient drop in demand	168
8.4(a)	The dynamic adjustment of the interest rate, inflation and the natural interest rate to a permanent drop in demand	169
8.4(b)	Dynamic adjustment of output to a permanent drop in demand	170

8.4(c)	Wage inflation, *ULC* and unemployment: response to a permanent drop in demand	170
8.5	Negative demand shock	171
8.6(a)	Active fiscal policy: interest rate, inflation and natural interest rate	172
8.6(b)	Active fiscal policy: output	172
8.6(c)	Active fiscal policy: wage inflation, *ULC* and unemployment	172
9.1	The adverse employment effects of inflation targeting	189
9.2	Inflation targeting with a fixed nominal interest rate	191
9.3	Inflation targeting under the Pasinetti rule	193
9.4	Inflation targeting and the 'stagnationist bonus'	194
10.1	Responses to policy shock: UK	205
10.2	Job matching and persistence	207
10.3	Responses of NK models to productivity shocks	214
10.4	Responses of NK models to monetary shocks	215
10.5	Responses of labour market models to productivity shock	217
10.6	Responses of labour market models to monetary shock	218

Acknowledgements

Chapter 5 is a revised version of a chapter in John McCombie, Maurizio Pugno and Bruno Soro, *Productivity Growth and Economic Performance: Essays on Verdoorn's Law*, Palgrave Macmillan (2002). Reproduced by permission of Palgrave Macmillan.

Extracts from the *Collected Writings of John Maynard Keynes* are reproduced with permission of Palgrave Macmillan.

An earlier version of Chapter 9 was presented at the Meetings of the Eastern Economic Association, New York, February 2007, the 'Unemployment: Past and Present' conference, Cambridge, August 2007, and the Third Biennial Canada/US Eastern Border Post Keynesian Workshop, Montreal, September 2007. Mark Setterfield is grateful to conference participants and in particular to Malcolm Sawyer for helpful comments. Any remaining errors are his own.

Notes on the Contributors

Philip Arestis is University Director of Research, Cambridge Centre for Economic and Public Policy, Department of Land Economy, University of Cambridge, UK.

Jagjit S. Chadha is Professor of Economics at the Department of Economics, University of Kent, Canterbury, UK.

Giuseppe Fontana is Professor of Monetary Economics at Leeds University Business School, University of Leeds, UK and Professor of Economics, University of Sannio, Benevento, Italy.

Eckhard Hein is Senior Researcher at the Macroeconomic Policy Institute (IMK) at the Hans Boeckler Foundation, Duesseldorf, Germany, and is Visiting Professor at Carl von Ossietzky University, Oldenburg, Germany.

Elias Karakitsos is Director and Partner at Guildhall Asset Management Ltd, and Associate Member of the Centre for Economic and Public Policy, University of Cambridge, UK.

John McCombie is Director of the Cambridge Centre for Economic and Public Policy, and Fellow in Economics at Downing College, University of Cambridge, UK.

Qi Sun is a research associate and PhD student at the Centre for Dynamic Macroeconomic Analysis at the Department of Economics, University of St Andrews, Scotland, UK.

Mark Roberts is Lecturer in Spatial Economics, Planning and Policy, Department of Land Economy, University of Cambridge, UK.

Malcolm Sawyer is Pro-Dean for Learning and Teaching and Professor of Economics at Leeds University Business School, UK.

Mark Setterfield is Professor of Economics at the Department of Economics, Trinity College, USA, and is an Associate Member of the Centre for Economic and Public Policy, University of Cambridge, UK.

Englebert Stockhammer is Assistant Professor at the Department of Economics, Vienna University of Economics and Business Administration, Austria.

A. P. Thirlwall is Professor of Applied Economics at the University of Kent, Canterbury, UK.

James Trevithick is Director of Studies at King's College, Cambridge, UK.

1
Introduction
Philip Arestis and John McCombie

Unemployment is an area that has been rather neglected in the recent past. This is because it has not been viewed as a real problem for many countries. But it is a problem to some countries; the European Union (more particularly Germany, France and Spain) is probably the best example in this regard. In an attempt to examine a number of issues that relate to unemployment, a conference was held in Cambridge at Downing College from 30 August to 1 September 2007 under the auspices of the Cambridge Centre for Economic and Public Policy. The proceedings are being published in two volumes, and this is the first of the two.

Malcolm Sawyer begins Chapter 2 by discussing Michał Kalecki on the causes of unemployment and on the policies to achieve full employment. Kalecki established that the lack of effective demand was the major cause of low economic activity and unemployment in the early 1930s. His main writings on the possibilities for a reduction and perhaps an elimination of unemployment date back to the mid-1940s. This chapter outlines his contribution on policies towards reducing unemployment, and evaluates their contemporary relevance. Three major aspects of Kalecki's writings are discussed. The first relates to the issue of establishing a sufficiently high level of aggregate demand to ensure full employment. Kalecki considered the possible roles of, for example, increased investment and consumer expenditure, and of government expenditure and taxation. Further, he considered and rejected the various arguments which were raised against the use of fiscal policy and budget deficits. The second aspect, represented in his paper on 'Political Aspects of Full Employment' (1943), focused on the political obstacles to the achievement of full employment in the long run. The third aspect, to which little attention has been given, relates to the size of the capital stock and whether it could support the full employment of labour and whether an inadequate capital stock has inflationary implications.

A. P. Thirlwall, in Chapter 3, turns to the relevance today of Keynes, with particular reference to unemployment in rich and poor countries. The purpose of his chapter is to argue that Keynes's ideas, formulated in the first half of the twentieth century, are as relevant today as they ever were when thinking about the nature of unemployment and how to reduce it. But the nature of unemployment differs between the two sets of countries and so does the particular challenge of reducing it. In the advanced countries, it is the concept of involuntary unemployment that needs to be resurrected and stressed, and the demand management used to reduce it. In developing countries, of prime importance is the role of government in raising the rate of capital accumulation and investing in labour-intensive projects. This chapter includes Thirlwall's work on unemployment over the past 40 years and the challenge of employment creation in advanced and developing countries. He reminds readers of pre-Keynesian (classical) employment theory and applies Keynes's concept of involuntary unemployment to the high rate of unemployment in the core countries of the European Union following the Maastricht Treaty in 1992. Thirlwall is critical of the idea that a high rate of unemployment somehow constitutes a 'natural' rate that has nothing to do with lack of demand. Finally, the role of deficit financing and the inflation tax in developing countries is considered, where the major task of employment creation is simultaneously to raise the rate of capital accumulation and to move towards more labour intensive techniques of production.

In Chapter 4, James Trevithick examines Keynesian involuntary unemployment and modern macroeconomics. N. Gregory Mankiw's *Macroeconomics* is probably the most influential book in the teaching of introductory macroeconomics in the English-speaking world and beyond. It is the set textbook for first year macroeconomics in Cambridge: it is a 'must buy' book. In North American universities, it is the set text for intermediate macroeconomics. It represents the distillation of a consensus which has emerged particularly in North America over the last three decades. Controversy and debate among various strands of macroeconomic thought has produced a convergence towards a framework of macroeconomic analysis, which is, or so it is claimed, almost universally accepted. In this mainstream consensus, the short run is dominated by Keynesian economics with sticky prices; the long run by old-style classical economics, where prices are, to use Pigou's description, 'plastic' or 'elastic'; and the very long run by the Solow/Swan model of economic growth, where prices are only implicitly included. Moreover, the process of transition from one 'run' to another is never analysed. James Trevithick regards Mankiw's text as deeply flawed in several ways, and in this chapter he takes issue with one aspect of this consensus. The aspect he chooses to question lies at the heart of Keynes's rejection of the classical theory of labour market adjustment and its replacement with Keynes's own, more satisfactory analysis of the relationship between money wages on the one hand and the absolute price level on the other. Although there are some sections of *Macroeconomics* where Mankiw appears to be approaching Keynes's analysis, in others he retreats so that money wages and prices are variables with a life of their own. Trevithick regards this separation as erroneous and he endeavours to correct it.

Mark Roberts in Chapter 5 examines growth and unemployment in an extended Kaldorian model. The 'standard' Kaldorian model of economic growth is one in which the existence of dynamic increasing returns generates a positive feedback mechanism from the demand-side of an economy to the supply-side. This ensures that the growth process is characterized by 'circular and cumulative causation', whereby any initial growth advantage tends to sustain itself. However, a deficiency of the standard model is that it implicitly assumes workers react passively to changes in their real wages when the rate of inflation changes. The model presented in this chapter relaxes this assumption by introducing a conflict theory of wage bargaining. With this theory, the model can explain growth and unemployment. Furthermore, in this extended model, not only is the positive feedback mechanism of the standard Kaldorian model enhanced, but an offsetting negative feedback mechanism is introduced. Thus, while faster labour productivity growth induced by faster growth in demand reduces workers' expected rate of inflation and leads to moderated wage demands, lower unemployment makes workers more militant when bargaining for wage increases. Overall, the extended model provides a better understanding of the codeterminants of an economy's rate of economic growth and unemployment.

Chapter 6 deals with Post Keynesian economics. Eckhard Hein and Engelbert Stockhammer, in monetary policy, wage bargaining, employment and inflation, provide a Post Keynesian (PK) alternative to the New Consensus Models (NCMs). They present a model that synthesizes several of the PK arguments and consists of three classes: rentiers, firms and workers. It has a short-run inflation barrier derived from distributional conflicts between these classes, which are endogenous in the medium run. Distributional conflict, however, not only affects inflation but income shares as well. On the demand side, the income classes have different savings propensities and only firms invest. The authors apply a Kaleckian investment function with expected sales and internal funds as major determinants of investment, which allows for the inclusion of real debt effects on firms' investment decisions. They analyse short-run stability and include medium-run endogeneity channels for the NAIRU (including hysteresis in the labour market, wage and profit aspirations based on conventional behaviour, investment and the capital stock, and the implications for costs from changes in the interest rate). The model is used to analyse NCM and alternative PK policy assignments and rules. Hein and Stockhammer attempt to show that improving employment without increasing inflation is possible if the Central Bank targets distribution; if wage bargaining targets inflation; and if fiscal policies are used for short- and medium-run real stabilization purposes.

In Chapter 7, Giuseppe Fontana analyses the 'unemployment bias' of the New Consensus View of macroeconomics and continues the critique of the NCM. His chapter reviews some of the main reasons for the success of the New Consensus View before highlighting some of its problems, including the replacement of fiscal policy with monetary policy as the main stabilization tool, and the exclusively short-run view of the role of aggregate demand. More importantly, drawing on the records of the FOMC meetings of the Federal Reserve System, the first part of this chapter discusses the 'unemployment bias' of the conventional policy strategy, namely the persistent tendency to keep the unemployment rate above the NAIRU, as long as the economy does not have stable prices. The second part of the chapter discusses a recently proposed amendment to the conventional or deliberate policy strategy of the New Consensus View, the so-called opportunistic strategy. This alternative policy strategy contains two original features, namely path dependency and a zone of discretion. These two features have the potential to eliminate, or at least contain, the 'unemployment bias' of the conventional or deliberate policy strategy of the New Consensus View. For this reason, Fontana closely scrutinizes the nature and implications of path dependency and a zone of discretion, before assessing the pros and cons of the opportunistic approach.

Philip Arestis and Elias Karakitsos, in Chapter 8, consider unemployment and the natural interest rate in a Neo-Wicksellian Model, sustaining the critique of the NCM. In these models, the natural interest rate is a constant and the emphasis on this variable has shifted from its original insight as the reward to capital (the real profit rate) to a real interest rate that defines the stance of monetary policy as neutral, tight or easy. The purpose of this chapter is to endogenize the natural interest rate and the supply of (potential) output in an otherwise Neo-Wicksellian model. They show that in the presence of transient shocks the system returns to its initial steady state. However, under long-lasting shocks the system converges to a different steady state. Thus, inflation, output and unemployment would converge to different long-run equilibrium values under longer-lasting shocks. Arestis and Karakitsos show that such a shock can be offset by fiscal policy, thereby reinstating fiscal policy as an important arm of demand management that affects unemployment. These results are different from the ones reached within the pure Neo-Wicksellian model. In the latter, although, under conditions of transient shocks, the system reverts to an exogenously determined NAIRU, no such mechanism prevails in the case of long-lasting shocks.

In Chapter 9, Mark Setterfield asks whether inflation targeting is the enemy of employment targeting and offers a further (Post Keynesian) critique of the NCM. Mainstream macroeconomic models portray capitalism as a real exchange economy, in which real outcomes are supply-determined and money is neutral (at least in the long run). The inevitable conclusion of these models is that inflation targeting is ultimately neutral with respect to real macroeconomic performance: any rate of inflation can be achieved that is consistent with the same (supply-determined) rate of employment. According to the Post Keynesian tradition, however, capitalism is properly conceived as a monetary production economy, in which real outcomes are demand-determined and money is non-neutral, even in the long run. It is shown that with the Post Keynesian approach, inflation targeting can be inimical to employment, neutral with respect to employment, or can even enhance employment depending on the macroeconomic policy architecture. The main conclusion to be drawn is that policy activism contributes to the social construction of the economy and that both competing characterizations of the workings of the economy, and consideration of the nature of macroeconomic policy interventions, are essential for understanding the properties of controversial policies like inflation targeting.

In Chapter 10, Jagjit S. Chadha and Qi Sun discuss labour market search and monetary shocks from a theoretical perspective. They are concerned with the implications for monetary policy and output dynamics of a general equilibrium business cycle model where prices are sticky and there are labour market rigidities. In the New Keynesian paradigm, key state variables behave somewhat like asset prices – jumping in price and quantity to clear quickly, and with expected deviations from the flex–price outcome. Following Walsh (2003) and Ravenna and Walsh (2007), the authors explore the implications of a labour search model in which employment is the outcome of a costly search process and the marginal employee is affected by monetary policy and productivity shocks. In this model output responds in a hump-backed and persistent manner to monetary shocks and the resulting Phillips curve seems to change the trade-off faced by monetary policy makers. This is because responding to output deviations may become more important than inflation alone when labour markets adjust slowly because (i) there are speed limit effects on the appropriate growth rate of output and (ii) 'interest rates directly impact firms' costs by increasing search time and, so it makes more sense to try and keep the economy near full employment'.

We would like to thank the authors for their stimulating contributions to the conference. Alec Dubber and Taiba Batool at Palgrave Macmillan, and their staff, have been extremely supportive throughout the life of this project. Finally, we are extremely grateful to Warren Mosler for his continuing support of the Cambridge Centre and for having made the conference possible.

2
Kalecki on the Causes of Unemployment and Policies to Achieve Full Employment
Malcolm Sawyer

Introduction

The purpose of this chapter is to review Michal Kalecki's contributions on understanding the causes of unemployment and his policy discussions relating to unemployment, and to evaluate their contemporary relevance.

There are three major aspects to Kalecki's writings in this respect on which I draw in this chapter. The first relates to the issue of establishing a sufficiently high level of aggregate demand to ensure full employment. Kalecki had established the lack of effective demand as the major cause of low economic activity and unemployment in the early 1930s, and it may be said that he did so about three years prior to Keynes (Kalecki, 1933; Keynes, 1936). However, Kalecki's main writings on the possibilities for the reduction and perhaps elimination of unemployment date to the mid-1940s, many arising from his work at the Oxford University Institute of Statistics. Deficient aggregate demand was a pervasive feature of capitalist economies, and Kalecki considered the possible roles of, for example, increased investment and consumer expenditure and of government expenditure and taxation as ways of securing adequate aggregate demand consistent with full employment of labour. Further, he considered and rejected the various arguments which were raised against the use of fiscal policy and budget deficits.

The second aspect, particularly represented in his 'Political Aspects of Full Employment' (Kalecki, 1943), focused on the political and social obstacles to the long term achievement of full employment. Specifically the idea that the economic and political power of the working class would be strengthened by prolonged full employment, and that pressures would build from capitalists to constrain that power and to bring full employment to an end.

The third aspect, to which little attention has been given, relates to the role of the size of the capital stock in terms of its ability to support full employment of labour and the ways in which the inadequacy of the capital stock has inflationary implications. When capacity is insufficient, then a relatively high level of demand would bring firms into operating where unit costs were rising, and as a consequence prices rising relative to wages, thereby depressing real wages. Workers may seek to raise money wages to catch up with prices, but that would be offset by further price rises, thereby generating rising inflation.

Aggregate demand and budget deficits

Kalecki considered that a reserve army of unemployed labour was a general characteristic of a capitalist economy. Under capitalism

> a considerable proportion of capital equipment lies idle in the slump. Even on average, the degree of utilization throughout the business cycle will be substantially below the maximum reached during the boom. Fluctuations in the utilization of available labour parallel those in the utilization of equipment. Not only is there mass unemployment in the slump, but average employment throughout the cycle is considerably below the peak reached in the boom. The reserve of capital equipment and the reserve army of unemployed are typical features of capitalist economy, at least throughout a considerable part of the cycle. (Kalecki, 1991, p. 311)

Kalecki adopted the optimistic view in the mid-1940s that, notwithstanding the pervasive nature of insufficient aggregate demand and unemployment of labour under capitalism, unemployment could now be overcome, at least at an intellectual level (as political obstacles to the sustained achievement of full employment remained). He wrote that 'a solid majority of economists is now of the opinion that, even in a capitalist economy, full employment may be secured by a government spending programme, provided there is in existence an adequate plan to employ all existing labour power, and provided adequate supplies of necessary foreign raw-materials may be obtained in exchange for exports' (Kalecki, 1990, p. 347). At least sufficient aggregate demand could be secured through government action, though as this quote suggests there can be supply-side constraints on the achievement of full employment.

Kalecki discussed 'three ways to full employment' in terms of government spending and subsidies to mass consumption (leading to a budget deficit), stimulation of private investment and redistribution (consideration of the foreign trade sector was left for another paper in the same volume of essays). He argued that there were limits to the stimulation of private investment for aggregate demand purposes but that the other methods were capable of securing a level of aggregate demand consistent with full employment. Kalecki (1990, pp. 377–86) raised the question of whether full employment could be achieved by stimulating investment and answered that there were severe limits to doing so. He argued that there would need to be continuing and cumulative stimulation of investment, and that the rate of interest, taxes on income and profits would have to be reduced continuously or subsidies to investment be continuously increased (cf. Kalecki, 1990, p. 377). The basis of the argument was that a high level of investment would lead to the capital–output ratio rising and the rate of profit declining, and to maintain a high level of investment would require measures to offset the effects of a declining rate of profit. However, as Laski (1983) claimed, this argument is not correct in that a high level of investment would indeed lead to a higher capital–output ratio but one which would eventually stabilize.[1]

Kalecki based his argument on the assumption that there would be a tendency for the level of aggregate demand to fall short of what was required for full employment. There was then a need for either a budget deficit to mop up the difference between full employment savings and investment, or for full employment savings to be reduced through a redistribution of income (from rich to poor). Kalecki was clear that a long-run budget deficit would generally be required to secure full employment, reflecting the perceived lack of private effective demand and tendency of savings to exceed investment. Some other Keynesian authors argued for the requirement for a budget deficit in this context. Lerner (1943) put the case for functional finance, which 'rejects completely the traditional doctrines of "sound finance" and the principle of trying to balance the budget over a solar year or any other arbitrary period' (p. 355). Kalecki's argument was essentially similar: a budget deficit is required to correct a deficiency of aggregate demand, and it is precisely in conditions of deficient aggregate demand that funds will be available for the budget deficit.

Domar (1944) noted that 'it is possible that private investment will be able to absorb all savings year in and year out, or that private investment will at least fluctuate around a sufficiently high average so that deficits which may be incurred by the government in some years will be offset by surpluses made in others'. But this could not be assured and he examined the case 'where private investment is insufficient to absorb intended savings over a relatively long period of time' (p. 798). He argued that 'since government is absorbing a part of savings, it is of course desirable that its expenditures be productive' (p. 820), where he interpreted 'productive' in a broad sense, including expenditure on education and health. However, if 'institutional forces prevent the government from spending money on anything but leaf-raking, it should still absorb the savings unused by private enterprise and spend them on leaf-raking' (p. 820).

Others adopted a more passive fiscal policy approach, whereby budget deficits emerged during slowdowns but with budget surpluses during upswings. In a proposal reminiscent of the present Stability and Growth Pact for the Economic and Monetary Union within the European Union, The White Paper on Employment Policy of 1944 stated that 'to the extent that the policies proposed in this Paper affect the balancing of the Budget in a particular year, they certainly do not contemplate any departure from the principle that the Budget must be balanced over a longer period'; and there was also concern in reducing 'that part of the public debt which is a dead-weight war debt' (Ministry of Reconstruction, 1944, p. 25). Kalecki argued that the White Paper on Employment Policy did not provide a programme for achieving lasting full employment, which would have to be based on a long-run budget deficit policy or the redistribution of income towards wages, thereby stimulating aggregate demand. He argued that even if policies after counter-cyclical were successful in stabilizing effective demand, it did not follow that full employment would be achieved. The simple reason was that the relatively stable level of private investment may well fall below the level required to match savings out of full employment income (Kalecki, 1997, pp. 243–4).

The manipulation of aggregate demand can take the form of fiscal policy (via budget deficits) and influence the distribution of income. But Kalecki also argued that

> the gap to be covered [to stimulate aggregate demand to reach full employment] may be so large that public investment will soon become entirely, or at least nearly, useless. In such a case it would be absurd to restrict the government spending programme to public investment when a higher standard of living can be achieved by devoting a part of this spending to increasing consumption. The general principle must be that social priorities decide the nature of the government's spending programme. (Kalecki, 1990, p. 368)

He then argued that the proper role of private investment was the provision of the means for the production of consumption goods, and not to ensure the full employment of labour. Investment, private or public, should only be carried out if it leads to useful outputs. The stimulation of consumption rather than investment should be used to generate sufficient effective demand for full employment.

When a budget deficit was required in order to sustain a high level of aggregate demand, Kalecki clearly set out the argument that the funding of a deficit did not constitute a problem. He argued (e.g. Kalecki, 1990, p. 358) that the budget deficit 'finances itself', by which he meant that a rise in the budget deficit generates a rise in income and changes in the distribution of income, leading to an exactly sufficient increase in savings to match the deficit and to provide the funds for government borrowing. He then set out, for a closed economy, the equality:

$$G + I = T + S \qquad (2.1)$$

(where G is government expenditure, T is tax revenue, I is investment expenditure and S is savings) and hence:

$$G - T = S - I \qquad (2.2)$$

which can be readily modified for the open economy as:

$$G + I + X = T + S + M \qquad (2.3)$$

(where X is exports and M is imports). This can be rewritten as:

$$(G - T) = (S - I) + (M - X). \qquad (2.4)$$

From this perspective, the budget deficit is to be used to mop up the 'excess' of private savings over investment, and the counterpart budget surplus is to be used when investment expenditure exceeds savings (at the desired level of economic activity). It is, of course, the case that the private savings (in excess of private investment) can only actually occur if the government runs a budget deficit. The alternative is that private savings decline (through a decline in income) until savings and investment are equal.

The question can be posed as to whether the propensity to save and to invest, the rates of taxation and the level of government expenditure, along with the foreign trade position, will be compatible with equation (2.3) holding at full employment. Kalecki's view was that it would generally only do so if government expenditure exceeded tax revenue, that is, the government ran a budget deficit. Clearly the resulting scale of budget deficit depends on the propensities to save (which in turn depends on the distribution of income) and to invest, and the foreign trade position. This suggests that a policy towards budget deficit should be formulated with knowledge of the relevant propensities etc., and should not be formulated by the imposition of some arbitrary number on the size of the deficit (relative to GDP). This would argue against not only policies such as the eurozone Stability and Growth Pact of a balanced budget over the cycle but also against any 'golden rule' that the current budget should be balanced, though borrowing can be undertaken to fund public investment.

The arguments against the use of fiscal policy and budget deficits are well-known. Kalecki, in my view, largely answered these arguments in his papers.[2] We shall now look at these arguments and summarize Kalecki's responses.

Unsustainable deficits?

A traditional argument (which continues to be heard) against the use of budget deficits is that they constitute a burden on future generations, and, as they lead to rising debt, are unsustainable. Kalecki (1990, pp. 362–4) argued that an increasing national debt did not constitute a burden on society as a whole, since it is largely an internal transfer, and that a rising national income would generate rising tax revenues with a progressive tax system (relative to GDP). He noted that if full employment is maintained by deficit spending, then the public debt expands and the resulting interest payments on the debt also rise. But the effects of that depend on the rate of growth of the economy. In the event that there was a problem of a rising debt to income ratio (and hence of interest payments to income), Kalecki advocated an annual capital tax, levied on firms and individuals, which would raise money to finance the interest payments on the national debt which would affect 'neither capitalists' consumption nor the profitability of investment' (Kalecki, 1990, p. 363; see also Kalecki, 1997, pp. 163–7).

Kalecki also noted that in the White Paper on Employment the argument was made 'that there will be no unfavourable effect if the debt increases not more than proportionately to the national income. They hope that the national income in this country will increase, but somehow they fail to draw the obvious conclusion that the public debt may be permitted to increase proportionately to the national income' (Kalecki, 1997, p. 243). Kalecki did not, as far as I am aware, work through the simple algebra which indicates that a continuous budget deficit (including interest payments) relative to GDP of b leads to a debt to GDP ratio which stabilizes at $d = b/g$, where g is the nominal growth rate if b is calculated in nominal terms. Domar (1944) considered a number of cases amongst which he produced and particularly emphasized this result. If the (post-tax) rate of interest on government debt r exceeds the growth rate g, then the primary budget will be in surplus, whereas when $r < g$ the primary budget will also be in deficit. (For further discussion, see Arestis and Sawyer, 2006.)

Monetary policy

In his discussion of 'three ways to full employment', Kalecki made no mention of the use of monetary policy. It can though be inferred that he did not consider monetary policy to be an effective means of raising demand to achieve full employment. As indicated above he did not see the stimulation of investment as a means of maintaining full employment, and since the effect of the interest rate would be on investment (if at all) this cuts out the use of lower interest rates to stimulate demand.

In a paper on monetary policy, Kalecki did argue that

> the only channel through which open-market [monetary] policy would stimulate consumption and investment is the consequent fall in the rate of interest, and in particular the long-term rate. The fall in the rate of interest would probably tend to stimulate consumption mainly through inflating capital values of the existing assets; feeling richer, the owners might consume more out of their income. This effect would be significant, most probably, only if the fall in the rate of interest were considerable, which would require open-market operations on a very large scale. Even when effective, this seems to me the wrong way, from the social point of view, to increase employment because the method boils down to the stimulation of capitalist consumption. (Kalecki, 1990, p. 403)

Kalecki also argued that in practice the long-term rate of interest is rather stable, and that the relatively small changes which occur in the long-term rate of interest would have little influence on investment activity (Kalecki, 1990, pp. 296–7). This led him to dismiss those theories of the business cycle which suggest that the end of a boom derives from an increase in the rate of interest.

In effect Kalecki played down the role of monetary policy along two lines. First, in practice the long-run rate of interest was the relevant one, but it did not vary much over time. Second, the effect of a change in interest rate could be rather small and hence the size of change in interest rates which would be required to have much effect was in some sense large. 'The reduction of the long-term rate of interest would stimulate investment by increasing its net profitability. Here again, a substantial fall in the rate of interest is necessary in order to make the effect significant.' Further, 'filling the deflationary gap ... by stimulating private investment would in the long-run create 'over-investment', i.e. reduce the rate of profit and thus prove a self-defeating measure. It also would create over-capacity, which is a sheer waste of resources' (Kalecki, 1990, p. 403).

Kalecki clearly expressed the view that aggregate demand sufficient to underpin full employment of labour could be secured through a redistribution of income and a long-term budget deficit. Fiscal policy rather than monetary policy was the route to full employment. Now that the deficient demand problem is understood it can be overcome. But other barriers remain and it is those to which we now turn.

Inflation, capacity and politics

Capacity and inflation

Kalecki's analysis is often portrayed with firms operating with excess capacity alongside labour being unemployed. There seems the implicit suggestion that there would be sufficient productive capacity to generate full employment if only there was sufficient effective demand. Most (perhaps all) representations of Kalecki's approach in models which are given the epithet Kaleckian involve the related notion that average costs of production are constant and firms operate with excess capacity, with the degree of capacity utilization determined by the level of aggregate demand. There have been debates as to whether some notion of the long run can be characterized by excess capacity (e.g. Dutt, 1987, 1994, 1995; Duménil and Lévy, 1995; Glick and Campbell, 1995).

This is a reasonable reflection of much of Kalecki's writings on capitalism, though as we will shortly argue not all. In a more general sense, in his comparison between capitalism and socialism, Kalecki characterized the level of economic activity in capitalist economies as demand constrained, whereas in planned socialist economies the level was supply (resource) constrained. In developing economies unemployment of labour largely arises from a shortage of capital equipment. Kalecki did consider insufficient capacity as a possible constraint on the achievement of full employment of labour. This aspect of Kalecki's work has been little recognized. It is also linked with aspects of his view on inflation (and I would claim that a model consistent with these views of Kalecki is developed in Sawyer (2001) and in Arestis and Sawyer (2005)). The achievement of full employment may be hampered by inflationary pressures which arise from relatively high levels of economic activity, though

> inflation will result only if effective demand increases so much that a general scarcity of labour or equipment (or both) arises. Up to a point, the short-period supply curves are horizontal or mildly rising for most commodities. But when effective demand increases significantly beyond this point, the steeply upward-sloping parts of the short-period supply curves become relevant. As a result, there is a general increase in prices out of proportion with average prime costs, and in this way the vicious spiral of prices and wages is started. In order to avoid inflation, the government must, therefore, be careful not to push its deficit spending beyond the mark indicated by full utilization of labour and equipment. (Kalecki, 1990, p. 361)

Kalecki's writing on inflation would suggest that he viewed a level of aggregate demand, which led to demand in some sectors being ahead of supply capacity in those sectors, as a major source of inflationary pressures. The shortage of supply capacity would lead to increasing unit costs, rising prices and declining real wages, which could generate a money wage response but one which cannot restore real wages (cf. Kalecki, 1997, pp. 83–8). 'The "vicious spiral" arises because, after a fall in real wage-rates, money wages cannot "catch up" with prices and restore the real wage-rates to the previous level. This is caused by the fact that in the periods in question the supply of consumption goods is for one reason or another inelastic' (Kalecki, 1997, p. 85). A clear implication of this view is that a plentiful capital stock (meaning one that could employ the available workforce under conditions of constant or declining real unit costs) is a powerful antidote to inflationary demand pressures.

Kalecki noted the role of *increases* in demand rather than that of a high level of demand when he wrote that 'the increases in prices and wages referred to above are not the result of the maintenance of a high level of effective demand but rather a phenomenon connected with the *rapid rise* in this level' (Kalecki, 1997, p. 573). Thus a high level of demand when combined with appropriate productive capacity need not be inflationary, though a rapid increase in demand may be.

Kalecki argued that the right balance between capital equipment and available labour, with sufficient capital equipment needs to employ all the available labour and to leave some capacity in reserve, would be needed to enable full employment without inflationary pressures:

> If the maximum capacity of equipment is inadequate to absorb the available labour, as will be the case on backward countries, the immediate achievement of full employment is clearly hopeless. If the reserve capacities are non-existent or insufficient, the attempt to secure full employment in the short run may easily lead to inflationary tendencies in large sections of the economy, because the structure of equipment does not necessarily match the structure of demand. (Kalecki, 1990, pp. 361–2)

The argument put here is that the extent to which countries are 'backward' (using the terminology of this quote) is more extensive than envisaged by Kalecki and that a shortage of capital and equipment is a more widespread phenomenon. Specifically, as we suggest below, a prolonged recession which wipes out substantial capacity, or a major shock such as a large oil price rise which makes substantial amounts of capacity unprofitable, can also be causes of a lack of productive capacity. Further prolonged periods of low demand which may not involve a recession can suppress investment, and have a gradual eroding effect on productive capacity.

Kalecki saw inflation as arising from growing demand which cannot be met by growing supply 'owing to scarcity of plant, labour, or raw materials' (Kalecki, 1997, p. 85). The 'characteristic of inflation ... [is] a rise in price of consumers' goods in relation to the relevant costs of labour and raw materials' (Kalecki, 1997, p. 86). What is relevant for inflation are conditions of supply: 'during inflation the steeply rising part of the supply curve comes into the picture', hence unit costs and prices rise relative to wages, and real wages decline. A general rise in prices comes through the rise of numerous individual prices. 'It follows directly that to prevent "inflation in general" one must deal with "inflations" in particular groups of commodities, and this may be done only by rationing: to avoid inflation it is necessary to cut purchasing power in those sectors of the economy where it is directed on goods in short supply' (ibid.). This was written under war time conditions, and hence Kalecki did not consider the possibilities of enhancing supply. There is a more general implication of this approach, namely that inflationary problems arise when demand runs ahead of capacity, even when there is unemployment of labour, for there simply may be an inadequate capacity to support the full employment of labour. When enterprises operate with high levels of capacity, they are faced with rising costs: real wages fall, but money wages cannot catch up with prices to restore the initial real wage.

Politics and inflation

The discoveries of Keynes and Kalecki in the 1930s on the principle of effective demand and the associated idea that governments could (*and* should) manipulate their budget stance to generate high levels of employment (rather than aim for a balanced budget) seemed to open up the way for the achievement of permanent *full employment* in capitalist economies. In a famous article, Kalecki (1943, 1990, pp. 347–56) raised a number of doubts about the possibilities of achieving prolonged full employment in a laissez-faire capitalist economy. In this article, Kalecki introduced an idea which later became known as the political business cycle. Economic activity and employment could be stimulated prior to elections to aid the chances of the governing party being re-elected. But the resulting high level of employment would not last, and at best full employment would only be achieved at the top of the cycle.

In his discussion of issues of full employment in the mid-1940s, Kalecki argued that under sustained full employment 'the social position of the boss would be undermined, and the self-assurance and class consciousness of the working class would grow. Strikes for wage increases and improvements in conditions of work would create political tensions' (Kalecki, 1990, p. 351). He suggested that 'discipline in the factories' and 'political stability' would also be undermined. Much may be read into these words, but I think it is reasonable to suggest that full employment may involve significant wage inflation and a fall in work intensity and labour productivity, along with a decline of 'discipline in the factories'. The volume of profits would be higher under full employment (and hence the rate of profit, though perhaps not the share), with money wage rises leading to rising prices (to protect profits) and a squeeze on rentier income. As the threat of dismissal ceases to play a role, work intensity may be lower at full employment, and labour productivity thereby lower than otherwise. This latter idea has been incorporated into a range of macroeconomic models in the past 20 years, notably Shapiro and Stiglitz (1984) and Bowles (1985), under the general heading of 'shirking' models. Kalecki clearly used rather different terminology, and as the quote above indicates he saw full employment in terms of raising the self-assurance of the working class, which was otherwise held back by unemployment. But the effects of 'shirking' in the Shapiro and Stiglitz approach have rather similar effects with regard to productivity as the 'loss of discipline in the factories'.

But, whatever the terminology, Kalecki saw laissez-faire capitalism as inconsistent with sustained full employment. He, in rather typical laconic style, concluded that '"full employment capitalism" will, of course, have to develop new social and political institutions which will reflect the increased power of the working class. If capitalism can adjust itself to full employment, a fundamental reform will have been incorporated in it' (Kalecki, 1990, p. 356). The fundamental reforms could range from coordinated wage bargaining with broad agreement over the distribution of income between wages and profits which may restrain inflationary pressures, through to the development of forms of work organization including worker participation which can achieve high levels of productivity without the threat of 'the sack'.

This discussion portrays two different angles on inflation, which can appear at first sight as in some contradiction – the first stresses lack of capacity and the second the effects of full employment of labour on wages and productivity. The argument I want to put is that they refer to different 'images' of where an economy is, indicate an approach to inflation which does not portray a unique cause of inflation, and which suggest the need for different policy regimes depending on the economic circumstances. It is then necessary to analyse the prevailing economic circumstances, and I would argue that currently most economies can be better characterized by insufficient productive capacity rather than sustained full employment.

I draw upon the model developed in Sawyer (2001). In that model, the interaction of price setting and wage determination was explored. A price curve (labelled p-curve) was derived in terms of real product wages and employment based on the decisions of firms with regard to prices, employment and output. The general approach is that in light of the demand conditions which they face, firms set their prices relative to a nominal wage in a manner which depends on market power and the level of output. This provides (for the given nominal wage) a relationship between price and output, and this can be translated into a relationship between real product wage and the level of employment. An important aspect of this model is that the position of the price curve depends on the amount of productive capacity: capital enhancing investment would shift the p-curve to the right, capital deepening investment would shift the p-curve upwards. The price curve is taken to be of an inverted U-shape in the real wage employment space, reflecting initially declining

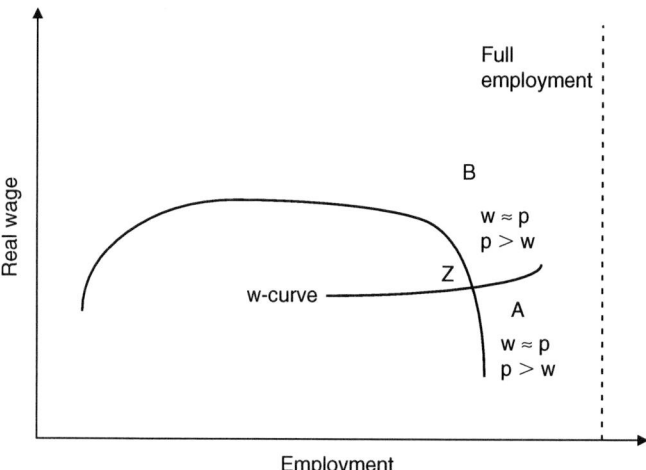

Figure 2.1 Relationship between *p*-curve and *w*-curve involving insufficient capacity

average costs, a range (possibly extensive) of constant costs and then a rising average cost.

A wage curve (labelled w-curve) was derived based on the outcome of wage determination. It was argued that a variety of approaches to wage determination (e.g. efficiency wages, bargaining models) give rise to an essentially similar equation which is a positive relationship between real wages and employment. For example a target real wage equation of the form $\dot{w} = a_1 + a_2 \dot{p}_{-1} + a_3 U + a_4(w_{-1} - p_{-1} - T)$ (the dot over the variable is the proportionate rate of change, w is the money wage, p is the price level, U is the unemployment rate and T is the target real wage), yields an equilibrium relationship of the form $a_1 + a_3 U + a_4(w - p - T) = 0$ (assuming for simplicity $a_2 = 1$).

The lack of capacity scenario can be portrayed in Figure 2.1. The p-curve is drawn with a shape and position to emphasize the lack of capacity in the economy relative to that required to support full employment. The w-curve is drawn as virtually horizontal around the intersection with the p-curve to indicate that workers will seek to maintain real wages but with little pressure to increase them. The price setting mechanism is such that above the p-curve prices will rise faster than wages (and hence the real product wage will fall) and below prices will rise more slowly than wages. For the w-curve, above it wages will rise less

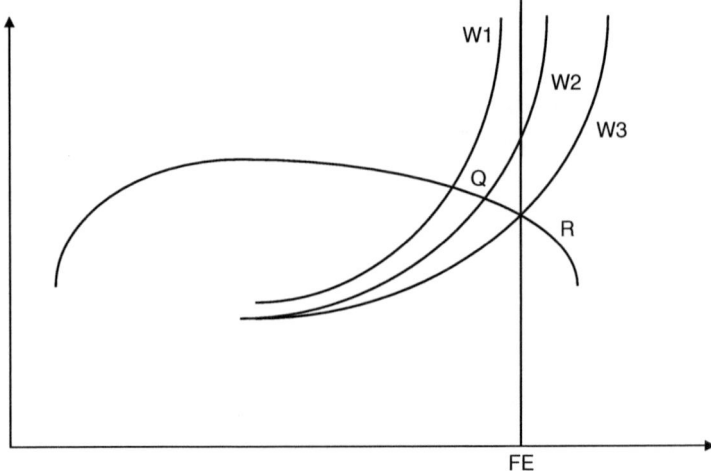

Figure 2.2 Range of w-curves and effects on unemployment

quickly than prices (hence the real product wage will decline) and below wages will rise faster than prices. The position of the economy on Figure 2.1 would depend on the level of aggregate demand (setting the level of employment) and the prevailing real wage (which will, of course, change as the inflationary process proceeds).

If the level of aggregate demand and the prevailing real wage are such that the economy is operating in the equivalent of zones A or B then firms would be raising prices faster than wages but workers would be seeking to maintain real wages. An inflationary spiral would develop, generated largely by firms' pricing behaviour, with some tendency for the real wage to decline. Inflation would stabilize if the economy reached a point such as Z. The point Z is viewed as an inflation barrier. There is no strong reason why the economy would actually operate at that point as it is not a strong (or even weak) attractor for the level of economic activity, which is demand determined.

The full employment scenario can be illustrated in alternative ways. In Figure 2.2 a range of possible w-curves are combined with a p-curve where lack of capacity is not an issue. The w-curve W1 corresponds to what may be termed the Shapiro-Stiglitz (1984) view that as employment approaches full employment then higher and higher real wages (relative to unemployment benefits) are required to maintain the cost of job losses. Full employment appears to be impossible. For a position of the curve such as W2 with an inflation barrier at Q, then a situation of full employment (FE) would involve inflationary pressures. However, the achievement of full employment could come from increased capital stock which shifts the p-curve upwards or from reductions in the bargaining strength of workers which shifts the w-curve outwards. A curve such as W3 would be required to reach full employment.

The interpretation of the different positions of the w-curve depends on the construction of the w-curve. In the cost-of-job-loss approach (Shapiro and Stiglitz, 1984; Bowles, 1985) the curve arises from the difficulties which firms have in monitoring the employment contract and overcoming the workers' tendency to shirk. Alternative modes of work organization (perhaps corresponding to a 'fundamental reform') would be required. In the target wage approach, the position of the w-curve depends on the coefficients of the wage equation, and specifically the degree to which unemployment restrains wage change and the degree of 'catch-up' of real wages towards the target real wage.

Implications for current situations

The rise in inflation in many industrialized countries during the 1960s and into the 1970s, after a decade or more of low unemployment, and then the rise in unemployment after 1973, again brought to the fore the issue of whether persistent full employment was possible under 'laissez-faire' capitalism. For many Western European countries, there had been a period of sustained full employment (though as Boltho (1982) indicated full employment was only reached around the late 1950s and lasted for only a decade). Inflation had tended to rise during the 1960s and into the 1970s and there was much discussion of a profit squeeze (e.g. Glyn and Sutcliffe (1971)). 'Fundamental reforms' had not been incorporated into capitalism, though various forms of corporatism, codetermination, and so on were developed which could arguably be seen as 'substantial reforms' which sought to contain the power of the working class in periods of high employment. But over the past two decades or more, the 'reforms' have been in the neo-liberal direction.

The rising unemployment from the mid-1970s onwards could be interpreted in this light, as could the subsequent (though long drawn out) reduction in inflation be interpreted as the reassertion of the role of the industrial reserve army of labour. How is the present situation of generally low inflation to be viewed, and to what extent does the fear of inflation limit the achievement of full employment?

Kalecki saw inflation as arising from growing demand which cannot be met by growing supply because of the scarcity of capital, labour or raw materials. A characteristic of inflation would be the price of consumer and other produced goods rising relative to the cost of labour and raw materials (cf. Kalecki, 1997, pp. 85–6). The conditions of supply are relevant for inflation when the rising portion of the cost curves are relevant and hence unit costs and prices rise relative to wages and real wages decline. Wages respond as workers seek to maintain real wages, leading to further increases in unit costs. As the wage–price ratio that firms are seeking conflicts with the previous real wage which workers sought to maintain, there is a conflicting inflation story to be told.

Kalecki portrayed a developing country as one in which there was insufficient capacity to sustain the employment of all who sought work. The portrayal of a capitalist economy as one of demand deficiency and plentiful capacity would match with the experience of the 1930s, and the situation of plentiful capacity would be generally relevant for the late 1950s and into the 1960s once post-war reconstruction had been largely completed. The oil price shock of 1973 had the effect of reducing effective capacity as oil-intensive industries became unprofitable. In the case of the UK, the high sterling rate of the early 1980s and the Thatcher monetarism wiped out substantial parts of UK manufacturing. Dow (1998) argued

> that in a major recession underemployment results in the deterioration and premature scrapping of physical equipment, and that disbandment or underemployment of a firm's workforce similarly results in the partial destruction of working practices and working relations. The latter constitute the intangible capital of a firm, the value of which is an important fraction of its market value as a going concern. The capital stock, physical and intangible, takes time to build up, and its destruction cannot be made good rapidly; in effect, therefore, the destruction is quasi-permanent. In this way demand shocks impact on supply. A major recession causes a downward displacement of the growth path of productivity (or potential or capacity output); after the recession, the 'stable growth' mechanism described by the first mechanism will in the absence of further shocks start to operate again, i.e. normal growth will be resumed from the low point of the recession. (p. 369)

Dow produces estimates of the impact of five major recessions in the UK, the significance of which is that it implies that substantial (negative)

Table 2.1 Unemployment rate and output gap for various countries, 2005

Country	Unemployment rate*	Output gap
Australia	5.1	−0.2
Austria	5.2	−2.2
Belgium	8.4	−1.6
Canada	6.8	0.0
Czech Republic	7.9	−0.6
Denmark	4.8	−0.7
Finland	8.4	−0.5
France	9.5	−1.8
Germany	9.5	−1.9
Greece	9.8	1.5
Hungary	7.2	−0.3
Ireland	4.3	0.5
Italy	7.7	−1.4
Japan	4.4	−0.8
Luxembourg	4.5	−1.7
Netherlands	4.7	−3.0
New Zealand	3.7	1.0
Norway	4.6	1.2
Portugal	7.6	−3.4
Spain	9.2	−0.8
Sweden (2004)	6.4	−0.7
Switzerland	4.5	−1.0
UK	4.7	−0.5
USA	5.1	0.0

Note: *Standardized unemployment rate.
Source: OECD *Economic Outlook* (July 2006), Paris: OECD.

changes in capacity can occur as the result of recession, which have long lasting effects.

The lack of capacity currently can be illustrated by comparing the estimates of the output gap with the prevailing level of unemployment. Some are given in Table 2.1 for a range of OECD countries for 2005. The output gap is intended to represent how current output compares with some notion of normal, average or trend output: though we may doubt whether trend output represents full capacity (in the sense that more output could be obtained even when the output gap is zero). It is self-evident from Table 2.1 that, according to these estimates and hence the underlying methodology in their construction, that full employment (say 2 per cent unemployment) would not be compatible with a zero

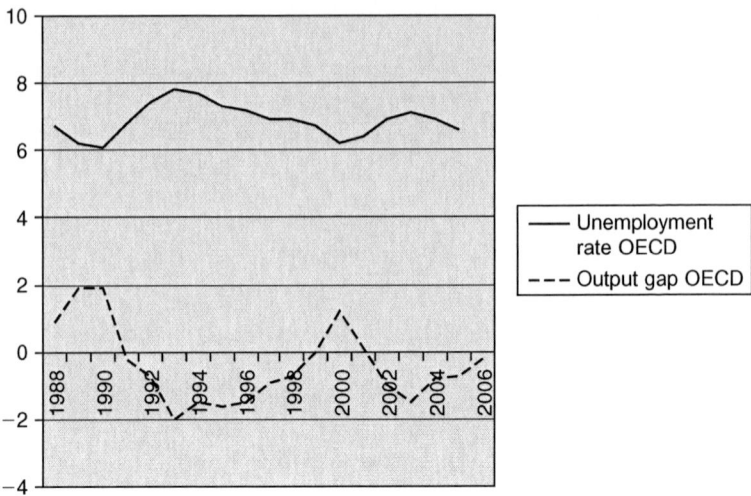

Figure 2.3 Time series on unemployment and output gap for OECD area
Source: OECD *Economic Outlook* (July 2006), Paris: OECD.

output gap, and would require in most countries for output to greatly exceed its trend level.

Figures 2.3–2.5 provide time series graphs for the OECD area, the UK and Greece. It is evident for the OECD as a whole that there has been no general trend in the rate of unemployment and that a calculated output gap of zero corresponds to an unemployment rate of around 7 per cent. For the UK a downward trend in unemployment goes alongside a trendless output gap, whereas for Greece an upward trend in unemployment goes with a trendless output gap. These movements indicate that the relationship between the rate of unemployment and the output gap changes over time. In the case of the UK, declining unemployment went alongside no general rise in capacity utilization (as far as that is indicated by the output gap), whereas in Greece, rising unemployment went alongside no general decline in capacity utilization.

The position in many European countries is a combination of significant levels of unemployment and output estimated to be close to trend. This is suggestive of a position portrayed by Kalecki in terms of a lack of capacity. This could mean that inflationary pressures would come from a sustained increase in demand, yet arising from a lack of capacity. This may be modified by the ready availability of competing imports, but it

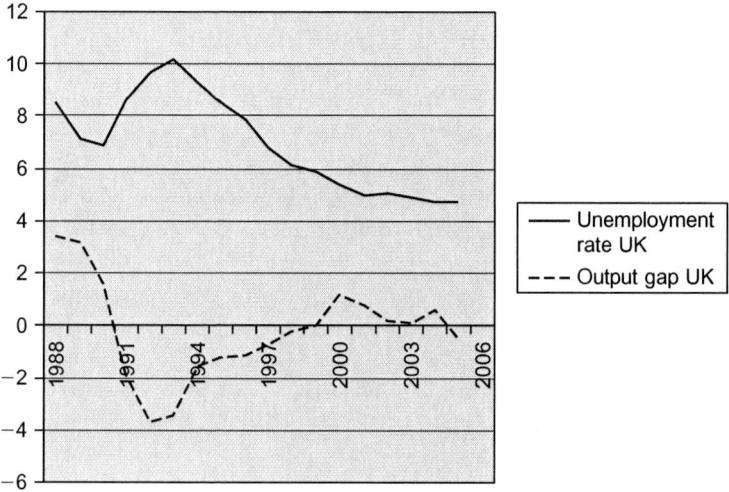

Figure 2.4 Time series on unemployment and output gap for UK
Source: OECD *Economic Outlook* (July 2006), Paris: OECD.

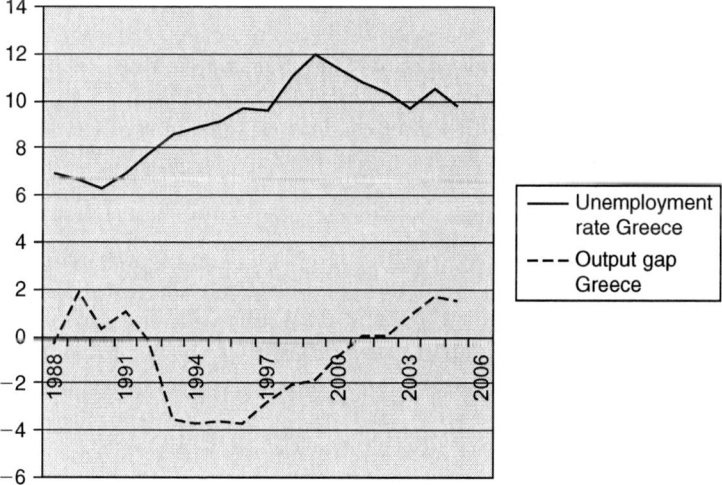

Figure 2.5 Time series on unemployment and output gap for Greece
Source: OECD *Economic Outlook* (July 2006), Paris: OECD.

would still mean that there are difficulties in reaching full employment through demand expansion due to a lack of capacity.

Conclusions

Although Kalecki is best-known for his discovery of the principle of effective demand and his analysis of the role of demand in the determination of the level of economic activity, he recognized the role of 'supply-side' factors on the level of employment. He argued that demand deficiency could overcome the scourge of unemployment through fiscal policy. He confronted many of the arguments which have subsequently been deployed against the effectiveness of fiscal policy. He did not, though, say much on the practicalities of ensuring that the fiscal stance could achieve full employment on a continuous basis, that is, issues of fine tuning.

Kalecki saw inflation as arising from growing demand which cannot be met by growing supply 'owing to scarcity of plant, labour, or raw materials' (Kalecki, 1997, p. 85) and the 'characteristic of inflation ... [which is] a rise in price of consumers' goods in relation to the relevant costs of labour and raw materials' (Kalecki, 1997, p. 86). Inflation arises when demand expands past the point of effective capacity. He did though suggest that such a lack of capacity was a feature of a 'backward economy' or one suffering the aftermath of war-time destruction. I have suggested that the lack of productive capacity is more pervasive than Kalecki suggested, and that for many Western European countries this may currently form a significant constraint on the expansion of economic activity.

Kalecki is well-known for his arguments that full employment capitalism would involve inflationary strains and the breakdown of 'discipline in the factories'. Industrialized countries have not had the luxury of testing the proposition during the past three decades. The experience of the 1960s and 1970s is suggestive that full employment capitalism would face these problems. Any 'fundamental reforms' since then have been in the form of repressing rather than liberating workers. These changes may have enabled capitalism in some Anglo-Saxon countries to approach, though not reach, full employment without inflationary pressures.

Notes

1. The change in the capital–output ratio is $d(K/Y)/dt = (1/Y)dK/dt - (K/Y)(1/Y)dY/dt$: the first term on the right-hand side is the net investment to output

ratio, and the second term is the capital–output ratio times the growth of output. Clearly a rise in the investment–output ratio leads to a rising capital–output ratio; but the condition for a stable capital–output ratio can readily be derived as the equality between the two terms on the right-hand side of the equation.
2. Recent work by Philip Arestis and myself on fiscal policy has restated and expanded the arguments advanced by Kalecki. See, for example, Arestis and Sawyer (2003, 2004, 2006).

References

Arestis, P. and M. Sawyer (2003) 'Reinventing Fiscal Policy', *Journal of Post Keynesian Economics* 26 (1): 4–25.
Arestis, P. and M. Sawyer (2004) 'On Fiscal Policy and Budget Deficits', *Intervention, Journal of Economics* 1 (2): 61–74.
Arestis, P. and M. Sawyer (2005) 'Aggregate Demand, Conflict and Capacity in the Inflationary Process', *Cambridge Journal of Economics* 29 (6): 959–74.
Arestis, P. and M. Sawyer (2006) 'Fiscal Policy Matters', *Public Finance* 54: 133–53.
Boltho, A. (ed.) (1982) *The European Economy: Growth and Crisis*, Oxford: Oxford University Press.
Bowles, S. (1985) 'The Production Process in a Competitive Economy: Walrasian, neoHobbesian and Marxian models', *American Economic Review* 75: 16–36.
Domar, E. D. (1944) 'The "Burden of the Debt" and the National Income', *American Economic Review* 34 (4): 798–827.
Dow, J. C. R. (1998) *Major Recessions: Britain and the World, 1920–1995*, London: Oxford University Press.
Duménil, G. and D. Lévy (1995) 'A post-Keynesian Long-term Equilibrium with Equalized Profit Rates? A Rejoinder to Amitava Dutt's Synthesis', *Review of Radical Political Economics* 27 (2): 135–41.
Dutt, A. K. (1987) 'Competition, Monopoly Power and the Uniform Rate of Profit', *Review of Radical Political Economics* 19 (4): 55–72.
Dutt, A. K. (1994) 'Classical Competition and post-Keynesian Monopoly Power: A Possible Synthesis', in M. Glick (ed.), *Competition, Technology and Money: Classical and Post-Keynesian Perspectives*, Aldershot: Edward Elgar: 40–51.
Dutt, A. K. (1995) 'Monopoly Power and Uniform Rates of Profit: A Reply to Glick-Campbell and Duménil-Lévy', *Review of Radical Political Economics* 27 (2): 142–53.
Glick, M. and D. A. Campbell (1995) 'Classical Competition and the Compatibility of Market Power and Uniform Rates of Profit', *Review of Radical Political Economics* 27 (2): 124–35.
Glyn, A. and R. Sutcliffe (1971) *The Profits Squeeze*, Harmondsworth: Penguin.
Kalecki, M. (1933) *Proba teorii koniunktury*, Warsaw: Institute of Research on Business Cycles and Prices. (English version appears in Kalecki (1990) pp. 66–108.)
Kalecki, M. (1943) 'Political Aspects of Full Employment', *Political Quarterly* 14 (4): 322–31.
Kalecki, M. (1990) *Collected Works of Michal Kalecki*, vol. 1, ed. J. Osiatyński, Oxford: Clarendon Press.

Kalecki, M. (1991) *Collected Works of Michal Kalecki*, vol. 2, ed. J. Osiatyński, Oxford: Clarendon Press.

Kalecki, M. (1997) Studies in Applied Economics 1940–1967; Miscellanea, Collected Works, vol. 7, ed. J. Osiatyński, Oxford: Clarendon Press.

Keynes, J. M. (1936) *The General Theory of Employment, Interest and Money*, London: Macmillan.

Laski, K. (1983) 'Kalecki's Political Aspects of Full Employment: Forty Years After', mimeo, Linz: Johannes Kepler Universitat.

Lerner, A. (1943) 'Functional Finance and the Federal Debt', *Social Research* 10 (1): 38–51; reprinted in W. Mueller (ed.) *Readings in Macroeconomics*, New York: Holt, Rinehart and Winston: 353–60.

Ministry of Reconstruction (1944) *Employment Policy*, Cmnd. 6527, London: HMSO.

Sawyer, M. (2001) 'The NAIRU, Aggregate Demand and Investment', *Metroeconomica*, 53 (1): 66–94.

Shapiro, C. and J. Stiglitz (1984) 'Equilibrium Unemployment as a Worker Discipline Device', *American Economic Review* 74 (3): 433–44.

3
The Relevance of Keynes Today with Particular Reference to Unemployment in Rich and Poor Countries

A. P. Thirlwall

It is worse in an impoverished world to provoke unemployment than to disappoint the rentier.

(J. M. Keynes, *Essays in Persuasion*, 1931, p. 103)

Introduction and personal reminiscences

The world has masses and masses of surplus labour. According to the International Labour Organization (ILO) in Geneva, over one billion workers, or one-third of the world's total labour force, are either openly unemployed with no work at all, or disguisedly unemployed in the sense that they work a suboptimal number of hours and would like to work more, but can't. Job creation for all those who want to work at the prevailing money wage is one of the great economic and social challenges of the twenty-first century. Not only is unemployment an economic waste, it is also a cause of poverty, stress-related illnesses, marriage breakdown and sometimes civil unrest. Indeed, for survival and basic human dignity, it could be argued that in a civilized society, everyone should have the right to work, just as Yunus Muhammad (2003), in the context of developing countries, has argued that everyone (not just the rich) should have the right to credit as a means of escaping from poverty.[1] This is not a new sentiment. Adam Smith (1776) expressed it in the *Wealth of Nations* thus:

> The property which every man has in his own labour, as it is the original foundation of all property, so it is the most sacred and inviolable. The patrimony of a poor man lies in the strength and dexterity of his

hands, and to hinder him from employing this strength and dexterity in what manner he thinks proper without injury to his neighbour, is a plain violation of this most sacred property. (p. 136)

I've had a long standing interest in unemployment and its causes, both in rich developed countries and in poor developing countries. Most of my research in the 1960s and 1970s was on the nature and types of unemployment in the UK, and on the causes of regional differences in unemployment (e.g. Thirlwall, 1966, 1969c, 1974b, 1975; Harris and Thirlwall, 1968; Dixon and Thirlwall, 1975). I have always reacted, as Keynes did in the 1930s (Keynes, 1936), to the view that most unemployment in most contexts is voluntary or 'natural' due to the laziness of workers or the malfunctioning of labour markets, and has nothing to do with the demand for labour in the aggregate. After all, in wartime, everyone is employed. My reading of economic history is that most episodes of high unemployment have been of an involuntary nature – a type of unemployment now largely forgotten by a younger generation of economists brought up on American textbooks full of the so-called 'new Keynesian' economics which attributes the major part of unemployment to institutional rigidities, particularly wage and price stickiness (see Mankiw, 2007), but which has nothing to do with Keynes's explanation of unemployment at all. To give one amusing illustration, recently I was an assessor of candidates for the Government Economic Service in the UK. One of the questions on the macroeconomics exam paper was: 'Why is Unemployment in the European Union so High?'. None of the candidates who answered the question mentioned 'a lack of demand'. All the answers centred around minimum wages, wage rigidity, labour immobility, high unemployment compensation payments and stubborn trade unions. When I asked one of the candidates in an interview whether he had heard of the Keynesian revolution, he replied, 'I've heard of Keynes, but not of the revolution'!

As a graduate student in the US, I took a course in the History of Economic Thought, and Keynes's *General Theory* was one of the set texts (along with Marshall's *Principles* and Chamberlin's *Monopolistic Competition*). For the first time, I studied the *General Theory* in depth, and appreciated more fully than ever before where all the important concepts in modern macroeconomics come from, which many of the younger generation of economists don't seem to be aware of.[2] The central message I learnt, of course (if I didn't know it already), was that in contrast to classical theory, not all unemployment in an economy is necessarily frictional, structural or voluntary due to a refusal of workers to accept a cut in their real wage. There can be such a thing as involuntary unemployment because:

1. Workers can be off their supply curve for most of the time because they are not in a position to equate the real wage with the marginal disutility of work, and certainly will not withdraw their labour in the event of a small rise in the price of wage goods, i.e. the supply of labour is not a function of the real wage as in classical theory, but the money wage.
2. An economy can get stuck at a point where workers would like to work more at the current *money* wage (and a lower real wage, if necessary) given the opportunity, but they cannot.
3. At the aggregate level, it is the level of employment, determined by effective demand, that determines the real wage, not vice versa.
4. A cut in money wages is no guarantee of a cut in real wages because wages are both a cost and a component of demand. Falling wages may mean falling prices, particularly in competitive markets.

The only way of analysing the effect of wage cuts on employment is by analysing the effect of wage cuts on the components of aggregate demand; namely consumption, investment and the foreign balance. Most important of all, Keynesian conclusions concerning the long-run breakdown of effective demand and involuntary unemployment do *not* depend on the assumption that money wages and prices are rigid, but rather depend on uncertainty associated with the existence of money, and what Keynes called 'the peculiar properties of money'; its 'zero elasticity of production' and its 'zero elasticity of substitution'. This means firstly that money is not like any other good because factors of production are not employed in its production (or money doesn't grow on trees as Paul Davidson (1978) would say), so that as economic agents switch from buying goods to holding money there is a net diminution in the demand for goods; secondly, even if the price of goods falls, and the rate of interest rises, agents still want to hold money.

My PhD was partly on regional differences in unemployment in the UK where I first formally identified a cyclical element, and that the cyclical component was higher in the high unemployment regions than in the low unemployment regions (Thirlwall, 1966). By definition, cyclical unemployment is demand-deficient unemployment. When I gave a paper to the British Association for the Advancement of Science in 1973 on the topic of 'Regional Economic Disparities and Regional Policy in the Common Market' (Thirlwall, 1974a) arguing the case for a demand stimulus in high unemployment regions of Europe, it elicited a very hostile (typically neoclassical) response from Harry Johnson who that year was President of the Economics Section of the Society (Section F). He wrote (Johnson, 1974):

> My main objection to the Thirlwall approach – is that a great deal of fairly high-powered theory is laid out in defending the need for regional policy and explaining why effective policy is likely to be much more difficult than it seems, without any questioning of the hypothesis that the source of regional disparities is to be found in demand and not in supply factors. After generations of regional disparities, going well back beyond the demand deficiency period of the 1920s and 1930s and involving pretty much the same regional disparity pattern in spite of tremendous changes in British industrial location and production structure, there is at least plausibility in the alternative hypothesis that regional social structures arrive at different preferred patterns as to unemployment rates and real wages while employed, the differences reflecting observable differences between the utility values of leisure time on the one hand and material standards of living on the other. If this is so, regional differences in unemployment rates may represent equilibrium and not disequilibrium regional social choices; and policy, if it seeks (perhaps socially wrongly) to equalise regional employment percentages, may have to tackle basic social attitudes on the supply side of work desires rather than employment opportunities made available by subsidy policies. (p. xviii)

This is long-hand[3] for the typical neoclassical view that the explanation of regional and national differences in unemployment is that work/leisure preferences differ spatially, or, more pejoratively, people in some locations are lazier than in others. This is also what typified the Thatcher view of high unemployment in Britain in the 1980s, summed up in the immortal words of one of her Ministers, Norman Tebbit, that unemployed workers should 'get on their bikes' – there is plenty of work out there to be done. Unfortunately, what this view of unemployment doesn't explain is why lazy people should all be concentrated in particular geographic locations, especially when institutional structures do not differ interregionally. Why are they not randomly distributed across the country?

As well as doing research on unemployment, I was also involved in the late 1960s in policy-making to reduce unemployment, working as an Economic Adviser in the newly created Research and Planning Division of the Department of Employment and Productivity, charged with the responsibility of providing the economic rationale for reform of the Employment Exchange system in the UK, which at that time had the dual function of dispensing unemployment compensation payments (hence its dole queue image) and finding work for people. We argued the case for separation of the two functions, and for the establishment of a network of modern, computer-connected, Job Centres across the country with the sole responsibility of matching the supply and demand for labour to reduce levels of frictional and structural unemployment. Such a network was created, with estimates of the conditions under which the benefits in terms of increased output would exceed costs (Thirlwall 1969b, 1972). Unemployment in the UK was rising at this time, and the Phillips Curve was also beginning to shift outwards. In fact, one of the arguments for 'more active manpower policies' was to improve the trade-off between inflation and unemployment because it was shown formally (and empirically) that the greater the degree of disequilibrium between occupational and regional labour markets, the more unfavourable the aggregate trade-off will be (Lipsey, 1960; Archibald, 1969; Thirlwall, 1969a). It is not easy to evaluate the success of active manpower policies because their effects at any one time tend to get swamped by aggregate demand changes. This was true in the UK in the 1970s and 1980s when unemployment rose unrelentingly, firstly as a result of the world recession following the oil price increase in 1973, and then as a result of demand deflation to squeeze inflation out of the economy, culminating in the ill-fated monetarist experiment of the early 1980s which led to unemployment rising to 3.4 million in 1986 (or 11.2 per cent of the workforce). Unemployment has never returned to the levels of 1.5 to 2.5 per cent, which were the norm in the 1950s and 1960s. The policies of the 1970s and 1980s, which devastated large sections of British industry, appear, in retrospect, to have done permanent damage to the ability of the economy to operate at such low levels of unemployment without causing inflationary pressure, despite the emasculation of the trade unions. The phenomenon of hysteresis has caused frictional and structural unemployment to rise in the UK, despite institutional changes to improve the functioning of labour markets.

But economists rarely talk about types of unemployment any more. They talk of 'natural' rates of unemployment; and Keynesian modes of thinking have disappeared almost entirely. There has been a return to pre-Keynesian, even anti-Keynesian, modes of thinking, particularly in the US and within the European Union. In an article entitled 'The Death of Keynesian Economics', written in 1980, Robert Lucas (later a recipient of the Nobel Prize for economics) went as far as to say 'one cannot find good under-forty economists who identify themselves or their work as "Keynesian". Indeed, people often take offence if referred to as Keynesians. At research seminars, people don't take Keynesian theorising seriously any more; the audience starts to whisper and giggle at one another'. For Lucas, and his followers, there is no such thing as involuntary unemployment, but as Frank Hahn (1982) once said, 'I wish he [Robert Lucas] would become involuntarily unemployed and then he would know what the concept is all about'!

In the rest of this chapter, I shall briefly discuss pre-Keynesian (classical) employment theory; I shall rehabilitate and resurrect Keynes's concept of involuntary unemployment; I shall apply the relevance of the concept to the high rate of unemployment in the core countries of the European Union, especially since the implementation of the Maastricht Treaty in 1992, leading up to monetary union in 1999. I am critical of the idea that this high unemployment somehow constitutes a 'natural' rate. Finally I will consider the relevance of Keynesian thinking in the context of developing countries, and particularly the role of deficit financing, and the inflation tax, where the major task of employment creation is to raise the rate of capital accumulation and move towards the use of more labour intensive techniques of production, simultaneously.

Classical employment theory

Keynes's understanding of the classical theory of employment (and unemployment), and his attack on it, was largely based on Arthur Pigou's book *The Theory of Unemployment*, published in 1933. According to Pigou, and the latter-day (neo-) classical economists that now dominate thinking and policy-making in the eurozone of the European Union:

> with perfectly free competition among work people and labour perfectly mobile, the nature of the relation (i.e. between the real wage rates for which people stipulate and the demand function for labour) will be very simple. There will always be at work a strong tendency for wage rates to be so related to demand that everybody will be employed. Hence in stable conditions everyone will actually be employed. The implication is that such unemployment exists at any time is due wholly to the fact that changes in demand conditions are continually taking place and that frictional resistances prevent

the appropriate wage adjustments from being made instantaneously. (p. 252)

If the demand for labour is a decreasing function of the real wage on the assumption of diminishing returns to labour (the first classical postulate), and the supply of labour is an increasing function of the real wage to compensate for the increasing marginal disutility of work (the second classical postulate), then what Pigou says is tautologically true; there must always be a real wage that clears the labour market. But as Keynes notes in the *General Theory* (p. 275), Pigou's book, *The Theory of Unemployment*, is a misnomer because it is not about *unemployment*, but about how much employment there will be, given the supply function of labour when the conditions for full employment are satisfied. The book is not capable of telling us what determines the *actual* level of employment, and has no bearing on involuntary unemployment. In fact, the two classical employment postulates admit the possibility of only two types of unemployment, 'frictional' and 'voluntary', and there are only four means of increasing employment: (i) by reducing frictions in the labour market; (ii) by a decrease in the marginal disutility of labour; (iii) by an increase in the marginal physical product of labour; and (iv) by an increase in the price of non-wage goods compared to the price of wage goods. But Keynes asks rhetorically, 'is it true that the above categories are comprehensive in view of the fact that the population generally is seldom doing as much work as it would like to do on the basis of the current wage?' (p. 7). Surely, says Keynes, 'more labour would, as a rule, be forthcoming at the existing money wage if it were demanded' (p. 7).

Here we come to the nub of the issue. Is the supply of labour a function of the real wage (as classical theory assumes) or the money wage? Keynes is in no doubt that it is the latter, firstly because workers do not normally withdraw their labour in the event of prices rising (with money wages constant), and, secondly, in any case, workers are not in a position to equate their real wage with the marginal disutility of work because they can only determine their money wage and have no control over prices. As Keynes remarks:

> it is important to emphasise that the whole of Professor Pigou's book is written on the assumption that any rise in the cost of living, however moderate, relatively to the money wage, will cause the withdrawal from the labour market of a number of workers greater than that of all the existing unemployed (p. 277)

and

> it is fantastically far removed from the facts to assume, at a time when statistical unemployment in Great Britain exceeded 2,000,000 (i.e. when there were 2,000,000 men willing to work at the existing money wage) that any rise in the cost of living, however moderate, relatively to the money wage would cause withdrawal from the labour market of more than the equivalent of all these 2,000,000 men. (p. 277)

Attempts to reduce real wages by cutting money wages would likely be resisted because workers are concerned with wage relativities, but

> it would be impractical to resist every reduction in real wages due to a change in the purchasing power of money which affects all workers alike; and in fact reductions in real wages arising in this way are not, as a rule, resisted unless they proceed to an extreme degree. (p. 14)[4]

Involuntary unemployment

By attacking the second classical employment postulate that the supply of labour is a function of the real wage, and instead making the supply of labour a function of the money wage, Keynes was able to identify a third type of unemployment, in addition to frictional and voluntary unemployment, which is involuntary. Keynes writes: 'we need to throw over the second postulate of the classical doctrine and to work out the behaviour of a system in which involuntary unemployment in the strict sense is possible' (p. 17). His definition of involuntary unemployment is worth repeating in full, if only to remind those of classical/neoclassical persuasion that it has nothing to do with rigid money wages:

> men are involuntarily unemployed if, in the event of a small rise in the price of wage goods relatively to the money wage, both the aggregate supply of labour willing to work for the current money wage and the aggregate demand for it at that wage would be greater than the existing volume of employment. (p. 15)

The definition is actually unnecessarily complicated, and one could simply say that a person is involuntarily unemployed if they are willing to work at the going money wage given the opportunity. This could be associated in the short run with a lower or higher real wage depending on whether there is diminishing or increasing returns to labour. Keynes assumed, like the classical theorists, that increased employment would be associated with a lower real wage because of diminishing returns,[5] but, as Dunlop (1938) and Tarshis (1939) first showed, employment and real wages tend to move together in the same direction, not inversely. Keynes's (1939) reaction to Dunlop and Tarshis was to say:

> it seems we have been living all these years on a generalisation which held good, by exception in the years 1880–1886, which was the formative period in Marshall's thought on this matter, but has never once held good in the fifty years since he crystallised it. (p. 38)

But he was pleased because he said that the inverse relation between employment and real wages was inconvenient for his theory because:

> it had a tendency to offset the influence of the main forces which I was discussing and made it necessary for me to introduce qualifications which I need not have troubled with if I could have adopted the contrary generalisation [i.e. of a *positive* relation between employment and the real wage]. (p. 40)

In particular: 'the practical case for a planned expansionary policy is considerably reinforced', because no reduction in the real wage is implied (p. 45).

To explain involuntary unemployment, Keynes resurrects Malthus's concept of 'effective demand', and he was puzzled why later classical economists forgot the concept. He blames Ricardo for accepting Say's Law of Markets that supply creates its own demand: 'Ricardo conquered England as the Holy Inquisition conquered Spain'. He goes on:

> the great puzzle of Effective Demand with which Malthus had wrestled vanished from economic literature. You will not find it mentioned even once in the whole works of Marshall, Edgeworth and Professor Pigou, from whose hands classical theory has received its most mature embodiment. It could only live furtively, below the surface, in the underworlds of Karl Marx, Silvio Gessell or Major Douglas. (p. 32)

Keynes might express his sentiment today as: 'the concept of effective demand with which I wrestled has vanished from the economics literature. You will not find it mentioned hardly at all in modern textbooks or in financial organisations such as the European Central Bank... it only lives on furtively in the underworld of Post Keynesian economics.'

Remember the quote from Robert Lucas that economists don't take my theorising seriously any more; the audience starts to laugh and giggle at one another'.

Keynes was also puzzled why contemporary economists continued to ignore the growing divorce between what classical theory predicted and the facts of experience:

> professional economists after Malthus, were apparently unmoved by the lack of correspondence between the results of their theory and the facts of observation ... a discrepancy which the ordinary man has not failed to observe, with the result of his growing unwillingness to accord the economists that measure of respect which he gives to other groups of scientists whose theoretical results are confirmed by observation when they are applied to the facts. (p. 33)

Keynes's only explanation was that:

> contemporary thought is still deeply steeped in the notion that if people do not spend their money in one way, they will spend it in another – [but] those who think in this way are deceived, nevertheless, by an optical illusion which makes two essentially different activities [i.e. saving and investment] appear to be the same. They are fallaciously supposing that there is a nexus which unites decisions to abstain from present consumption with decisions to provide for future consumption; whereas the motives which determine the latter are not linked in any special way with the motives that determine the former. (pp. 20–1)

Here lies the heart of the Keynesian revolution: that for the first time the schedules of saving and investment are divorced from one another; there is no price that necessarily equilibrates the two at full employment, so there can be a deficiency of aggregate demand; output is not necessarily self-financing; supply does not necessarily create its own demand; Say's Law is buried once and for all.

In place of Say's Law, we have the principle of effective demand, or more precisely the point of effective demand which determines the aggregate level of employment in the economy, and which has a *unique* value. This is determined (see Figure 3.1(a)) where the expected receipts schedule (DD), from the employment of N number of workers, composed of consumption (D_1) and investment expenditure (D_2), cuts from above the necessary proceeds schedule (ZZ) determined by the cost of

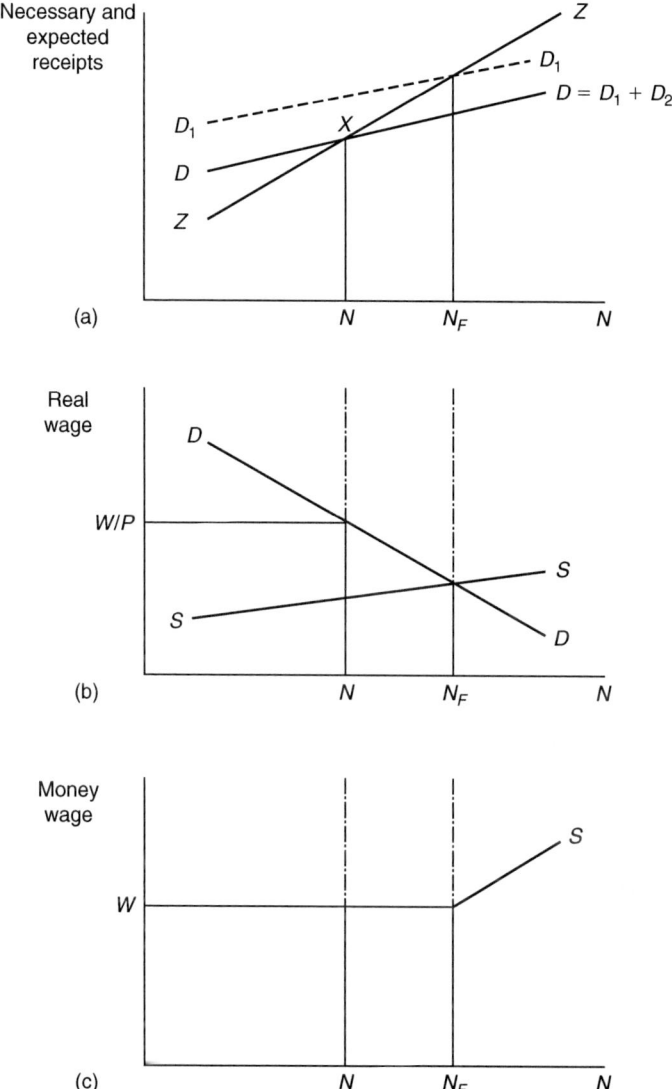

Figure 3.1 Keynesian involuntary unemployment

employing N number of workers at point X. DD is flatter than ZZ because as employment and income increases, consumption increases but not by as much as income. By contrast, in classical theory (or with Say's Law) there is no unique point of effective demand because aggregate demand (expected receipts) always accommodates itself to aggregate supply (necessary receipts) through the interest rate mechanism. In effect, DD and ZZ are coincident with one another; or as Keynes puts it:

> that is to say effective demand, instead of having a unique equilibrium value, is an infinite range of values all equally admissible; and the amount of employment is indeterminate except in so far as the marginal disutility of labour sets an upper limit. (p. 26)

In other words:

> Say's Law that the aggregate demand price of output as a whole is equal to its aggregate supply price for all volumes of output, is equivalent to the proposition that there is no obstacle to full employment. If, however, this is not the true law relating the aggregate demand and supply functions, there is a vitally important chapter of economic theory which remains to be written and without which all discussions concerning the volume of employment are futile. (p. 23)

Once the point of effective demand is determined in Figure 3.1(a), giving an employment level N, this determines the level of the real wage in Figure 3.1(b). Keynes says explicitly:

> for every value of N there is a corresponding marginal productivity of labour in the wage-goods industries; and it is this which determines the real wage... The propensity to consume and the rate of new investment determine between them the volume of employment, and the volume of employment is uniquely related to a given level of real wages – *not the other way round*. (emphasis added) (p. 29)

The level of employment, N, is below the full employment level, N_F, where the supply and demand for labour are equal, but the cause is not real wage resistance. Many workers are off their (classical) supply curve, and at least NN_F workers would be willing to work at a lower real wage given the opportunity with an expansion of aggregate demand in the economy, i.e. with an upward shift in the DD curve to D_1D_1 in Figure 3.1(a). Figure 3.1(c) shows the same number of workers willing to work at the same money wage, but at a lower real wage, and this is Keynes's measure of involuntary unemployment. Figures 3.1(a) to 3.1(c) can be summed up in Keynes's own words:

> Hence the volume of employment in equilibrium depends on (i) the aggregate supply function [ZZ]...(ii) the propensity to consume

$[D_1]$... and (iii) the volume of investment $[D_2]$... This is the essence of the General Theory of Employment. (p. 29)

Unemployment in the European Union

How does all this relate to the unemployment currently prevailing in the European Union (EU)? It is directly related because policy-makers in the EU, and particularly the European Central Bank (ECB), effectively deny that unemployment existing beyond point N can be reduced by policies of demand expansion without creating excessive inflationary pressure (or, more precisely, without accelerating inflation). The current unemployment rate in the core EU and eurozone countries of Germany, France and Italy is close to 8 per cent. Apparently, none of the unemployed are willing to work at the going money wage given the opportunity. In other words point N (92 per cent employment) is regarded as a 'natural' rate of employment, determined by structural factors and the characteristics of the labour market. There is no involuntary unemployment. This is what needs challenging, which it is not difficult to do. Firstly, there is the empirical evidence of what has happened to unemployment in the EU countries since the 1960s, and in the eurozone countries since the Maastricht Treaty was signed in 1992, paving the way for monetary union in 1999. Secondly, the concept of a 'natural' rate of employment (or unemployment) is so flawed in its underlying assumptions, and in the way that it is measured, as to be virtually useless as a guide to the conduct of economic policy for the achievement of full employment without inflation, as the performance of the US economy has demonstrated over the last decade or so (see below).

Applied labour economists seem to be divided over the precise causes of the rise in unemployment in the EU countries since the 1960s, but none of the serious studies attributes it solely to structural or institutional changes in the labour market. How could they, because as Blanchard and Wolfers (2000) point out: 'Explanations (of high unemployment) based solely on institutions... run... into a major empirical problem: many of the institutions were present when unemployment was low... Thus, while labour market institutions can potentially explain cross-country differences today, they do not appear able to explain the general evolution of unemployment over time'. Similarly, Oswald (1997) remarks: 'Despite conventional wisdom, high unemployment [in Europe] does not appear to be primarily the result of things like overgenerous benefits, trade union power, taxes or wage "inflexibilities"'. Nickell *et al.* (2005) provide, perhaps, the most thorough (econometric) and eclectic story that, of the 6–7 percentage point rise in the unemployment rate between 1960 and the mid-1990s, one-half can be attributed to institutional changes in the labour market, such as the unemployment compensation payment system, the system of wage determination, employment protection, labour taxes and barriers to labour mobility, and the other half can be attributed to demand deficiency. The high level of unemployment has persisted, and even increased in some countries since the mid-1990s, so that at least 3–4 percentage points of unemployment in the EU can be described as involuntary, or approximately seven million workers.[6]

In the big core countries of the EU, the situation worsened in the 1990s because to qualify to participate in monetary union, the Maastricht Treaty required that countries meet certain convergence criteria relating to interest rates, inflation, government budget deficits and government debt relative to GDP. The achievement of the latter three targets all required deflation as far as the major countries of the potential eurozone were concerned, and it is no wonder unemployment rose. Table 3.1

Table 3.1 Average levels of unemployment and consumer price inflation before and after 1992 (%)

Eurozone countries	Unemployment (%)			Inflation (%)		
	1980–1991	1992–2006	Change	1980–1991	1992–2006	Change
Austria	–	4.2[a]	–	4.2	2.4	−1.5
Belgium	8.8	8.4	−0.4	5.6	2.3	−3.3
Finland	5.3	11.4	+6.1	8.9	1.6	−7.3
France	8.5	10.2	+1.7	8.2	1.9	−6.3
Germany	5.6	8.3	+2.7	3.1	2.3	−0.8
Ireland	15.0[b]	8.2	−6.8	5.9[b]	3.5	−2.4
Italy	8.0	9.6	+1.7	15.2	3.5	−11.4
Luxembourg	2.5[b]	2.9	+0.4	5.4	2.5	−2.9
Netherlands	7.1	4.5	−2.6	2.9	2.7	−0.2
Portugal	6.9[c]	5.9	−1.0	24.0[c]	5.1	−18.9
Spain	14.3	12.9	−1.4	14.3	4.5	−9.8
Sweden	2.6	7.3	+4.7	11.6	1.7	−9.9
Non-euro countries						
Denmark	6.8[b]	5.8	−1.0	5.3[b]	2.4	−2.9
UK	9.2	6.6	−2.6	8.4	2.2	−6.2
USA	9.2	6.6	−2.6	5.9	3.2	−2.7

Notes: [a] 1973–2006; [b] 1982–1991; [c] 1983–1991.
Source: OECD Standardised Unemployment and Inflation Statistics (Paris: OECD).

shows the average level of unemployment (and the rate of consumer price inflation) in the eurozone countries plus, for comparison, Denmark and the UK outside the eurozone, and the US (outside the EU), in the 12 years before the Maastricht Treaty was signed and 15 years after. It is true that unemployment has fallen in some of the smaller countries, such as Belgium (marginally); Ireland (dramatically); the Netherlands and Portugal. Spain also shows a slight fall, but unemployment rose significantly for seven years between 1992 and 1999. But in the big eurozone countries of Germany, France and Italy, unemployment has increased significantly, and so too in Finland and Sweden – more than doubling in both cases. This is a very poor record for a monetary union which promised increased trade, faster growth and job creation. In Denmark and the UK, which took the decision not to be part of the eurozone, unemployment has fallen; so, too, in the US.

There is very little evidence that the *increase* in unemployment in the major eurozone countries is of the 'structural' (non-demand deficient) variety. If it was, unemployment and inflation would have risen together, but it can be seen from Figure 3.2 (constructed from the data in Table 3.1) that in Germany, France, Italy, Finland and Sweden unemployment rose as inflation fell, suggesting a conventional negative trade-off between

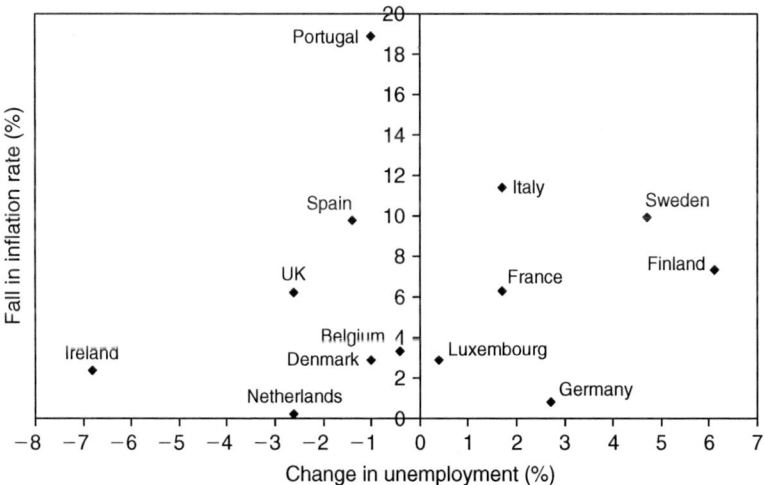

Figure 3.2 The relationship between the change in unemployment and the change in the inflation rate, 1980–91 to 1992–2006
Source: Table 3.1.

Figure 3.3 The relationship between inflation and unemployment across countries, 1992–2006
Source: Table 3.1.

these two variables. The price of attempting to achieve price stability in the eurozone has been the sacrifice of jobs. Also across countries, at least in the period 1992–2006, there is a suggestive negative relation between the rate of inflation and the level of unemployment, as can be seen in Figure 3.3. There are outliers on the graph – Portugal, Ireland, Spain and Italy – but ten of the countries lie almost on a straight line showing that the lower the inflation rate, the higher the unemployment rate, and vice versa.

In some smaller countries where unemployment has fallen, inflation has also fallen, suggesting an improvement in the trade-off between inflation and unemployment. This is to be welcomed, but the fact remains that in the big countries of the eurozone, which account for over 70 per cent of the workforce, there has been a chronic deficiency of demand for labour.

The reason for this demand deficiency is that both fiscal and monetary policy have been deflationary through the Growth and Stability Pact on the one hand, and by the actions of the European Central Bank (ECB) on the other, whose only remit is to keep the rate of inflation below 2 per cent per annum without regard to the growth of output, employment or unemployment. The Growth and Stability Pact, agreed at the Dublin Summit in 1996, restricted government budget deficits to 3 per cent of

GDP, regardless of the nature of the deficits and whether or not they were structural or cyclical. Romano Prodi, former President of the European Commission, was later to describe the Pact as the Growth and Stupidity Pact, and he was right to do so. As John Williamson (1980) once said of the target for the Public Sector Borrowing Requirement (PSBR) in the UK, introduced by the Thatcher government in 1979: 'to treat a nominal, inflation unadjusted, cyclically unadjusted PSBR target as a constraint on economic policy (let alone as an objective) is economic barbarism'. The Pact now seems to have fallen into abeyance, but the damage has been done by governments cutting expenditure to try to meet the target, even in recessions.

While a fixed deficit to GDP ratio pays no regard to demand management, neither does the ECB in setting interest rates. In fact, the ECB does not believe in demand management, as if the Keynesian revolution had never happened. Unemployment is the outcome of the characteristics of the labour market; rigid wages and labour immobility. It has nothing to do with the level of demand in the economy. The only remit of the ECB is to keep the rate of inflation in the eurozone below 2 per cent per annum, despite any scientific evidence that 2 per cent is an 'optimal' rate of inflation for maximizing growth and employment.[7] The instrument it uses is the interest rate which it threatens to raise if there is any sign that inflation might exceed the 2 per cent target, which then sends damaging signals to the private sector, particularly investors. This is voodoo economics. Apart from the fact that the eurozone is not an optimal currency area, which no-one disputes (not even the 'father' of optimal currency areas, Robert Mundell), the interest rate set by the ECB will always be some compromise rate which suits no one country in particular: too low for countries overheating and too high for countries that are stagnant. The interest rate also affects, of course, the euro exchange rate, which can damage growth if monetary policy is 'too tight' and the currency becomes overvalued. Mr Eddie George, former governor of the Bank of England, once famously declared: 'the Bank's job is to maintain macro-stability for the whole country, and discrepancies between regions and industries were regrettable but inevitable'. A less polite way of saying the same thing would have been 'high unemployment in the north of England (and elsewhere) is a price worth paying for "southern stability"'. Equally the President of the ECB could say the same for the countries of the eurozone; high unemployment in Germany, France and Italy is a price worth paying for price stability in the eurozone as a whole. It is not an attractive scenario, especially in view of the ECB's stubbornness to consider any alternative stance. Is it a 'price worth paying'? How does it know in advance that if it is more relaxed in its monetary policy, unemployment will not come down without inflation rising? The Reagan government in the US had the same attitude to monetary policy and unemployment in the early 1980s when unemployment approached 10 per cent, but look what happened there. *Faut de mieux*, Reagan became the greatest Keynesian ever to occupy the White House. Expansionary policies were continued by the Clinton administration in the 1990s. Unemployment fell to below 5 per cent without accelerating inflation, when the majority consensus in the 1980s was that the 'natural' rate of unemployment was 7–8 per cent (the average level then prevailing). Now the US Federal Reserve officially believes that it can operate with unemployment of 4.5 per cent in the long term without generating extra inflation. In fact, the forecasts for 2007 and 2008 are that unemployment will be 4.5 to 4.75 per cent, while inflation will *fall* from 2 to 2.5 per cent in 2007 to 1.75 to 2 per cent in 2008. So much for the concept of a 'natural' rate of unemployment if it can change so quickly. The staff at the Federal Reserve describe the natural rate as 'imprecise and time-varying', which is reminiscent of Friedman's description of the relation between changes in the money supply and inflation as 'long and variable'. At least the Fed is honest, but Keynesian economists could have told it four decades ago that there is nothing natural about the 'natural' rate of unemployment. As I showed in a paper in 1983 (Thirlwall, 1983), estimates of the natural rate of unemployment from an expectations-augmented Phillips curve will always mirror the actual rate of unemployment because the determinants of the so-called natural rate (i.e. the level of structural unemployment and labour productivity growth in a growing economy) depend on the strength of aggregate demand in the economy as a whole. In other words, the concept of the natural rate of unemployment is a theoretical construct with no operational significance. It cannot be known in advance. The ECB needs to remove its classical blinkers, and to test the water as the US did. Unemployment is too serious to be dictated by voodoo economics.

Unemployment in poor countries

While unemployment in rich developed countries is serious, particularly in some of the big countries of the EU, its magnitude is dwarfed by the level of unemployment and underemployment in poor developing countries. Most of the one billion workers identified by the International Labour Organization (ILO) as unemployed or underemployed reside in the rural and petty service sectors of the Third World. The nature of this surplus labour is complex, and so is its solution. It has both 'structural' and Keynesian features, and its solution requires a combination of a faster rate of capital accumulation, more labour intensive techniques of production, Keynesian policies to maintain aggregate demand in the face of shocks, and deliberate government policies to promote employment by investment in labour intensive public infrastructure projects which absorb surplus labour and at the same time increase the capacity of the economy to produce. Keynes would recognize the role of the State in developing countries, as he did in the case of demand-deficient unemployment in developed countries, although the nature of the recommended policies would differ.

One major component of surplus labour in poor countries is disguised unemployment on the land, which takes the form of too many workers working too few hours (a suboptimal day), at least outside of the harvest season. This depresses labour productivity and is a major cause of poverty. It is no accident that the ILO's estimate of one billion unemployed and underemployed is approximately the same as the World Bank's estimate of one billion living in extreme poverty on less than $1 per day. The underlying cause of underemployment, or disguised unemployment, on the land is the imbalance between the growth of demand for land-based products and the growth of supply. It is difficult for the growth of demand to keep pace with the growth of supply because the income elasticity of demand for most basic agricultural products is less than unity – otherwise known as Engel's Law. If the natural growth of the agricultural labour force is 2 per cent per annum (p.a.), and labour productivity through technical progress rises by 3 per cent p.a., the potential growth of agricultural supply is 5 per cent p.a. If the income elasticity of demand for agricultural products is, say, 0.7, an economy would have to grow at approximately 7 per cent p.a. for labour to be retained in the agricultural sector. Most poor developing countries do not grow at that rate. Either the surplus labour stays in the rural sector, and depresses average product, or it migrates to the cities. Migrants who cannot find work in the formal sector of the economy crowd into the petty service sector, or informal sector of the economy, depressing average product there too. This underemployment in cities is another major source of surplus labour. In fact, for the first time this year (2007) in the history of the world, it is estimated that more people now live in urban areas than in the rural sector, with the possibility that there is now as much surplus labour in the cities as there is in the countryside.

This is the source of unemployment and underemployment on the supply side, but what about the demand side? Why can't redundant rural workers find jobs in the modern industrial sector? The problem lies in the fact that the rate of new job creation is not sufficient to absorb all the labour becoming available, and this has two, not mutually exclusive, explanations. Firstly, for a given set of production techniques (or a given capital to labour ratio), the problem is an imbalance between the rate of growth of capital and the rate of growth of the effective labour force (the natural growth of the labour force plus the growth of labour productivity). The only solution is an increase in the rate of capital accumulation. Secondly, however, it could be argued that techniques of production are too capital intensive. If techniques of production are flexible, the challenge is to find more labour intensive ways of producing output without sacrificing efficiency, or the level of saving.[8] Here the Keynes-Harrod model of the relation between the natural rate of growth and the warranted rate of growth becomes a useful pedagogic device. The terms 'natural rate of growth' (g_n) and 'warranted rate of growth' (g_w) are normally associated with Harrod's 'An Essay in Dynamic Theory' (1939), where he first coined them, but I deliberately put Keynes's name first because, in fact, the concepts were anticipated by Keynes in his lecture to the Eugenics Society in 1937 on 'Some Economic Consequences of a Declining Population'. Consider, he says, a society with a savings ratio of 8–15 per cent and a capital-output ratio of 4, giving a rate of capital accumulation which will absorb savings of 2 to 4 per cent. With a constant capital-output ratio, this is also the required growth of output. But can this growth rate be guaranteed? Historically, it appeared to Keynes that one-half of the increase in capital accumulation could be attributed to population growth; the other half to increased living standards (or growth of labour productivity). Now suppose population growth falls to zero. Since the standard of life cannot be expected to grow at more than 1 per cent p.a., this means the demand for capital will only grow at 1 per cent p.a., while the supply of capital grows between 2 and 4 per cent p.a. – a clear and worrying imbalance which would have to be rectified either by reducing savings or reducing the rate of interest to raise the capital-output ratio. This discussion is exactly analogous to Harrod's discussion of divergences between g_w and g_n. The required rate of growth of output to absorb savings (the savings ratio divided by the required incremental capital-output ratio) is the warranted growth rate (g_w), and the growth determined by population and labour productivity growth is the natural rate of growth (g_n). Keynes was anticipating $g_w > g_n$ in developed countries, and the possibility of secular stagnation, but the situation is exactly the opposite in poor developing countries. If population growth plus productivity growth is approximately 5 per cent; the net savings

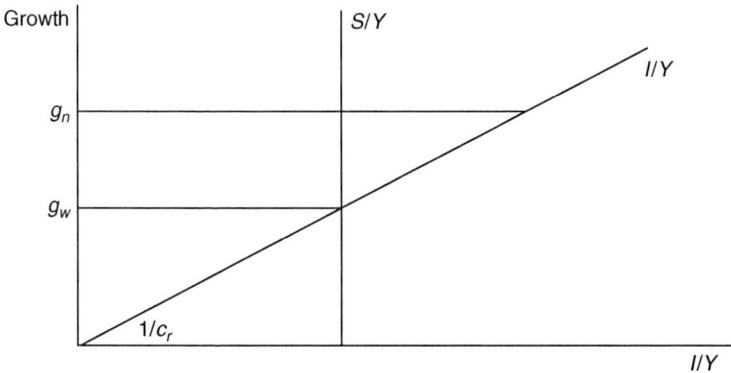

Figure 3.4 Reconciling the natural and warranted growth rates

ratio (S/Y) is 10 per cent, and the required capital-output ratio (c_r) is 4, this gives $g_n = 5$ per cent and $g_w = 10/4 = 2.5$ per cent. This discrepancy has two major consequences. Firstly, the growth of effective labour supply exceeds the growth of demand. Secondly, planned investment will exceed planned saving leading to inflationary pressure because with a potential growth rate of 5 per cent, there will be profitable investment opportunities greater than the amount of planned saving. This is why, in poor developing countries, the coexistence of high unemployment and inflation is not a paradox. To rectify this inequality between g_n and g_w there are four policy options, which are illustrated in Figure 3.4, which depicts an economy where $g_n > g_w$.

The first possibility is to reduce g_n by reducing the growth of the labour force, but this is not feasible in the short run, but it gives a justification for population control policies. The second possibility is to reduce g_n by reducing the growth of labour productivity, but this means slowing down the growth of living standards for those who work (for a given growth of output there is always a trade-off or conflict between employment growth and the growth of living standards). Thirdly, g_w can be increased by an increase in the savings ratio (an outward shift of the S/Y schedule). Lastly, g_w can be increased by reducing the required capital-output ratio (c_r) – a pivoting leftwards of the I/Y schedule – using more labour intensive techniques of production. In practice, only the last two options are feasible for generating more employment and reducing unemployment. I will concentrate here on the role of government in increasing the rate of capital accumulation through 'inflationary' finance and promoting the use of more labour-intensive techniques of production.

Governments can save and invest on society's behalf and invest in labour intensive public projects. Two scenarios need distinguishing: the first where the Keynesian multiplier is able to work; the second where there is no Keynesian demand-deficient unemployment. In the latter case, the inflation tax becomes relevant. If resources are unemployed or underused due to a genuine deficiency of demand (after a deflationary demand shock, for example), real output and saving can be increased by government spending, financed either by issuing bonds to the public or by printing money (or borrowing from the banking system, which amounts to the same thing). If the multiplier can work, any tendency towards inflation should burn itself out as the supply of goods increases to match the additional expenditure incurred. In addition, some deficit-financed projects may have considerable secondary repercussions on output if they eliminate production bottlenecks. In the agricultural sector of developing countries there are many opportunities for investment that can yield output several times the money value of the capital invested in a short space of time. Credit expansion for the use of fertilizers, irrigation and transport facilities are good examples. Credit expansion for specific employment-generating schemes in the public sector is another means of employment expansion. The capacity-generating effects of government expenditure and credit creation need to be considered alongside the demand effects.

If labour is unemployed, or underutilized, because of a lack of cooperating factors of production (mainly capital), and not demand deficiency, the direct multiplier effects of government expenditure will be small, and deficit financing is likely to be inflationary, notwithstanding the potential capacity-creating effects of investment. This brings us to the topic of the inflation tax, and how much extra resources governments can squeeze out of the economy for capital formation and employment creation without excessive inflation.

The inflation tax[9]

In his *Tract on Monetary Reform* (1923), Keynes described inflation as: 'a form of taxation that the public find hardest to evade and even the weakest Government can enforce, when it can enforce nothing else'. (p. 41) This is not an apologia for inflation, but it makes the point that if a government wishes to divert more of a country's resources to investment, and it is difficult to raise tax revenue by conventional means, one of the ways it can do so is to invest on society's behalf, financing the investment by expanding the money supply. In conditions where existing capital is fully employed, and the economy is static, money expansion will be inflationary. Inflation is the mechanism by which resources are redistributed from the private sector to the government because inflation imposes a tax on money holdings which consists of the reduction in the real purchasing power of money and of the real resources that the holders of money must forego to restore the real value of their money holdings (otherwise known as the real balance effect). The inflation tax is a form of forced saving. The base of the tax is the level of real cash balances (M/P), and the tax rate is the rate at which the real value of money is deteriorating, which is equal to the rate of inflation (dP/P). The real yield from the tax (R) is the product of the tax base and the inflation rate, i.e. $R = (M/P)(dP/P)$, which will be maximized, as in standard tax theory, when the elasticity of the base with respect to the tax rate is -1.[10] If the rate of inflation is equal to the rate of monetary expansion, the real tax yield (R) will equal the real value of the new money issued, i.e. $R = (M/P)(dM/M) = dM/P$.

The real yield from the inflation tax available for investment as a proportion of national income (R/Y) will be the product of the money-income ratio, $(M/P)/Y$, the rate of monetary expansion, dM/M, and the proportion of the increase in the real money supply used for investment, $R_I/(dM/P)$:

$$\frac{R_I}{Y} = \left(\frac{M}{PY} \cdot \frac{dM}{M} \cdot \frac{R_I}{dM/P} \right) \tag{3.1}$$

To give an example, suppose the money-income ratio is 0.4, and one-half of the new money issued is devoted to investment, then a 10 per cent increase in the money supply would yield 2 per cent of national income for investment purposes and job creation. If all the new money is used for investment purposes, the real yield from the tax is simply the ratio of the real value of new money issued to income (our earlier result), which in this example would be 4 per cent of national income.

These calculations assume that the desired ratio of money holdings to income remains the same regardless of the rate of inflation. In practice, the base of the tax is likely to fall because the opportunity cost of holding money rises, but empirical studies of the demand for money show that the elasticity of the base with respect to the rate of inflation is quite low, even in high-inflation countries, and certainly not in excess of -1. This suggests that the inflation tax can work even in countries that have been experiencing high inflation rates for many years. This is not necessarily to endorse the inflation tax in these circumstances, but Arthur Lewis

(1955) is theoretically correct when he says: 'inflation which is due to the creation of money for the purpose of accelerating capital formation results in accelerated capital formation' (p. 405).

It should also be remembered that inflation is not necessarily inegalitarian if the capital accumulation is used to help the poor by investment in labour intensive projects which, by reducing the overall capital-output ratio of the country, raises the warranted rate of growth towards the natural rate. As Keynes (1930) says in Volume 2 of the *Treatise on Money*:

> the working class may benefit far more in the long run from the forced abstinence which a Profit Inflation imposes on them than they lose in the first instance in the shape of diminished consumption – so long as wealth and its fruits are not consumed by the nominal owner, but are accumulated.[11] (pp. 162–3)

Keynes (1931) also described inflation as unjust and deflation as inexpedient, but 'it is worse in an impoverished world to provoke unemployment than to disappoint the rentier' (p. 103). Keynes's concave indifference curve between inflation and unemployment would be tangential to any conventional convex trade-off between inflation and unemployment far to the left of the point of tangency of most policy-makers today in both rich and poor countries.

Summary and conclusions

In this chapter I have tried to argue that Keynes's ideas formulated in the first half of the twentieth century are as relevant today as they ever were in thinking about the nature of unemployment, and how to tackle it, in both developed and developing countries. Employment for all those who want to work is one of the hallmarks of a civilized society, and should be possible. The task is not necessarily easy, but employment creation should be one of the top economic priorities of any government in the twenty-first century, where unemployment (and underemployment) is a serious phenomenon. But the nature of unemployment differs between developed and developing countries, and so does the challenge. In the rich developed countries, it is the concept of involuntary unemployment that needs resurrecting and stressing, and the important role of demand management. In the poor developing countries, it is the role of government in raising the rate of capital accumulation, and investing in labour intensive public projects, which is of prime importance.

The Keynesian counter-revolution, which started in the US in the 1960s, and spread to Europe, has gone too far in denying the existence of involuntary unemployment. The concept of a 'natural' rate of unemployment, and its empirical measurement, is seriously flawed. Two decades ago in the US, academic economists and policy-makers believed that the 'natural' rate of unemployment was 8–10 per cent, but now that unemployment is below 5 per cent with inflation steady, the natural rate theorists resemble the emperor with no clothes. The concept of a natural rate of unemployment still dies hard in Europe, however, particularly in the policy-making thinking of the European Central Bank. But the best economic research suggests that at least half of the high unemployment in the EU, or 3 to 4 percentage points, is of the involuntary variety, and could be reduced by more enlightened economic policies, which gives growth a chance. The prevailing orthodox view among policy-makers that all unemployment is the result of 'rigidities in the labour market' (the parrotlike mantra), and the denial of a role for demand management in reducing unemployment, needs seriously challenging. Full employment in the Keynesian sense would be possible in the EU with more flexible monetary and fiscal policy, but economic management in Europe has been made much more difficult by monetary union. The noble goal of greater European integration and cooperation has been bought at a heavy economic price. As Tinbergen (1955) taught us a long time ago, more than one policy goal requires more than one policy instrument. But in the eurozone there is only one policy instrument, the interest rate, and only one policy goal – price stability. As long as this is the case, the prospect for unemployment looks bleak.

The prospects for unemployment in poor developing countries also look bleak. The unemployed in the rural sector will continue to migrate to the cities, and the fear of inflation will reduce the rate of job creation. To paraphrase Keynes: 'the IMF and World Bank have conquered the developing countries as the Holy Inquisition conquered Spain'. The policy of 'structural adjustment' foisted on developing countries was always a euphemism for deflation, and has stifled investment, growth and employment creation, as well as inflation. There is really no solution to unemployment in developing countries without an increase in the rate of capital accumulation to match the effective growth of labour supply and a move towards more labour intensive techniques of production. This should be the prime focus of economic policy in these countries.

Notes

1. Interestingly, Yunus Muhammad received a Nobel Prize in 2006 for peace, not for economics.
2. I recently informed a young colleague with a PhD from a prestigious UK university that the term 'liquidity preference' was first coined by Keynes. It came as a revelation to him!
3. Harry Johnson was always verbose, and he holds the record for the longest sentences ever written in the literature of economics.
4. This difference in behaviour according to how the real wage reduction comes about has nothing to do with money illusion.
5. It is not entirely clear that Keynes based his belief in diminishing returns to labour on the law of variable proportions because in some sections of *The General Theory* (e.g. p. 295) he mentions that if labour was homogeneous there would be constant returns. This would imply a belief in diminishing returns based on the use of 'inferior' labour, the greater the volume of employment.
6. J. Cornwall (2007) presents a convincing aggregate demand model explaining the successive cyclical rises in unemployment in the OECD countries since the 'golden age' of the 1950s and 1960s.
7. The international evidence is, in fact, to the contrary. See Thirlwall (2005).
8. For a detailed discussion of this issue, see Thirlwall (1995).
9. This section draws on Thirlwall (1974, 2006).
10. The yield will be maximized when the rate of change of the yield $(dR/R) = 0$. $dR/R = d(M/P)/(M/P) + d(dP/P)/(dP/P)$. Setting $dR/R = 0$, gives $d(M/P)/(M/P) = -d(dP/P)/(dP/P)$. Dividing through by $d(dP/P)/(dP/P)$, gives $d(M/P)/(M/P) \div d(dP/P)/(dP/P) = -1$.
11. Admittedly, Keynes was referring to the redistribution of income within the private sector between wages and profits, but the principle is the same.

References

Archibald, G. C. (1969) 'The Phillips Curve and the Distribution of Unemployment', *American Economic Review*, May: 124–34.

Blanchard, O. J. and J. Wolfers (2000) 'The Role of Shocks and Institutions in the Rise of European Unemployment: The Aggregate Evidence', *Economic Journal* 110: C1–33.

Cornwall, J. (2007) 'A Keynesian Model of Unemployment Growth: Theory', in P. Arestis, M. Baddeley and J. McCombie (eds), *Economic Growth: New Directions in Theory and Policy*, Cheltenham: Edward Elgar.

Davidson, P. (1978) *Money and the Real World*, 2nd edn, London: Palgrave Macmillan.

Dixon, R. and A. P. Thirlwall (1975) *Regional Growth and Unemployment in the United Kingdom*, London: Macmillan.

Dunlop, J. (1938) 'The Movement of Real and Money Wage Rates', *Economic Journal*, September: 413–34.

Friedman, M. (1968) 'The Role of Monetary Policy', *American Economic Review*, April: 1–17.

Hahn, F. (1982) *Money and Inflation*, Oxford: Blackwell.

Harris, C. P. and A. P. Thirlwall (1968) 'Interregional Variations in Cyclical Sensitivity to Unemployment', *Bulletin of the Oxford Institute of Economics and Statistics* 30 (1): 55–66.

Harrod, R. (1939) 'An Essay in Dynamic Theory', *Economic Journal*, March: 14–33.

Johnson, H. G. (1974) 'Introduction', in H. G. Johnson (ed.), *The New Mercantilism*, Oxford: Blackwell.

Keynes, J. M. (1923) *A Tract on Monetary Reform*, London: Macmillan.

Keynes, J. M. (1930) *Treatise on Money*, vol. 2, London: Macmillan.

Keynes, J. M. (1931) *Essays in Persuasion*, London: Rupert Hart-Davis.

Keynes, J. M. (1936) *The General Theory of Employment, Interest and Money*, London: Macmillan.

Keynes, J. M. (1937) 'Some Economic Consequences of a Declining Population', *Eugenics Review*, April.

Keynes, J. M. (1939) 'Relative Movements of Real Wages and Output', *Economic Journal*, March: 34–51.

Lewis, A. (1955) *Theory of Economic Growth*, London: Allen and Unwin.

Lipsey, R. G. (1960) 'The Relation Between Unemployment and the Rate of Change of Money Wage Rates in the UK. 1862–1957: A Further Analysis', *Economica* 27 (February): 1–31.

Lucas, R. (1980) 'The Death of Keynesian Economics', *Issues and Ideas*, Winter: 18–19.

Mankiw, N. G. (2007) *Macroeconomics*, 7th edn, New York: Worth Publishers.

Muhammad, Y. (2003) *Banker to the Poor: Micro-Lending and the Battle Against World Poverty*, London: Aurum Press.

Nickell, S., L. Nunziata and W. Ochel (2005) 'Unemployment in the OECD since the 1960s: What do we Know?', *Economic Journal*, January: 1–27.

Oswald, A. (1997) 'The Missing Piece of the Unemployment Puzzle', Inaugural Lecture, University of Warwick, November.

Pigou, A. C. (1933) *The Theory of Unemployment*, London: Macmillan.

Smith, A. (1776) *An Inquiry into the Nature and Causes of the Wealth of Nations*, London: Straham and Caddell.

Tarshis, L. (1939) 'Changes in Real and Money Wages', *Economic Journal*, March: 150–4.

Thirlwall, A. P. (1966) 'Regional Unemployment as a Cyclical Phenomenon', *Scottish Journal of Political Economy* 13 (June): 205–19.

Thirlwall, A. P. (1969a) 'Demand Disequilibrium in the Labour Market and Wage Rate Inflation in the United Kingdom', *Yorkshire Bulletin of Economic and Social Research*, May: 66–76.

Thirlwall, A. P. (1969b) 'On the Costs and Benefits of Manpower Policies', *Department of Employment and Productivity Gazette*, November: 1–5.

Thirlwall, A. P. (1969c) 'Types of Unemployment: With Special Reference to "Non Demand-Deficient" Unemployment in Great Britain', *Scottish Journal of Political Economy* 16 (February): 20–49.

Thirlwall, A. P. (1972) 'Government Manpower Policies in Great Britain: Their Rationale and Benefits', *British Journal of Industrial Relations* 10 (2): 165–79.

Thirlwall, A. P. (1974a) 'Regional Economic Disparities and Regional Policy in the Common Market', *Urban Studies* 11 (February): 1–12.

Thirlwall, A. P. (1974b) 'Types of Unemployment in the Regions of Great Britain', *Manchester School*, December: 325–39.

Thirlwall, A. P. (1974c) *Inflation, Saving and Growth in Developing Economies*, London: Macmillan. p. 54 (n 9).
Thirlwall, A. P. (1975) 'Forecasting Regional Unemployment in Great Britain', *Regional Science and Urban Economics* 5 (August): 357–74.
Thirlwall, A. P. (1983) 'What are the Estimates of the Natural Rate of Unemployment Measuring?', *Oxford Bulletin of Economics and Statistics* 45 (2): 173–80.
Thirlwall, A. P. (1995) 'Reconciling the Conflict Between Employment and Saving and Employment and Output in the Choice of Techniques in Developing Countries', in *The Economics of Growth and Development: Selected Essays of A.P. Thirlwall*, Chelmsford: Edward Elgar.
Thirlwall, A. P. (2005) 'The Determinants of Saving in Developing Countries and the Impact of Financial Liberalisation', in P. Arestis, M. Baddeley and J. McCombie (eds), *The New Monetary Policy*, Chelmsford: Edward Elgar.
Thirlwall, A. P. (2006) *Growth and Development: With Special Reference to Developing Countries*, 8th edn, London: Palgrave Macmillan.
Tinbergen, J. (1955) *On the Theory of Economic Policy*, Amsterdam: North-Holland.
Williamson, J. (1980) 'Memorandum to Treasury and Civil Service Committee of the House of Commons', *Memoranda on Monetary Policy, 17th July 1980*, London: HMSO.

4
Aggregate Supply in the New Consensus

James Trevithick

Introduction

N. Gregory Mankiw's *Macroeconomics* is perhaps the most influential book in the teaching of macroeconomics in the English-speaking world, and probably beyond. It is the set textbook for first-year macroeconomics in Cambridge. It is one of those 'must buy' books. In North American universities it is the set text for intermediate macroeconomics. It is the distillation of a consensus which has emerged, particularly in North America, over the last three decades. Controversy and debate among various strands of thought have produced a convergence towards a framework of macroeconomic analysis which is, or so it is claimed, almost universally accepted. In this mainstream New Consensus (I shall be using capitals throughout), the short run is dominated by Keynesian economics with sticky prices, the long run by old-style classical economics where prices are, to use Pigou's description, 'plastic' or 'elastic', and the very long run by the Solow/Swan model of economic growth where prices are barely mentioned at all, although they are there implicitly. Moreover, the process of transition from one 'run' to another is never analysed. My use of 'consensus' is the one presented in Mankiw, and also in David Romer's *Advanced Macroeconomics*, which is technically more demanding and therefore less well known.

I regard Mankiw's text as deeply flawed in several respects, but in this chapter I should like to take issue with just one aspect of this consensus as encapsulated there. The aspect I should like to question lies at the heart of the Keynesian rejection of the classical theory of labour market adjustment and its replacement with his own, more satisfactory analysis of the relationship between money wages on the one hand and the absolute price level on the other. Although there are some sections of Mankiw

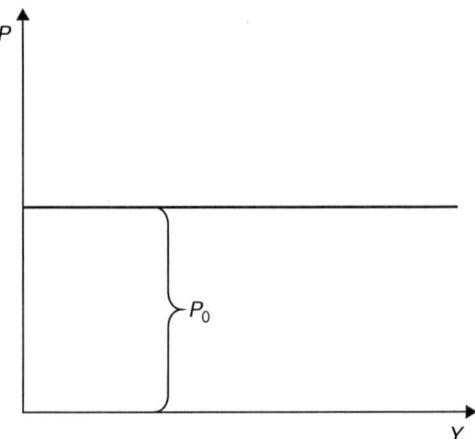

Figure 4.1 The textbook version of the Keynesian fix-price model

where he appears to be approaching Keynes's analysis, he appears to advance a model of sticky wages, not only to explain the sluggishness of adjustment to full employment at the natural level of output, but also to explain the phenomenon of general unemployment itself. Not only do money wages move sluggishly, but when they do move they adjust in such a way as to obstruct the attainment of full employment. Parallels are drawn with the treatment of the origins of general unemployment in the works of that pre-eminent classical economist, A. C. Pigou.

In what follows the framework of analysis is the familiar *AS/AD* structure. Obviously I shall be concentrating principally upon the '*AS*' part of this framework, but I shall also slip in a few sceptical words concerning the '*AD*' part.

Two simple approaches to aggregate supply in the New Consensus

Mankiw first approaches the question of aggregate supply in a pretty standard, rather old-fashioned way. In the short run the aggregate supply function in price/output space can be represented by Figure 4.1 (see Mankiw, 2007, p. 267). The absolute price level, P, is exogenously given at a level P_0, and alterations in the level of real national income, Y, are given so as not to provoke any changes in prices.

Over the relevant range before full employment is reached, the aggregate supply function resembles the horizontal line in Figure 4.1.

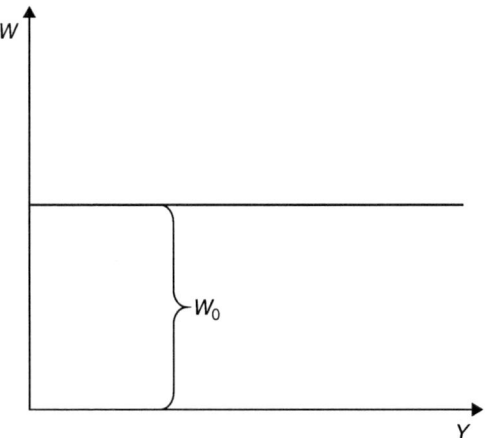

Figure 4.2 The initial *General Theory* assumption of fixed money wages

This is a very close relative to Figure 4.2, which represents diagrammatically the simplifying assumption of the first 18 chapters of *The General Theory*, namely that the level of money wages (but *not* the absolute price level, P) is constant at a level W_0.

This aid to exposition was, of course, abruptly and necessarily abandoned in Chapter 19 of *The General Theory*, the chapter entitled 'Changes in Money-Wages', in which Keynes relaxed the convenient assumption that the level of money wages was exogenously given by outside forces. His aim in that chapter was to explore the indirect routes by which falling money wages and consequent falling prices might act as a stimulus to output and employment.

All of this is familiar territory, and I have no wish to pursue this approach to aggregate supply any further. What I wish to examine below is one of the three approaches to aggregate supply which has emerged in the American New Consensus as summarized in Mankiw's influential book.

Three approaches to aggregate supply

Before we embark on an examination of the New Consensus, let us point briefly to an aspect of aggregate supply upon which all macroeconomists – Keynesian, New Keynesian, New Classical – agree. This is the form of the long-run aggregate supply schedule ($LRAS$) in (P, Y) space.

60 Aggregate Supply in the New Consensus

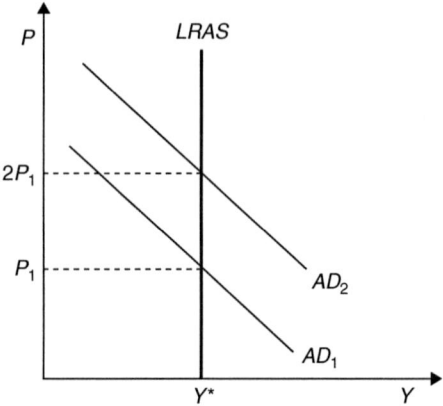

Figure 4.3 Aggregate supply in the long-run

Let us assume that, as a result of a large increase in aggregate demand, all nominal prices double. In terms of Figure 4.3, the shift in the aggregate demand schedule (*AD*) from AD_1 to AD_2 raises the price level from P_1 to $2P_1$. All relative prices and all real quantities remain unchanged. In particular the full employment level of aggregate supply will remain unchanged at Y^*. This echoes Keynes's definition of full employment output in the very early parts of *The General Theory*:

> In the previous chapter we have given a definition of full employment in terms of the behaviour of labour. An alternative, though equivalent, criterion is that at which we have now arrived, namely a situation in which aggregate employment is inelastic in response to an increase in the effective demand for its output. (Keynes, 1936, p. 26)

For Keynes, Y^* constitutes an absolute, unbreachable ceiling on the level of output in the economy. It could never be exceeded, even temporarily. Attempts to use monetary policy to raise output above Y^* would result in a situation of what he termed 'true inflation':

> When a further increase in the quantity of effective demand produces no further increase in output and entirely spends itself on an increase in the cost-unit [the level of money wages, *W*] fully proportionate to the increase in effective demand, we have reached a condition which might be appropriately designated as one of true inflation. (ibid., p. 303)

Broadly speaking there are three approaches to aggregate supply in the modern New Consensus. All three produce the same final equation, but the manner in which they do so differs substantially among them. The resultant equation is:

$$Y_t = Y^* + \alpha(P_t - P_t^e) + \varepsilon_t \qquad (4.1)$$

where ε_t is a randomly distributed disturbance term. (For simplicity we shall suppress reference to ε_t in what follows.) The other variables are Y_t, the actual level of real income; Y^*, the full employment (natural) level of real income; P_t, the actual value for the absolute price level; and P_t^e, the expected value of that variable.

In the New Consensus, there are three distinct explanations for equation (4.1). The first is new classical, the second and third are new Keynesian.

The 'imperfect information' model is quite simple to grasp in principle, though it is very hard to relate to the actual working of a modern economy. The economy comprises a large number of individual suppliers who produce their own individual goods in isolation from other suppliers. Mankiw refers to these individual suppliers as 'farmers', though the same analysis could apply to any self-employed, solitary producer of any type of good. The farmer who produces the ith crop has a perfect knowledge of the market price of that crop, P_i, but he has a very imperfect knowledge of the other absolute prices P_j, $j = 1, \ldots, n, j \neq i$. In other words he has very good information about P_i, but much more limited information concerning all of the other prices that go to make up the absolute price level, P. And the same argument goes for his interpretation of changes in the price level. In an environment in which all prices are changing at the same proportional rate, usually as a result of a rise in the supply of money, the farmer knows what is happening to P_i, but he is less sure about what is happening to P_i/P. The hypothesis is that, being more impressed at the rise in the price of the good he produces than the possible general rise in all prices, he responds by producing more, working longer hours to supply what he perceives to be an enhanced demand for his product over that of other products.

There are several important points to note in this approach. For a start, since the supplier only employs himself, he has no demand for labour function. He has his own labour supply function, of course, but the principal argument of this function is the simple ratio P_i/P. There is no recognizable real wage rate and there is no conventional interaction between L^d and L^s. Markets always clear – this is, after all, a new classical model. The fact that $(Y_t - Y^*)$ can be positive does not contradict this proposition. Market clearance at $Y_t > Y^*$ is the result of imperfect information, whereas market clearance at Y^* is the result of perfect information. Obviously the same reasoning applies, *mutatis mutandis*, to a situation where $Y_t < Y^*$ is the initial state.

The 'sticky-prices' model has been proposed by Mankiw to explain why prices respond sluggishly to alterations in demand conditions. This is very clearly explained in his text and little further need be said here. Suppose there is an increase in aggregate demand which is across the board, affecting all firms similarly. Some firms will react immediately by raising prices, while others will be sluggish in their reaction as a result of 'menu costs' which, though they may appear to be rather small at the micro level, turn out to be significant at the macro level. For an explanation of this particular rationale behind equation (4.1), see Mankiw (2007, pp. 375–6).

The principal thrust of this chapter will be to explore the third major rationale for equation (4.1). This is the *sticky-wages* model, a model which has been in circulation in one form or another for many decades both before and after the publication of *The General Theory*. Unlike the analysis of cases (a) and (b), where the initial state was assumed to be one of full employment at the natural level of output Y^*, Mankiw interestingly assumes an initial state of what used to be called underemployment equilibrium, i.e. a state in which $Y_t < Y^*$. The chain of reasoning runs as follows. The money wage rate at time t, W_t, is fixed by a contract between workers and employers in the light of what prices are expected to be over the life of the contract. Let us assume that the contract period is one year, though typically money wage contracts tend to cover longer periods of time. Workers form a forward looking estimate of what prices are likely to be over the duration of the contract. That is, they form an expectation of P_t, namely P_t^e. There is 'an unexpected change in the price level' (p. 379, line 2), hence $P_t > P_t^e$, and, assuming that workers do not renege on their contracts, W/P falls. Since the initial state is one where $Y < Y^*$, it follows that $L < L^*$, where L is the actual level of employment, and that L is demand-determined, i.e. $L = L^d$. The fall in W/P induces employers to employ more workers. Output and employment both rise. (Once again recall the central importance of the marginal productivity theory of the demand for labour, not only in this model, but also in Keynes's own model.) However, if workers, at the end of their contract period, retaliate at the erosion of their real wage by demanding proportionately higher money wages, W/P will rise back to its original level, as will output and employment.

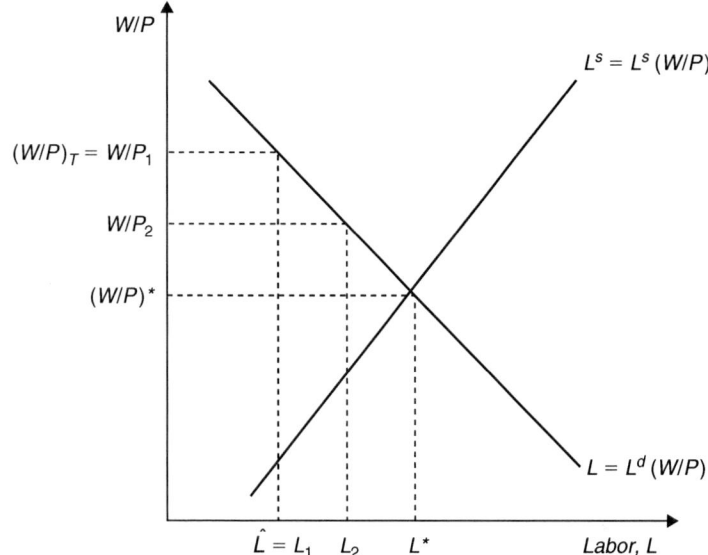

Figure 4.4 The level of employment when the target real wage exceeds the market-clearing real wage

Several aspects of this story remain mysterious. For a start we are given no clue to the origin of the unexpected rise in P. Presumably it lies in an increase in aggregate demand which, for Mankiw, is the product of an unexpected increase in the money supply. Secondly, and of quite fundamental importance, it appears that workers have it within their power to dictate what their 'target' real wage will be. If workers are prepared to accept the erosion of their target real wage rate in response to the unexpected increase in P, then the rises in Y and L will not be temporary at all: they will be lasting.

If one were to superimpose a labour supply function on Mankiw's Figure 13.1(a), the gist of this model becomes clearer. Figure 4.4 is, in all but three respects, identical to Mankiw's figure 13.1a – even the American spelling of 'labor' is the same! The first respect in which my figure differs is the explicit inclusion of a labour supply function. The second respect stems from the first: we are able to read off the market-clearing real wage rate, $(W/P)^*$, and the market-clearing level of employment, L^*. The third respect is that we are able to show how the target real wage rate, $(W/P)_T$, is equal to the initial real wage rate, W/P_1.

The implications of the Mankiw version of the sticky-wage model yield a model which appears to be the same as equation (4.1) in every respect but one. Whereas Y^* is usually interpreted as the full employment (natural) level of real income, if workers persist in pursuing a target real wage $(W/P)_T > (W/P)^*$, and if they are successful in this pursuit, then the actual level of employment can never, in the long run, equal L^*. As a result, Y^* is also unattainable. Equation (4.1) should be rewritten as:

$$Y_t = \hat{Y} + \alpha(P_t - P_t^e) + \varepsilon_t \qquad (4.2)$$

where $\hat{Y}$ is now the level of real income corresponding to a level of employment $L_1 = \hat{L}$, which in turn corresponds to the particular target real wage $(W/P)_T$.

It is hard to overestimate how far-reaching are the ramifications of the sticky-wage model. In the enhanced version of Mankiw's Figure 13.1(a), summarized in Figure 4.4, it is clear that the origin of general unemployment resides in an excessively high $(W/P)_T$. If $(W/P)_T = (W/P)^*$, there would be no general unemployment. If only workers, or their union representatives, could be persuaded to reduce their target real wages, all would be well. The labour market would clear, and there would be no Keynesian unemployment. This was precisely the view taken by pre-Keynesian economists such as Pigou. If only 'prices', which included money wages, were sufficiently 'plastic' in responding to market forces, then no general unemployment could persist. Where such general unemployment did persist – the phenomenon of general unemployment was clearly a stark fact of life recognized by all of the classical economists of the time – then the blame lay squarely at the door of the workers themselves. Workers were responsible for their own, self-inflicted misery.[1] In terms of Figure 4.4, the fact that L falls short of L^* and, as a consequence, that Y falls short of Y^*, is entirely attributable to the fact that workers have succeeded in pegging the target real wage at a level in excess of its market clearing value, $(W/P)^*$.

But before we can engage in a compare-and-contrast exercise of the sticky-wage model as expounded by Mankiw, we must highlight the salient features of the analysis of the labour market as set out in Keynes's *General Theory*. In particular we must explore the 'involuntariness' of Keynesian unemployment.

Keynes's involuntary unemployment

The General Theory gets off to a dreadful start. Keynes's legendary prose style seems to have deserted him almost at the first hurdle. As early on as page 15, he sets about defining involuntary unemployment in the most

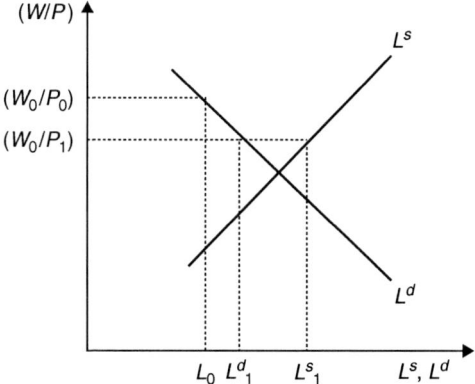

Figure 4.5 Testing for the presence of involuntary unemployment

convoluted language. The definition was so important to Keynes that he wrote the whole sentence, five and a half lines long, in italics, a stylistic device which he normally used sparingly. I shall attempt to aid exposition by using square brackets to interpolate modern language into the text, and by trying to explain what he was driving at by means of a very simple diagram.[2] The definition is as follows:

> *Men are involuntarily unemployed if, in the event of a small rise in the price of wage-goods* [a rise in P] *relatively to the money-wage* [W], *both the aggregate supply of labour willing to work for the current money-wage* [W_0] *and the aggregate demand for it at that wage* [after P has risen] *would be greater than the existing volume of employment* [L_0].

Small wonder that few economists, if they have made the effort to read *The General Theory*, have made it much beyond this excruciating definition. Nevertheless I shall try to make sense of it with the aid of Figure 4.5. When quoting from the above definition, I shall retain Keynes's italics.

The real wage, W/P, is measured along the vertical axis, and the supply of and demand for labour, L^s and L^d, respectively, are measured along the horizontal axis. The real wage is initially (W_0/P_0), and the corresponding level of employment – '*the existing volume of employment*' – is L_0. The price level now rises from P_0 to P_1, while the money wage rate remains at W_0. The real wage rate falls to (W_0/P_1). Quite clearly, even though '*the current money-wage*' remains unchanged at W_0, not only is '*the aggregate supply of labour willing to work for the current money-wage ... greater than the existing volume of employment* [L_0]' but so too is '*the aggregate demand for it at that wage*'. In other words, both $L_1^d > L_0$ and $L_1^s > L_0$. In fact inspection of the diagram reveals that $L_1^s > L_1^d > L_0$.

Although Keynes attached great significance to his italicized definition, it really does not take us as far as he imagined. The definition simply furnishes us with a hypothetical test of the presence of involuntary unemployment: if the real wage is in excess of its market-clearing value, and if it is eroded slightly by a small rise in the price level, and if the inequalities $L_1^s > L_1^d > L_0$ persist, albeit to a lesser extent, then we still have involuntary unemployment. If he had overcome his hostility to mathematical and diagrammatic techniques, he would have been able to draw the very simple diagram above without all of the verbiage.

The classical economists of the time insisted that, in a truly competitive labour market, there would be automatic tendencies at work in driving down the real wage rate. In the first instance, of course, there would be downward pressure on money wages, but this would feed through to the all-important reductions in the real wage rate. Commenting in 1937 on the connection between money wages and employment in Keynes's *General Theory*, Pigou, the foremost classical economist of his day, wrote: 'Until recently no economists doubted that an all-round reduction in the rate of money wages might be expected to increase, and an all-round enhancement to diminish, the volume of employment' (Pigou, 1937).

It should be noted in passing that Pigou was singled out for savage treatment by Keynes for one sole reason: Pigou had the particular courage, in retrospect the misfortune perhaps, to commit to print what his other classical contemporaries had simply taken for granted. Pigou's *The Theory of Unemployment* (1933) was the only systematic treatise on the theory of employment and unemployment to be found in the classical literature. It was turgidly written and, I suspect, little read. But at least it was there to be deconstructed by Keynes. And the irony is that both Keynes and Pigou were fellows of the same Cambridge college, King's, and of necessity came into contact with each other on a daily basis. One must presume that when, for example, they were dining together on High Table – Pigou was senior to Keynes in the pecking order of the Fellowship, and therefore would have presided at dinner quite frequently – they avoided talking about economics. And in any case, 'talking shop' at dinner was frowned upon in those days.

So why did Keynes dismiss the idea that money wage cuts would stimulate employment? His answer ran as follows. Pigou and the other classical economists were rather cavalier in their treatment of changes in money wages and changes in real wages. They tended to associate the one with the other: for example reductions in money wages would put downward pressure on real wages. This, quite simply, is wrong.

But why did an economist of Pigou's deserved eminence tend to conflate movements in W with movements in (W/P)? To Keynes's eye, this conflation was mysterious, but there are two possible explanations for it. Firstly the quantity theory of money was never very far from the minds of the classical writers. The absolute price level was first and foremost determined by the quantity of money in circulation. For a constant nominal supply of money, the price level was 'anchored' by this magnitude. It follows that, if P is determined by the money supply, a reduction in W would necessarily result in a reduction in (W/P). Secondly there may have been a fallacy of composition: what may hold true in the small did not necessarily hold true in the large. A money wage cut in a particular industry may reduce the real wage in that industry. *Ceteris paribus* may be invoked in this circumstance, but not in the large, that is, at the level of the macroeconomy. Cuts in money wages will simply lead, in Leijonhufvud's phrase, to a process of 'balanced deflation', i.e. a spiral in which successive reductions in money wages lead to equiproportionate reductions in prices, leaving the real wage rate unchanged.

In order to understand how a process of balanced deflation works, consider the essential element of classical and neo-classical labour market analysis, the marginal productivity theory of the demand for labour. Recall also that this was one of the aspects of classical macroeconomics which Keynes embraced wholeheartedly. Indeed he went so far as to describe it as 'indefeasible'. If the initial state is one of general unemployment, the demand for labour determines the actual employment of labour. The condition that the marginal physical product of labour be continuously equal to the real wage rate formed an integral part of Keynes's theory of employment.

This equilibrium condition can be quite simply stated as $W/P = MPPL$, where $MPPL$ is the marginal physical product of labour. Rearrangement of this equilibrium condition yields: $P = W/MPPL$. Keynes thought he was treading faithfully in Marshall's footsteps by positing marginal-cost pricing, so that the above equilibrium relationship yielded an aggregate supply curve which was the marginal cost curve for output as a whole. Hence $MC = P = W/MPPL$, where MC is the marginal (labour) cost for output as a whole. For a given value for the money wage rate, W_0, we are able to locate the position of the MC curve in (P,Y) space. This is illustrated in Figure 4.6.

The shape of the $MC(W)$ curve is, of course, determined by the shape of the $MPPL$ curve. The position of the MC curve is entirely determined

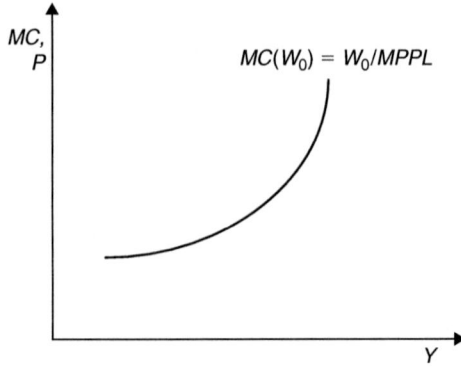

Figure 4.6 Aggregate supply at less than full employment

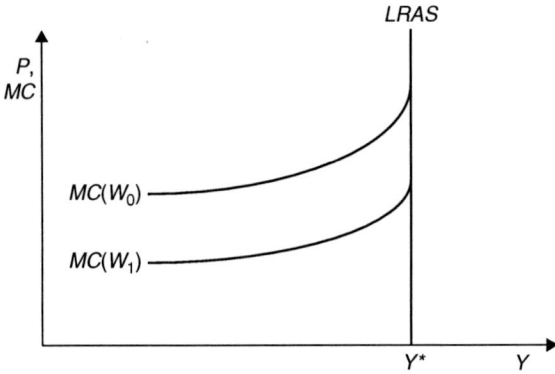

Figure 4.7 Aggregate supply at two different money wage rates

by the level of money wages, W. In fact there is an infinite set of MC curves, each one corresponding to a different value for W. Two such curves are illustrated in Figure 4.7.

Note that the notion that the aggregate supply curve is identical with the $MC(W)$ curve only applies when the initial state of the economy is one of underemployment equilibrium, i.e. where $Y < Y^*$. At full employment the relevant supply curve is $LRAS$, as in Figure 4.3.

Let us assume that we know the level of money wages so that we can pin down the position of the MC curve in (P,Y) space. If the level of money wages is W_0, then the resulting curve is $MC(W_0)$, as in Figure 4.8.

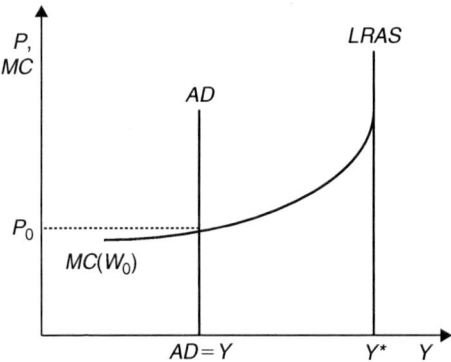

Figure 4.8 Aggregate supply, aggregate demand, and the determination of the absolute price level

The question now arises, where along the MC curve will the economy settle down? The answer is quite simple. The level of effective demand determines the level of real income when the initial state is one in which $Y < Y^*$. The level of aggregate demand, AD, is determined off-stage by the income-expenditure model. Following the orthodox Marshallian principle that, in perfect competition, $P = MC$, we can read off from Figure 4.8 that the absolute price level will be P_0. The resulting real wage rate will be (W_0/P_0).

Thus far we have assumed that money wages are sticky. As was said earlier, this was the simplifying assumption of the first 18 chapters of *The General Theory*. In Chapter 19, however, this assumption was relaxed and money wages were allowed to fall. In the presence of excess supply in the labour market, it is plausible to assume that the price of labour will fall. But which price? The classical writers were far from ignorant of the distinction between money wages and real wages, that is between W and (W/P), but, for the reasons hazarded by Keynes, they tended to conflate movements in the two:

> It is admitted [by the classical writers], of course, that the bargains [over wages] are actually made in terms of money, and even that the real wages to labour are not altogether independent of what the corresponding money-wage happens to be. Nevertheless it is the money-wage thus arrived at which is held to determine the real wage. Thus the classical theory assumes that it is always open to labour to reduce its real wage by accepting a reduction in its money-wage. (Keynes, 1936, pp. 10–11)

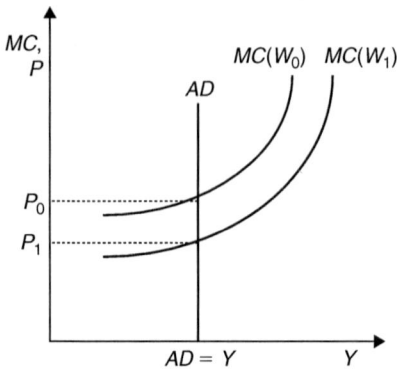

Figure 4.9 Balanced deflation

And again:

> Traditional [classical] theory maintains, in short, that the wage bargains between the entrepreneurs and the workers determine the real wage. (ibid., p. 11)

In other words the classical writers took it for granted that movements in W were matched by sympathetic movements in (W/P). For Keynes this was an absolutely fundamental error.

Consider Figure 4.9. Output is fixed by aggregate demand, and is represented by the vertical line AD. The initial level of money wages is W_0, and the corresponding absolute price level is P_0. Suppose now that the presence of excess supply in the labour market puts downward pressure on the money wage so that it falls to W. The aggregate supply curve is displaced downwards from $MC(W_0)$ to $MC(W_1)$. Following the $P = MC$ principle, the absolute price level falls from P_0 to P_1, and that fall is *equiproportionate* to the fall in W_0. In other words $(W_0/P_0) = (W_1/P_1)$: in the face of a substantial reduction in the money wage rate, the *real* wage rate remains unchanged. Price deflation has been a 'balanced' process.

In this vein Keynes wrote:

> The traditional [classical] theory maintains, in short, *that the wage bargains between the entrepreneurs and the workers determine the real wage*; so that, assuming free competition amongst employers and no restrictive combination amongst workers, the latter can, if they wish, bring their real wages into conformity with the marginal disutility of

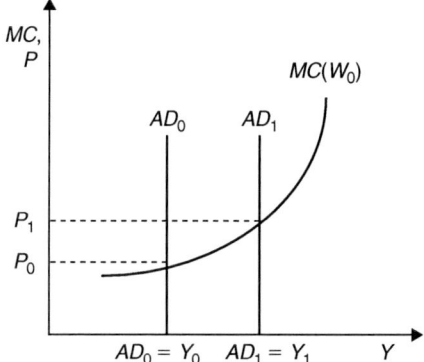

Figure 4.10 An increase in aggregate demand reduces the real wage

employment offered by the employers at that wage. (ibid., italics in the original)

What he was saying here was that, even if the labour market were highly competitive, the only 'price' directly capable of revision either upwards or downwards was the level of money wages. The origins of involuntary unemployment reside in the impotence of both employers and workers to have any influence whatsoever over the real wage rate. Workers are prepared to work at lower real wages – their unemployment would not be *in*voluntary if they were not – but the only price over which they have any control is the level of money wages. They can exert no control over the level of real wages.

The question thus arises: what *does* determine the real wage? Consider Figure 4.10. Once again the assumption of a given money wage affords enormous expositional assistance, enabling us to draw a fixed *MC* curve corresponding to a money wage of W_0.

Let there now be an off-stage increase in aggregate demand from AD_0 to AD_1 which raises real income from Y_0 to Y_1. The price level rises from P_0 to P_1 while, by hypothesis, W remains constant at W_0. The real wage rate falls from (W_0/P_0) to (W_0/P_1). In terms of the labour demand schedule, the economy slides down the *MPPL* schedule. If there is no money wage retaliation by workers, as there should not be if the unemployment is truly involuntary, then the boost to aggregate demand will have been validated by the fall in the real wage rate which Keynes's retention of the marginal productivity theory of the demand for labour required.

Tying the above analysis together we are now in a position to state what determines the real wage rate in Keynes's *General Theory*. Firstly there is the state of technology as summarized in the short-run production function $F(L)$, and its first derivative, $F'(L)$, which is the schedule of the marginal physical product of labour. In perfect competition this is identical to the demand for labour schedule, L^d. The shape of the *MPPL* schedule determines the shape of the $MC(W)$ schedule, and the magnitude of W determines the location of this schedule in (P,Y) space. Secondly there is the essential Keynesian component, the level of effective demand, or, as we would call it nowadays, the level of aggregate demand, *AD*. A knowledge of *AD* enables us to ascertain precisely where the economy is along the given $MC(W)$ curve, thereby enabling us to read off what the absolute price level is for a given magnitude for the money wage rate. All of this is rather wordily summarized by Keynes thus:

> [T]he wage-unit [W], can thus be regarded as the essential standard of value; and the price-level, given the state of technique and equipment, will depend partly on the cost-unit and partly on the scale of output, increasing, where output increases, *more* than in proportion to any increase in the cost-unit, in accordance with the principle of diminishing returns in the short period. (1936, p. 302, italics in original)

This is a much-overlooked aspect of Keynes theory of prices. At first sight the claim that the level of money wages 'can thus be regarded as the essential standard of value' seems harmless enough. Harmless, that is, until one realizes the theory which it is aimed at replacing, namely, the quantity theory of money. Starting off with general unemployment, the price level was no longer determined by the quantity of money in circulation, but by the level of money wages. The problem for Keynes was that, whereas the quantity of money was usually regarded as exogenous, the factors determining the level of money wages were unknown. The system was over-determined. As Keynes remarked, 'we are one equation short'.

So for Keynes, when the initial state is one where $Y < Y^*$, the real wage rate was determined by three factors: (a) the money wage rate, W; (b) the state of technology, summarized in the short-run production function, $F(L)$, and its first derivative, $F'(L)$, which is identical to the demand curve for labour in perfect competition; (c) the level of effective demand, *AD*, which determines Y, which in turn determines L. An increase in *AD* raises Y and L, which raises P in relation to W, the rise in L producing the concomitant fall in $F'(L)$. At each stage in this process equality is continually maintained between (W/P) and $F'(L)$. Some *tour de force* on Keynes's part!

Compare and contrast

So how does the sticky-wages model, as expounded in Mankiw, compare and contrast with *The General Theory* model expounded, accurately I hope, above? There are many points of similarity. The assumption of fixed money wages is common to both models. For Keynes it was a simplifying assumption, but it nevertheless was an assumption which formed the basis for two thirds of *The General Theory*. And, of course, Keynes muddied the waters totally unnecessarily by making a series of empirical asides throughout his great book to the effect that, in practice, in Britain in the interwar period, money wages did appear to be rigidly downwards. If any single person was culpable for the hoary old canard that Keynesian economics was based on the assumption of fixed money wages and prices, then it was Keynes himself![3] He should have shunted all of that material, incisive though his speculations were on the sources of money wage rigidity, into a separate article to avoid further confusing the already confused among his readership.

For Mankiw, money wages are indeed fixed, but are fixed only for the period of the wage contract between workers and employers. Once the contract expires, then everything is up for renegotiation in the light of changed circumstances, and particularly changed circumstances surrounding the price level. For Keynes in Chapter 19 there are no such considerations to worry about. Once one allows for the fact that money wages will succumb to competitive pressures and fall, potentially going into freefall, with prices tumbling not far behind, then the scene is set for all nominal prices to tend asymptotically towards zero. The search was then on for the indirect routes by which falling money wages and prices could stimulate aggregate demand, the two most best known routes being via the Keynes effect and the Pigou effect (see below and also Trevithick (1992), Chapter 5).

Most of the fixed wage model has already been analysed above, but there are a few ramifications which still need to be explored. Workers and employers agree on a particular real wage rate, the target real wage rate, what we have referred to as $(W/P)_T$. Workers and employers agree only on the money wage rate which corresponds to a particular expected real

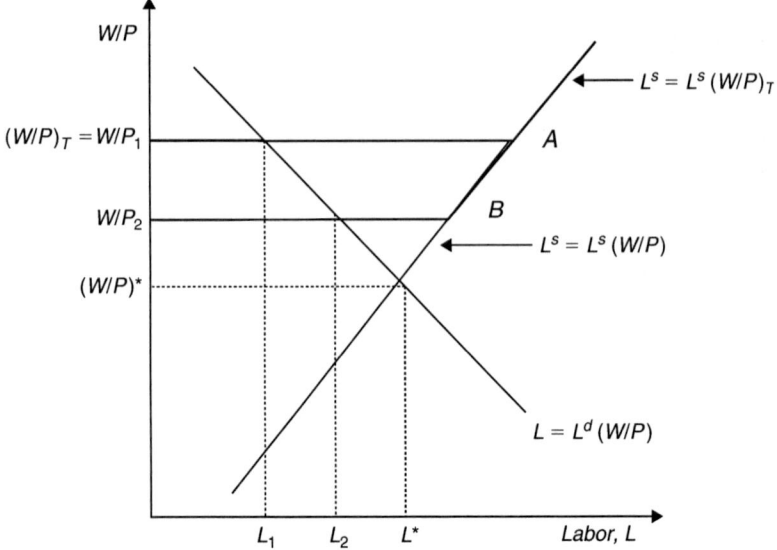

Figure 4.11 Real wage stickiness

wage rate, not on the amount of labour to be supplied. Mankiw addresses the question of the supply of labour at the bargained money wage rate:

> The final assumption of the sticky-wage model is that employment is determined by the quantity of labor that firms demand. In other words, the bargain between the workers and the firms does not determine the level of employment in advance; instead, the workers agree to provide as much labour as the firms wish to buy at the predetermined wage. (Mankiw, 2007, p. 378)

The essence of this proposition is illustrated in Figure 4.11.

The target real wage rate is $(W/P)_T$, but, as a result of an offstage rise in the price level, the realized real wage turns out to be (W/P_1). Even in these circumstances, workers are willing to supply as much of their labour as the employers demand, which means that the actual level of employment will be determined by where along the MPPL schedule, which is the demand for labour schedule, the actual value of the real wage rate indicates.

This analysis points to the existence of two sorts of supply of labour schedule. The first is the schedule indicated by the thinner line and by the lower arrow in Figure 4.11. This may be regarded as the 'true' labour supply schedule in the sense that it accurately reflects the aggregated preferences of workers between work and leisure in the absence of considerations of, for example, trade union monopoly power. The second, indicated by the bolder line and by the higher arrow in Figure 4.11, is that labour supply schedule which is the outcome of non-competitive behaviour in the labour market. The mere notion of a target real wage flies in the face of considerations of competition. Clearly at all points above the kink at point A, this labour supply schedule coincides with the 'true' schedule, but at all points below point A, the 'true' supply schedule is merely a curiosity. It is of no operational significance.

After the real wage rate has fallen as a result of the unexpected rise in the price level, the level of employment rises, and the bold section of the 'true' labour supply function now lies below A. The new kink occurs at B but, to the extent that the target real wage rate remains intact and is agreed to by both workers and employers, workers will renegotiate at the expiry of the wage contract and the money wage will rise to a level at which $(W_2/P_2) = (W/P)_T$ once again.

Although in Mankiw's text the source of the unexpected rise in price is not specified, it turns out to have been an unexpected increase in the supply of money. For Keynes the source could have been any factor, including monetary factors, which serves to raise the level of aggregate demand, AD. In all events, in both models, something must have happened to the level of aggregate demand to raise the price level relatively to the level of money wages. So here is a point of agreement between the two models.

But is the unemployment which persists in the sticky-wage model the involuntary unemployment of *The General Theory*? If Figure 4.11 is an accurate representation of the sticky-wage model, then the answer must be no. For Keynes, if aggregate demand rises sufficiently, and hence if the price level rises sufficiently, then there will be no barrier to the attainment of full employment at $(W/P)^*$, at L^* and Y^*. Certainly there will be no barrier on the part of the suppliers of labour, be they centralized or decentralized, to obstruct this process. At no stage in the progress to full employment will there be any form of retaliation against rising prices which necessarily accompany increases in aggregate demand. For Keynes there were no horizontal segments to the labour supply function as there are to the left of points A and B in the sticky-wage model. The most important relative price from the point of view of the labour market is obviously the real wage rate, and considerations of marginal productivity require that it fall to $(W/P)^*$. If the process gets stuck as a result of money wage retaliation before L^* is attained, then the remaining unemployment might be called something else, but it cannot be called involuntary in the sense of Keynes. In the sticky-wage model, the process does indeed get stuck at a level of unemployment where $(L^* - \hat{L}) > 0$ as a result of the successful pursuit of a target real wage rate $(W/P)_T > (W/P)^*$, but the resulting unemployment is definitely not involuntary. Such unemployment harks back to the analysis of Pigou and his interwar contemporaries. Organized labour, with the acquiescence of employers, manages to fix the real wage rate above its market-clearing level. At the risk of repetition, Keynes totally rejected the view *'that the wage bargains between the entrepreneurs and the workers determine the real wage rate'* (once again, Keynes's italics).

And while I'm at it: misgivings on the aggregate demand schedule

Although this chapter is principally devoted to an analysis of aggregate supply in the New Consensus on macroeconomics, questions regarding aggregate demand continue to surface, particularly as it is one of the two determinants of the real wage rate, the other being the state of technology.

Why does the aggregate demand schedule slope downwards? In virtually every exposition, from textbooks upwards, the standard reason given is that the lower the price level, the higher will be the real supply of money, and the higher will be the demand for output. This proposition is derived from the income version of Irving Fisher's equation of exchange, $MV = PY$, where M is the nominal supply of money (assumed to be equal to the demand for money), V is the income velocity of circulation of money, and Y is real national income. Rearranging and inserting the symbol AD, we obtain:

$$AD = P = MV/Y \qquad (4.3)$$

For given values of M and V, this equation yields a rectangular hyperbola. This is inconvenient in a model which deals mainly in straight lines, so the logarithm of the above is normally taken, yielding:

$$ad_t = p_t = m_t + v_t - y_t \qquad (4.4)$$

where ad_t, y_t, m_t, p_t, v_t are the logarithms of aggregate demand, real income, the nominal money supply, the absolute price level, and the income velocity of circulation of money, respectively.

We shall not wander down the logarithmic road at this stage. We shall simply assume that the *AD* schedule is fairly linear. Nothing of importance hangs on linearity. There are reasons for believing that the *AD* schedule is downward sloping, but these reasons are far more subtle than the naïve explanation contained in equations (4.3) and (4.4). Once again our journey takes us back to the question which Keynes initially posed in his Chapter 19. In the presence of excess supply in the labour market, it is reasonable to infer that money wages will fall. Once they start falling, so too will prices (see Figure 4.9 above). As prices fall, are there any forces at work which will raise the level of aggregate demand?

Yes, answered Keynes. As the real supply of money rises, interest rates will fall and interest rate-sensitive expenditures – most notably investment, but perhaps also consumption – will rise. The multiplier will kick in and income and employment will rise. The much-maligned but, in this context, very useful *IS-LM* model casts light on the phenomenon. The *LM* curve will shift to the right as a result of the *Keynes effect*. And Pigou also gains an honourable mention. He suggested that, as prices fall, the real value of the net worth of the private sector would rise. Consumption would rise as a direct result of this wealth effect. In the *IS-LM* model, this is represented by a rightward shift of the *IS* curve. This is known as the *Pigou effect*.

The combined forces of the Keynes effect and the Pigou effect are obviously complementary. Both of them serve to boost aggregate demand in the wake of falling prices. One of them works through the rate of interest (the Keynes effect) and the other works directly, requiring no intermediation via interest rates (the Pigou effect). Both of these effects are illustrated in Figure 4.12(a). Two snapshots of the economy are taken, one with a price level P_0, and the other with a considerably lower price level, P_1. The nominal supply of money remains constant at M_0. There is comparative-static equilibrium at point *A* with a price level P_0, and another equilibrium at point *B* with a price level P_1.

In Figure 4.12(b), the vertical axis now measures the absolute price level rather than the rate of interest. The absolute price level is now the principal focus of attention of the *AS/AD* framework. The *AD* schedule in panel (b) can be regarded as a collapsed version of the flex-price *IS-LM* model in panel (a). For example, points *A* and *B* in panel (a) correspond exactly to points *A'* and *B'* in panel (b). The *AD* schedule in (*P*, *Y*) space is far less cumbersome than the flex-price *IS-LM* system, but its lineage should never be forgotten. Both the position and the slope of the *AD* schedule are determined by factors far more complex – the interest elasticities of various expenditures, wealth effects, etc. – than

78 Aggregate Supply in the New Consensus

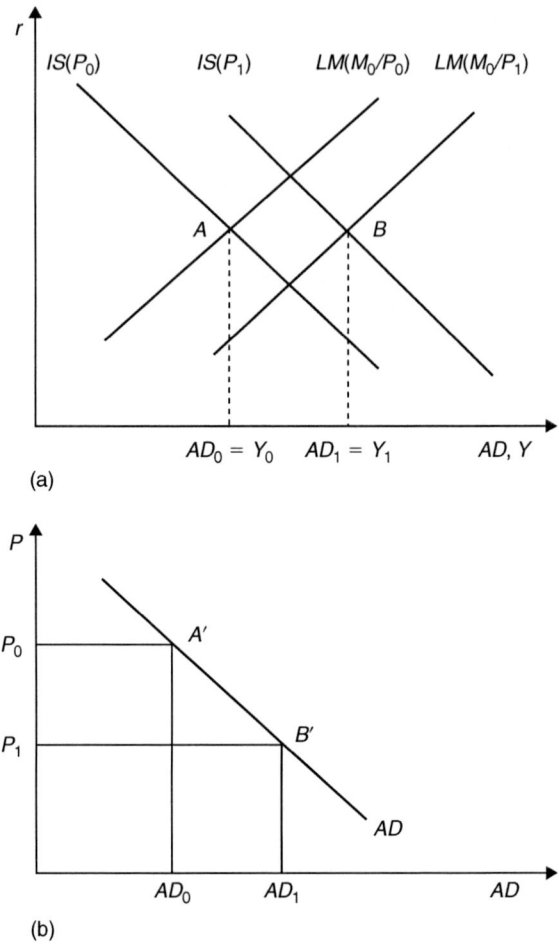

Figure 4.12 The Keynes effect, the Pigou effect, and the downward slope of the aggregate demand schedule

the naïve $MV = PY$ formulation of crude monetarism would be capable of handling.

But why did Mankiw, one of the pioneers of New Keynesianism in America, succumb to such a simplistic model of aggregate demand? To answer this question, one must cast one's mind back three or four decades. Monetarism reigned supreme in the 1970s and the early 1980s. Variants of equations (4.3) and (4.4) were frequently wheeled out to explain how an increase in aggregate demand would normally occur.

The idea became so embedded in the minds of the public and of the economics profession that inflation was 'always and everywhere a monetary phenomenon' that they became convinced that an increase in the money supply was the principal, probably the exclusive, cause of an increase in the price level. They accepted that ΔAD was caused by ΔM. So successful has the rhetoric of monetarism been in pervading the language of macroeconomics that it is now taken almost as axiomatic that an increase in the money supply will, perhaps after a few lags, raise all nominal prices equiproportionately. There is no longer any need to explore the various transmission mechanisms. That can be left to the specialist journals on monetary economics. Simplistic monetarism has gone to the very heart of mainstream macroeconomics. It is hard to conceive of an approach to aggregate demand that is *more* monetarist than equations (4.3) and (4.4).

Its success in shifting the language of discourse in macroeconomics is in stark contrast with the conspicuous failure of monetarism when it was applied to particular economies, most notably the British economy under Mrs Thatcher. With only a few dissenting Keynesian voices, soon to be silenced by expulsion from government, the British economy was subjected to the ferocious blast of the previously untested theory of monetarism. As John Kenneth Galbraith repeatedly pointed out, Friedman could not have wished for a more favourable laboratory for testing his ideas. Britain was a long-standing, stable democracy, with little taste for revolution or social unrest. A sense of reasonableness and deference to authority was widespread. However, with the passage of time, it became clear that the experiment was breaking down on so many fronts that all but a handful of its most diehard apologists came to regard the experiment as deeply flawed. But that is a much, much longer story. The mysterious fact remains that equations such as (4.3) and (4.4) continue to be replicated in textbooks despite the weight of practical experience.

Concluding remarks

Reading the macroeconomics literature as it has evolved since the early 1970s with the works of Lucas and others, one readily discerns a departure from Keynes's proposition that the level of money wages is 'the essential standard of value', along with technology and aggregate demand. For the emerging Consensus, movements in money wages on the one hand and prices on the other had become separated, occupying different, though interconnected, rooms. This view was taken to an extreme in the works of the French Keynesians (e.g. Malinvaud, (1977)), where W and P were prices to be administered separately from each other by some central planning agency. The New Consensus never went to that extreme, but the distinct impression remained that W and P, although not completely divorced but merely separated, to a large extent led lives of their own.

We saw earlier how the classical writers found it very difficult to extricate themselves from the clutches of the quantity theory of money. Keynes accepted that the quantity theory was perfectly valid when applied to an economy which was already fully employed, but that its validity evaporated when the initial state was one of chronic unemployment. At full employment, an increase in the supply of money would lead to what he termed 'true inflation', but this was categorically *not* the case where $Y_t < Y^*$. In the latter case, P was determined by W, by $F(L)$, and by AD. For a given technology and a given level of aggregate demand, movements in P were determined *exclusively* by movements in W. It followed that any talk of a change in the supply of money having any direct influence on the price level is erroneous except to the extent that it influenced the level of aggregate demand. Changes in the money supply only mattered to the extent that they altered the rate of interest, and hence the level of aggregate demand. 'The primary effect of a change in the quantity of money on the change in the quantity of effective demand is though its influence on the rate of interest' (Keynes, 1936, p. 298). The money supply in itself was of no intrinsic importance.

Not so in the New Consensus. Partly this is due to the fact that the starting point for most New Consensus models is full employment, i.e. $Y_t = Y^*$ initially. In these circumstances an increase in the money supply, anticipated or otherwise, will have an effect on P via the level of aggregate demand. For the New Consensus, an unanticipated increase in the money supply will also have repercussions for Y_t as a result of the $(P_t - P_t^e)$ term in equation (4.1). As we saw in the previous section, the question of how an increase in the money supply affects aggregate demand is nearly always short-circuited.

In the New Consensus AS/AD framework, an increase in the money supply is neutral at Y^*. Keynes did agree with that proposition. All nominal prices (P and W in our highly aggregated framework) should rise *pro tanto*. The difference between models (b) and (c) is that in model (b) prices are more sluggish than wages in responding to the rise in the money supply, whereas in model (c) the opposite is the case. Unlike *The General Theory* model, where adjustments appear to be frictionless,[4] these models explicitly incorporate sluggishness of response of nominal prices. As Stanley Fischer (1977) wrote in his seminal paper on sticky money-wage contracts:

> Because the money stock is changed by the monetary authority more frequently than labor contracts are renegotiated, and, given the assumed form of the labor contracts, monetary policy has the ability to affect the short-run behavior of output, though it has no effects on long-run output behavior.

And the same reasoning could be applied to Mankiw's interpretation of equation (4.1) in the form of the sticky-prices model. Because of significant menu costs, prices are changed less frequently than the Central Bank changes the supply of money. And presumably there are ways of combining models (b) and (c) to produce super-sluggish adjustment in a model with sticky wages *and* sticky prices. But that has probably been done already.

But let us end on a more positive note. The New Consensus does not follow Friedman (1975, pp. 20–1) down the return road to Pigovian labour market analysis. Friedman's basic model was that of Pigou, with bits of the market-clearing imperfect-information model thrown in for good measure. Workers and employers *did* exert powerful, direct influences over the real wage rate. By contrast the New Consensus *does* properly separate out movements in money wages from movements in real wages, though this is not always made very specific in particular models.

Notes

1. Hayek persisted in this view to the end, though Pigou eventually recanted in his *Keynes' General Theory* (1950).
2. Keynes and Marshall, both accomplished mathematicians in their own right, eschewed the use of mathematics in economics. This hostility carried over to an aversion to using diagrams as aids to exposition. Indeed *The General Theory* contains only one diagram (on page 180) and the inclusion of this solitary diagram was the result of intense pressure from Roy Harrod. Odd...
3. For a treatment of Keynes's views on money wage rigidity, see Trevithick (1976). I think I let Keynes off too lightly in that piece. His analysis was, I think, a correct description of what in fact happens in the process of wage bargaining, but it is by no means universally true, pertaining, as it did, to a particular country at a particular period in time. Where he went wrong was including this material within the body of an already difficult book. In the process, of course, he yielded an unfortunate hostage to fortune, giving his critics yet more ammunition in their claim that *The General Theory* relied on the assumption of given money wages.

4. Keynes's failure to deal with a whole raft of lags in adjustment exposed him to relentless criticism from his former pupil, D. H. [later Sir Denis] Robertson.

References

Fischer, S. (1977) 'Long-Term Contracts, Rational Expectations, and the Optimal Money Supply Rule', *Journal of Political Economy*, February 1:191–206

Friedman, M. (1975) *Unemployment versus Inflation? An Evaluation of the Phillips Curve*, London: Institute of Economic Affairs.

Keynes, J. M. (1936) *The General Theory of Employment, Interest and Money*, London: Macmillan.

Leijonhufvud, A. (1968) *On Keynesian Economics and the Economics of Keynes*, Oxford University Press.

Malinvaud, E. (2007) *The Theory of Unemployment Reconsidered*, Oxford: Blackwell.

Mankiw, N. G. (2007) *Macroeconomics*, 6th edn, New York: McGraw-Hill.

Pigou, A. C. (1933) *The Theory of Unemployment*, London: Macmillan.

Pigou, A. C. (1937) 'Real and Money Wage Rates in Relation to Unemployment', *Economic Journal*, September.

Romer, D. (2006) *Advanced macroeconomics*, 2nd edn, New York: McGraw-Hill.

Trevithick, J. A. (1976) 'Money Wage Inflexibility and the Keynesian Labour Supply Function', *Economic Journal*, June.

Trevithick, J. A. (1982) *Involuntary Unemployment: Macroeconomics from a Keynesian Perspective*, London: Harvester Wheatsheaf.

5
Growth and Unemployment in an Extended Kaldorian Model
Mark Roberts

Introduction

This chapter seeks to relax the implicit assumption of the 'standard' Kaldorian model of economic growth (attributable to Dixon and Thirlwall, 1975) that workers are passive to the implications of firms' pricing decisions for their real wages. To achieve this relaxation, the model is extended to include a conflict theory of wage bargaining. In doing so, the positive feedback mechanism from the demand- to the supply-side of the economy, which generates its characteristic feature of circular and cumulative growth, is reinforced. At the same time, however, the extension also introduces into the model an offsetting negative feedback effect from the demand- to the supply-side. This is because faster demand growth generates a tighter labour market which encourages worker militancy in wage bargaining. As this discussion implies, the extended Kaldorian model is, therefore, not just one of growth, but also of unemployment. This being the case, it is able to shed new light on the joint determinants of a (regional or national) economy's rates of economic growth and unemployment, as well as on possible sources of impure hysteresis in the labour market. It furthermore challenges the explanation which the standard unemployment literature provides as to the causes of the persistent disparities in unemployment rates between OECD countries that have been observed since the 1970s. Not only this, but it also challenges the conventional wisdom as to the potential role of the productivity slowdown in explaining the rise in OECD unemployment over recent decades.

The structure of the rest of this chapter is as follows. In the next section, the standard Kaldorian model of economic growth is outlined and its implicit assumption of worker passivity highlighted. The structure of an extended Kaldorian model which relaxes this assumption is then outlined. Following this, the extended model's equilibrium solution and dynamics are considered, which involves a discussion of both sources of impure labour market hysteresis in the model and the joint determinants of an economy's equilibrium rates of growth and unemployment. At this point, the relationship of the model's predictions with the conventional wisdom regarding OECD unemployment is also considered. This precedes a discussion of the potential existence of short- and long-run trade-offs between growth and unemployment. In the course of this discussion, the standard view of the role of the productivity slowdown in the general rise of OECD unemployment that has occurred since the 1970s is challenged. Finally, the chapter is brought to a conclusion with a summary of both the model and its implications for the standard story of OECD unemployment.

The standard Kaldorian model and worker passivity

The standard Kaldorian model of Dixon and Thirlwall (1975) assumes a small economy in which growth is export-led. This small economy competes via prices on international or interregional markets in the sale of a diversified range of goods with prices being determined via the application of a mark-up on unit labour costs. In turn, production of these goods is subject to increasing returns to scale, where, following Young (1928) and Kaldor (1966), these increasing returns are assumed to be primarily 'dynamic' in nature. These features of the model enter via the following set of four structural equations:

$$y_t = \gamma x_t \tag{5.1}$$

$$x_t = \eta \pi_{h,t} + \delta \pi_c + \varepsilon y_c \tag{5.2}$$

$$\pi_{h,t} = w_t - r_t + \tau \tag{5.3}$$

$$r_t = r_e + \lambda y_t \tag{5.4}$$

where y denotes the rate of real output growth, x the rate of real export growth,[1] π_h the rate of price inflation of home-produced goods, π_c the rate of price inflation of competitor economy exports, y_c a measure of the rate of growth of real income in the home economy's main export markets, w the rate of nominal wage inflation, r the rate of labour productivity growth, τ the rate of mark-up growth and r_e the rate of exogenous labour productivity growth.[2] Meanwhile, η represents the own-price elasticity of demand for exports ($\eta < 0$), δ the cross-price elasticity of demand for exports, ε the income elasticity of demand for exports and λ the Verdoorn coefficient. Equation (5.4) is Verdoorn's Law. By capturing the assumed presence of dynamic increasing returns, this equation generates a positive feedback from the demand-side of the economy to the supply-side, thereby ensuring growth is circular and cumulative.

To see the passivity of workers implicit in the standard Kaldorian model, note that equation (5.3), which describes the pricing decisions of domestic firms, can be rewritten as:

$$w_t - \pi_{h,t} = r_t - \tau \quad (5.5)$$

It therefore follows that, when domestic firms decide how to change the prices of their goods given changes in unit labour costs and in their feasible mark-up, a rate of growth of the real product wage is implied. This implied rate of real wage growth may be thought of as the *price-determined rate of real product wage inflation* (PDWI). Given that the model assumes that w_t is exogenously determined it therefore follows that it implicitly assumes that domestic workers passively accept this PDWI regardless of its consequences for their real consumption wages. For example, if changing competitive conditions in export markets resulted in an increase in τ then the PDWI would decline. In the standard Kaldorian model workers simply accept this decline despite the fact that, *ceteris paribus*, it also implies a fall in the rate of growth of their real consumption wages.[3]

Growth and unemployment in an extended Kaldorian model

The set-up of the model

Relaxing the standard Kaldorian model's implicit assumption of worker passivity requires endogenizing the rate of nominal wage inflation.[4] To achieve this, it is first necessary to supplement equations (5.1)–(5.4) of the standard model with the following two structural equations:

$$w_t = a - bu_t + \pi_t^e \quad (5.6)$$

$$\pi_t^e = \phi \pi_{h,t} + (1 - \phi)\pi_c \quad (5.7)$$

Equation (5.6) states that the negotiated rate of nominal wage inflation in period t is a decreasing linear function of the period's unemployment rate, u_t, and an increasing linear function of both exogenous wage-push factors (a) and the rate of inflation that workers expect for the period for the basket of goods they consume, π_t^e.[5] The negative dependence on u_t arises because workers are less likely to push for real wage increases both in the aggregate and relative to one another when the labour market is weaker (see, *inter alios*, Layard et al., 1991, p. 13; Rowthorn, 1977, p. 219). Capturing the strength of this negative dependence is the parameter b. Meanwhile, equation (5.7) specifies π_t^e as a weighted average of the actual inflation rates for home-produced goods and imported final consumption goods in period t.[6] The weights, which, for simplicity, are assumed to be exogenously determined, are the respective shares of home-produced goods and of imports in the consumption expenditure of workers. Assuming that w_t is negotiated at the very outset of period t,[7] the fact that π_t^e has been specified as a weighted average of *actual* inflation rates implies an assumption of rational expectations on the part of workers.

To show that the addition of these two equations to the standard Kaldorian model implies that workers will no longer passively accept the PDWI implied by the pricing decisions of firms, substitute equation (5.7) into equation (5.6) and subtract $\pi_{h,t}$ from both sides to give:

$$w_t - \pi_{h,t} = a - bu_t + (1 - \phi)(\pi_c - \pi_{h,t}) \tag{5.8}$$

From equation (5.8), it follows that not only do the pricing decisions of firms imply a rate of growth of the real product wage, but so too does the bargain struck by workers with their employers in wage negotiations. This *bargained rate of real product wage inflation* (BRWI) is declining with u_t and increasing with both a and the term $(1 - \phi)(\pi_c - \pi_{h,t})$, which may be thought of as the 'wedge' that exists between the growth rate of the real product wage ($w_t - \pi_{h,t}$) and the (expected) growth rate of the real consumption wage ($w_t - \pi_t^e$).[8]

In comparing equation (5.8) with equation (5.5), it can be seen that, for any given rate of unemployment, there is no reason why the BRWI need coincide with the PDWI. In other words, workers no longer passively accept what their employers try to impose upon them. Rather, conflict exists within the labour market. This conflict is resolved through the unemployment rate, which acts as a disciplining device to overcome the dissatisfaction of workers, subduing their militancy to a point where they are willing to accept the real product wage that firms implicitly wish to impose upon them. Indeed, given the assumption that workers possess rational expectations, the unemployment rate in the extended model will always be such as to ensure the BRWI is consistent with the PDWI. This implies that the labour market is always in 'equilibrium' in the sense that inflation is not redistributing income between domestic workers and firms.[9]

In order to complete the endogenization of the rate of nominal wage inflation it is necessary to link the unemployment rate in equation (5.6), to the rate of real output growth in equation (5.1). To do this, the following three structural equations may be introduced:

$$u_t = u_{t-1} + n_t - e_t \quad (5.9)$$

$$e_t = -r_e + (1-\lambda)y_t \quad (5.10)$$

$$n_t = n_e + \rho(e_t - e_c) - \nu(u_t - u_c) \quad (5.11)$$

Equation (5.9) defines the unemployment rate in period t as equal to the unemployment rate in the previous period, u_{t-1}, plus the rate of labour-force growth in period t, n_t, net of the rate of employment growth in period t, e_t.[10] Meanwhile, equation (5.10) specifies e_t as a negative linear function of r_e and a positive linear function of y_t. This equation follows directly from Verdoorn's Law, equation (5.4), and the definition of labour productivity growth as $r_t \equiv y_t - e_t$.[11] It implies that employment growth is quantity-constrained by output growth and, therefore, that all unemployment in the model should be thought of as being both involuntary and arising from a deficiency of demand. Finally, equation (5.11) gives the rate of labour-force growth with n_e denoting the exogenous rate of labour-force growth in the economy.[12] The fact that n is specified as increasing with e and decreasing with u reflects evidence that increases in perceived employment opportunities are likely to encourage increased labour-force participation, particularly amongst women (see, *inter alia*), McCombie and Thirlwall, 1994; McCombie, 1998, p. 216; León-Ledesma and Thirlwall, 2002).[13] Meanwhile, the inclusion of measures of the rate of employment growth, e_c, and the unemployment rate, u_c, in competitor economies is intended to capture the idea that, in a regional setting, it is relative employment opportunities rather than real wages per se that are important in driving migration. Within the context of a national economy it is appropriate to set $e_c = u_c = 0$. In such a setting, this can be done whilst still maintaining that a buoyant domestic labour market will result in induced immigration and also the possible presence of 'guest workers'.[14]

Equations (5.6)–(5.7) and (5.9)–(5.11), taken together with equations (5.1)–(5.4), provide the structural equations of the extended

Kaldorian model. In this extended model, the positive feedback from the demand- to the supply-side of the economy that arises in the standard model from the assumed existence of dynamic increasing returns is enhanced. Thus, not only does faster demand growth directly lower the rate of inflation for home produced goods by stimulating labour productivity growth and, therefore, slowing the growth of unit labour costs, but it also indirectly lowers this rate of inflation. This is because workers factor the stimulated labour productivity growth into their expectations, thereby leading them to moderate their nominal wage demands in wage negotiations. However, against this, the introduction of a conflict theory of wage bargaining into the standard model also introduces an offsetting negative feedback effect from the demand- to the supply-side of the economy. In particular, the lowering of the unemployment rate which results from faster demand growth makes workers more militant in the wage bargaining process. As a consequence, there is a tendency for the positive impact of faster labour productivity growth on the rate of inflation for home produced goods to be counteracted, although this, in turn, is itself partly offset by any stimulated increase in labour-force growth.

To introduce transitional dynamics into the extended model it is necessary to introduce, in addition to the lag that already exists in equation (5.9), a lag in one or more of the eight structural equations. An outstanding candidate for the inclusion of such a lag is equation (5.2).[15] Quite apart from the recognition and order-delivery lags identified by Hooper and Marquez (1995, p. 109), the reaction to relative price movements typically involves discrete shifts to new suppliers. However, because they are costly, such shifts occur only gradually (Landesmann and Snell, 1989, p. 4; Carlin and Soskice, 1990, p. 293). In view of this, real export growth will be assumed to react to changes in relative prices with a single lag of one period. Assuming one period of logical time to be equivalent to one calendar year, such a specification is reasonably consistent with empirical work (see, in particular, Krugman, 1989; Landesmann and Snell, 1989).[16]

Solution of the model

For empirically plausible ranges of its exogenous variable and parameter values, the extended Kaldorian model possesses a stable equilibrium solution (y^*, u^*) in which both the rate of real output growth and the unemployment rate are strictly positive. This is illustrated in Figure 5.1 using a phase diagram. In this diagram the $\Delta y_t = 0$ schedule shows all combinations of y_t and u_t for which y_t is constant. Its upward slope

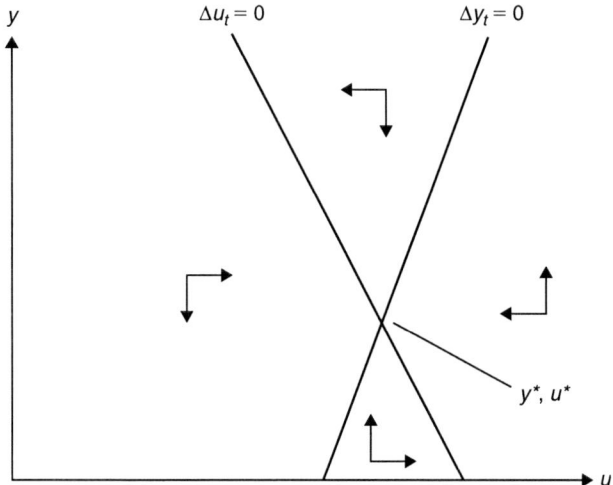

Figure 5.1 Phase diagram for the extended Kaldorian model

reflects the fact that a higher rate of unemployment lowers the negotiated rate of nominal wage inflation. This occurs both directly through the negative dependence of w_t on u_t and indirectly via reducing π_t^e, the rate of inflation that workers expect for the basket of goods they consume. Given the use of mark-up pricing by firms, lower nominal wage inflation in turn implies a fall in the rate of inflation of home-produced goods and therefore faster real output growth through increased relative export price competitiveness. Meanwhile, the $\Delta u_t = 0$ schedule shows all combinations of y_t and u_t for which u_t is constant. Its downward slope is a result of the fact that, from equation (5.10), a faster rate of real output growth leads to a faster rate of employment growth which, from equation (5.9), reduces the unemployment rate. From equation (5.11), the faster rate of employment growth and the lower unemployment rate also induce an increased rate of labour-force growth. However, provided $\rho < 1$, the increase in the rate of labour-force growth is not large enough to completely reverse the fall in u_t. As the figure shows, the intersection of the $\Delta y_t = 0$ and $\Delta u_t = 0$ schedules defines the equilibrium solution (y^*, u^*) of the model. The arrows in the phase diagram depict the dynamics of y_t and u_t. If y_t lies above (below) the $\Delta y_t = 0$ schedule then y_t tends to fall (increase). Meanwhile, if u_t lies to the right (left) of the $\Delta u_t = 0$ schedule then u_t tends to decline (increase). Thus, overall, if y_t and u_t are disturbed from their equilibrium values, the system tends to oscillate around (y^*, u^*). For ranges of exogenous variables and parameter values that are plausible for the UK, these oscillations are damped and therefore the extended model's equilibrium solution is stable.[17]

Notably, the above dynamics imply that the labour market in the extended model is characterized by impure hysteresis. This is despite the earlier noted fact that the labour market is in continual 'equilibrium' in the sense that the BRWI is always equal to the PDWI. At the heart of this impure hysteresis lies the reinforced positive feedback mechanism of the extended model. In the event of a shock that pushes the unemployment rate away from u^*, this positive feedback mechanism ensures that the effects of this shock only dissipate slowly over time. The speed of dissipation, and, therefore, the severity of impure hysteresis, is related to the strength of the positive feedback mechanism as determined by, for example, the size of the Verdoorn coefficient. It is also related to the strength of the negative feedback mechanism that exists in the extended model from the demand-side of the economy to the supply-side. That is to say, to the strength of the reaction of the negotiated rate of nominal wage inflation to a change in the unemployment rate. This is because it is this negative feedback mechanism that is responsible for helping to stabilize the model's dynamics.

From the above, it follows that the parameter b in equation (5.6) is a crucial determinant of the strength of impure hysteresis in the model. This parameter can be thought of as measuring workers' degree of real wage growth flexibility.[18] This is because it measures the degree to which the BRWI in equation (5.8) responds to changes in the unemployment rate. In turn, workers' degree of real wage growth flexibility varies with wage bargaining institutions and with the search 'effectiveness' of the average unemployed job seeker, which itself can be related to the average duration of unemployment and such determinants of the average duration as the length of entitlement to benefits. More specifically, with regard to wage bargaining institutions, workers' degree of real wage growth flexibility can be expected to be high both for economies in which bargaining is very decentralized and unions are very weak, and for economies where bargaining takes place at the national level between strong unions and strong employers' organizations (Layard et al., 1991). Meanwhile, a higher average duration of unemployment caused by, amongst other things, a longer duration of benefits is associated with a lower degree of real wage growth flexibility (ibid.). This is because the higher the average duration of unemployment, the lower the search 'effectiveness' of the average unemployed job seeker is likely to be. Whilst, however, the result that the severity of impure hysteresis is related to the flexibility of workers is one that the extended model shares with the standard unemployment literature, the insight that the extent of hysteresis also depends on the strength of the cumulative causation mechanism is new.

Whilst Figure 5.1 is helpful in illustrating the existence of a stable equilibrium solution, it provides no direct information as to the determinants of y^* and u^*. For this, it is necessary to explicitly state the model's equilibrium solution.[19] This is as follows:

$$y^* = \left[\frac{\gamma\eta b}{\upsilon(1 - \phi + \gamma\eta\lambda) - \gamma\eta b(1 - \rho)(1 - \lambda)}\right][(1 - \rho)r_e + n_e - \rho e_c + \upsilon u_c]$$
$$+ \left[\frac{\gamma\upsilon}{\upsilon(1 - \phi + \gamma\eta\lambda) - \gamma\eta b(1 - \rho)(1 - \lambda)}\right][(\delta + \eta)(1 - \phi)\pi_c$$
$$+ (1 - \phi)\varepsilon y_c - \eta(r_e - a - \tau)] \tag{5.12}$$

$$u^* = \left[\frac{1 - \phi + \gamma\eta\lambda}{\upsilon(1 - \phi + \gamma\eta\lambda) - \gamma\eta b(1 - \rho)(1 - \lambda)}\right][(1 - \rho)r_e + n_e - \rho e_c + \upsilon u_c]$$
$$- \gamma\left[\frac{(1 - \rho)(1 - \lambda)}{\upsilon(1 - \phi + \gamma\eta\lambda) - \gamma\eta b(1 - \rho)(1 - \lambda)}\right][(\delta + \eta)(1 - \phi)\pi_c$$
$$+ (1 - \phi)\varepsilon y_c - \eta(r_e - a - \tau)] \tag{5.13}$$

One point that arises from this explicit solution is that if the exogenous variables r_e, n_e, e_c, u_c, π_c, y_c, a and τ are all set equal to zero then $y^* = 0$. Therefore, strictly speaking, growth in the model is exogenous. However, this is *not* to say that government policy cannot influence y^*. In particular, as shown below, structural reforms that influence such parameters as λ are able to influence y^*. Furthermore, given the presence of Verdoorn's Law in its structural setup, there is evidently an element of endogeneity about any technological progress that does occur in the model. Another point to emerge is that, not only is the degree of impure hysteresis negatively related to b, but so is the equilibrium unemployment rate. Again, this is a result that is shared with the standard unemployment literature. Indeed, variations in wage bargaining institutions and the treatment of the unemployed which affect the parameter b are held by Layard *et al.* (1991) to be responsible for most of the cross-sectional, if not the time-series, variation in unemployment rates across OECD countries that has existed over the previous 30 to 35 years.[20]

However, the explicit equilibrium solution of the extended Kaldorian model again provides a possible challenge to this conventional wisdom.

This is because the solution indicates that the heterogeneity in OECD unemployment rates that has been witnessed over recent decades may also be due to other factors. Thus, perhaps most notably, because u^* is decreasing in ε in equation (5.13) the model predicts that OECD countries that have benefited from higher income elasticities of demand for their exports over recent decades should, *ceteris paribus*, have experienced lower unemployment rates. This is significant because the main determinant of the income elasticity of demand for a country's exports is its relative level of non-price competitiveness and such competitiveness has become ever more important in determining export success in the post-Second World War period (see, *inter alia*, Landesmann and Snell, 1989, p. 1; McCombie, 1998, p. 220; Petit, 1999, p. 159). The extended model therefore suggests that the standard literature's emphasis on the heterogeneity of labour market institutions as the cause of OECD unemployment rate disparities may be overstated.[21]

The possibility of a growth–unemployment trade-off

The negative effect of an increase in ε upon u^* discussed above is hardly surprising given that an increase in ε also has, from equation (5.12), a positive effect on y^*. However, other parameter and exogenous variable changes that increase y^* do not necessarily reduce u^*. In particular, consider an increase in either λ or r_e such as might result from structural reforms implemented in the economy. In particular, structural reforms that might be expected to affect λ include anything that affects the quality of industrial management or the prevalence of stifling regulations. Thus, for example, a removal of overly burdensome planning restrictions in a regional economy might cause an increase in λ. This is because such restrictions can inhibit the industrial expansion that is necessary to allow for an increased subdivision of the production process and therefore the full exploitation of dynamic increasing returns. Meanwhile, structural reforms that might increase r_e include measures that increase an economy's receptiveness to knowledge spillovers from other economies, that enhance the quantity and quality of human capital accumulation, and that improve the spillovers into the economy occurring from government-sponsored research and development (R&D).[22]

Regardless of the precise nature of the structural reform, it follows from equations (5.12) and (5.13) that, while an increase in r_e and/or λ will increase y^*, it will only also reduce u^* if:[23]

$$(1 - \rho)(1 + \gamma\eta - \phi) < 0 \tag{5.14}$$

Assuming, for the time being, $\rho < 1$, this condition reduces to $-\gamma\eta + \phi > 1$ (remember, $\eta < 0$). To understand the intuition behind this condition consider Figure 5.2, which depicts the effects of an increase in r_e.[24] As can be seen, this shifts the $\Delta y_t = 0$ schedule upwards. This is because for every level of u_t a higher r_e implies a lower rate of home price inflation and thus a faster rate of real export and real output growth. The lower rate of home price inflation is both a direct consequence of firms' practice of setting their prices as a mark-up on unit labour costs, and an indirect consequence of the rate of negotiated nominal wage inflation falling as workers revise their expectations of inflation downwards. Consequently, the upwards shift in the $\Delta y_t = 0$ schedule can be attributed to both a *direct price effect* and an *expectations effect*. The higher is $-\gamma\eta$ the stronger is the direct price effect because the greater is the impact of any given fall in $\pi_{h,t}$ on y_t. Meanwhile, the higher is ϕ the greater is the expectations effect because the more does π_t^e fall in response to a given fall in $\pi_{h,t}$. In contrast, the increase in r_e shifts the $\Delta u_t = 0$ schedule outwards. This is because, from equation (5.10), a higher r_e implies a slower rate of employment growth for every level of y_t. Given that it may provide grounds for worker dissatisfaction, this effect may be termed the 'Luddite effect'. Only if the direct price and expectations effects outweigh the Luddite effect will the upwards shift in the $\Delta y_t = 0$ schedule be large enough relative to the outwards shift in the $\Delta u_t = 0$ schedule to ensure that the unemployment rate is lower in the new equilibrium. Whilst this is the case in Figure 5.2, it is not so in Figure 5.3.

From the above it is clear that structural reform of an economy designed to work through r_e and/or λ brings with it the possibility of a long-run trade-off between growth and unemployment. Where such a trade-off does exist, it provides policy-makers with a dilemma. Moreover, the oscillatory dynamics of the model, evident from Figure 5.1, are such that even where such a trade-off does not exist, structural reform that increases r_e and/or λ still entails a short-run trade-off between growth and unemployment. The intuition for this is that whilst, from equation (5.10), the Luddite effect of structural reform comes into immediate effect, the countervailing direct price and expectations effects take time to kick-in. In turn, the delayed kicking-in of the direct price and expectations effects is a result of, in equation (5.2), x_t only responding to improvements in relative price competitiveness with a lag. From this it is clear that, even when structural reform that increases r_e and/or λ entails no long-run growth–unemployment trade-off, policy-makers will still be faced with a dilemma. In particular, is higher unemployment

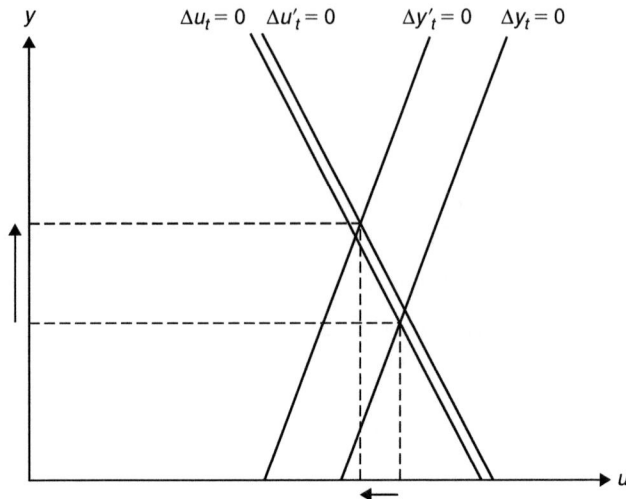

Figure 5.2 Absence of a long-run growth–unemployment trade-off $(-y\eta + \phi > 1)$

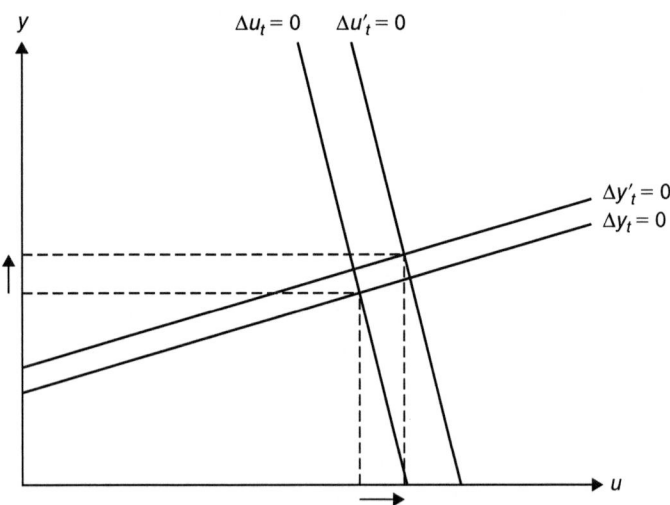

Figure 5.3 Existence of a long-run growth–unemployment trade-off $(-y\eta + \phi < 1)$

in the short run a price worth paying for faster growth and, ultimately, lower unemployment? From the government's viewpoint, the answer to this question will depend upon electoral and political economy considerations.[25]

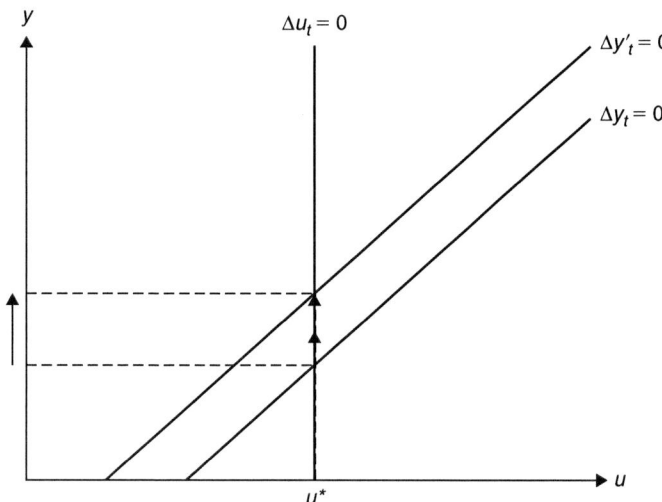

Figure 5.4 Absence of a growth–unemployment trade-off, even in the short run ($\rho = 1$)

There is, however, one special case of the model where structural reform working through r_e and/or λ entails neither a long-run nor a short-run trade-off. This is when $\rho = 1$, i.e. when the elasticity of labour-force growth with respect to employment growth is unity. As can be seen from Figure 5.4, in this case the $\Delta u_t = 0$ schedule has an infinite gradient with the result that u_t never deviates from $u^* = (n_e - e_c + \nu u_c)/\nu$. Thus, an increase in r_e that shifts the $\Delta y_t = 0$ schedule upwards increases y^*, whilst leaving, even during the transition to the new equilibrium, the unemployment rate unchanged. The intuition behind this result is that with $\rho = 1$, both the direct and indirect changes in the rate of employment growth that result from changes in r_e and/or λ are perfectly offset by countervailing movements in the rate of labour-force growth. In particular, the Luddite effect of structural reform, from which arises the possibility of trade-offs between growth and unemployment, is choked-off at source. This being the case, there can be no effect on the unemployment rate.[26]

However, even in this special case of $\rho = 1$, the absence of either a short-run or a long-run trade-off between growth and unemployment may be more apparent than real. This follows from the discussion of the rationale behind equation (5.11). Specifically, that discussion implies that the fall in the rate of labour-force growth that works to immediately choke-off the Luddite effect will be partly attributable to reduced labour-force participation. Consequently, whilst when $\rho=1$, no increase in the measured rate of unemployment will ever result, a decline in the proportion of working-age people in employment may nevertheless occur.[27]

The above discussion of the effects of changes in r_e and/or λ is interesting not just in its own right, but also because it implies that changes in the rate of labour productivity growth can be associated with changes in the model's equilibrium unemployment rate, u^*.[28] This is contrary to the view that dominates the standard unemployment literature. In particular, the standard view is that changes in the rate of labour productivity growth are *not* associated with, and, especially, do not cause, changes in an economy's equilibrium unemployment rate, i.e. in its NAIRU (see, inter alia, Layard et al., 1991; Blanchard and Wolfers, 2000, pp. C4–C6).[29] The origin of this view seems to be the somewhat weaker empirical observation that whilst labour productivity has been trended upwards over the broad sweep of history, the unemployment rate has been untrended (see Layard et al., 1991, p. 5; Blanchard and Katz, 1997, p. 56). To capture this feature of reality standard NAIRU models have found it necessary to assume that workers possess a reservation wage and that this reservation wage adjusts to any changes that occur in the level of labour productivity. However, as a corollary of this assumption, standard NAIRU models produce not only the empirically consistent result that the equilibrium unemployment rate is constant in the face of labour productivity growth, but also the much stronger result that it is constant in the face of *changes* in the rate of labour productivity growth.

However, in the model presented there is no reservation wage that is linked to the level of productivity. If there were, the rate of labour productivity growth would enter in equation (5.6) as a determinant of the negotiated rate of nominal wage inflation. Yet, despite this, the model still possesses an equilibrium unemployment rate that is constant in the face of labour productivity growth without producing the much stronger result of an equilibrium unemployment rate that is invariant to changes in the rate of labour productivity growth. In particular, whilst productivity growth shocks do not affect u^*,[30] structural changes that influence y^*, and thus, by extension, the equilibrium rate of labour productivity growth, do. Moreover, even if the model is modified to make w_t dependent upon r_t it still transpires that changes in productivity growth can be associated with changes in u^*. In this case, structural reform that leads to an increase in r_e and/or λ not only pushes up y^*, and, hence, the rate of labour productivity growth, but also increases u^* (see the mathematical appendix of Roberts, 2002).

The fact that changes in the rate of labour productivity growth can be associated with shifts in the equilibrium unemployment rate has potential implications as to the diagnosis of the causes of the large rises in unemployment that have occurred throughout the OECD, and, in particular, OECD Europe, since the 1960s.[31] Thus, whilst the theoretical conclusion that changes in productivity growth cannot affect the equilibrium unemployment rate has led the standard literature to downplay the productivity slowdown as a direct cause of the large rises in unemployment,[32] the model presented suggests that this downplaying may be a mistake. Therefore, the extended Kaldorian model suggests that the standard literature may have misdiagnosed not only the causes of the cross-sectional variations that have existed in OECD unemployment rates, but also the causes of the general rise in OECD unemployment. If this is indeed the case then the policy implications are profound. In particular, it would suggest that policies to reduce unemployment should focus not just on labour market reform, but also on implementing structural reforms that aim to influence the long-run rate of labour productivity growth. Most notably, from the discussion of this section it follows that, provided the condition in equation (5.14) holds, reforms that increase r_e and/or λ will both increase y^* and reduce u^*, whilst from the discussion of the previous section it follows that reforms that increase ε will also have the same effect. The latter being the case, it can be concluded that perhaps the best route to lower unemployment is not labour market reform, but the implementation of measures that aim to enhance the non-price competitiveness of exports.[33]

Summary and conclusions

To summarize, the standard Kaldorian model of economic growth implicitly assumes that workers are passive to the implications of firms' pricing decisions for their real wages. In this chapter, an extension of the standard model that relaxes this assumption through the introduction of a conflict theory of wage bargaining has been presented. This model is suggestive of possible shortcomings in the standard story of OECD unemployment over the last 30 to 35 years. First, in this standard story, the large cross-sectional variations in unemployment rates that have been, and continue to be, observed are explained by the heterogeneity of labour market institutions – in particular, by variations in wage bargaining institutions and the treatment of the unemployed. The extended Kaldorian model presented suggests that other factors – most notably, variations in the income elasticities of demand for exports reflecting variations in relative *non*-price competitiveness – may also have been important in explaining the heterogeneity of experience. Second, the standard story also sees labour market institutions as the key to explaining impure hysteresis in the labour market. Yet the extended model is suggestive of additional channels through which unemployment persistence may have been working, with the corollary that non-labour market institutions may be more important in the generation of persistence than has hitherto been realized. Third, and finally, in the standard story, the productivity slowdown is only indirectly associated with the general rise in OECD unemployment. However, the extended model suggests that this downplaying of the productivity slowdown may have been a mistake.

Notes

1. For simplicity equation (5-2) abstracts from possible movements in the nominal exchange rate, which might be present in applying the model to a national economy.
2. Variables without a time subscript are assumed to be exogenously determined in the extended Kaldorian model of the next section.
3. A further assumption implicit in equation (5.3), which can again best be seen from equation (5.5), is that the PDWI has no direct dependence upon the demand conditions faced by domestic firms in their product markets. This assumption seems reasonable (see Carlin and Soskice, 1990, especially, p. 140).
4. Pugno (1998) also endogenizes the rate of nominal wage inflation within a Kaldorian-style model.
5. Some support for the linear dependence of w_t on u_t comes from the finding for the OECD that 'the average response [of wage inflation] to unemployment is not strongly nonlinear' (Grubb, 1986, p. 72).
6. It is assumed that the same rate of inflation for competitor economy exports is relevant to imports of final consumption goods into the home market.
7. This assumption makes sense because equation (5.3) of the standard Kaldorian model implicitly assumes that in choosing π_h for period t domestic firms know what w_t will be and therefore do not have to form an expectation of it. In particular, the two assumptions are consistent if domestic firms set $\pi_{h,t}$ immediately after w_t has been set.
8. This follows from the fact that, from equation (5.7), $w_t - \pi_t^e = w_t - \pi_{h,t} - (1-\phi)(\pi_c - \pi_{h,t})$. It may be thought that reducing this wedge must, because it reduces the BRWI, necessarily reduce the equilibrium rate of unemployment in the model presented. However, this is not the case. This is because a fall in $\pi_c - \pi_h$ also leads to a slower rate of increase or faster rate of decline in the relative price competitiveness of home exports. In turn, this feeds through

to produce a slower rate of real output growth. Changes in payroll taxes will also drive a wedge between the growth rate of the real product wage and the (expected) growth rate of the real consumption wage. For simplicity, such changes are abstracted from here.
9. With the BRWI always equal to the PDWI it follows, from equations (5.5) and (5.8), that the unemployment rate at any moment in time is given by $u_t = [(a+\tau) - r_t + (1-\phi)(\pi_c - \pi_{h,t})]/b$. The result that the labour market is always in equilibrium could be altered by relaxing the assumption that workers possess rational expectations. In particular, if equation (5.7) is respecified as $\pi_t^e = \phi\pi_{h,t}^e + (1-\phi)\pi_c$, so that workers no longer have perfect knowledge of what $\pi_{h,t}$ will be when they enter wage negotiations, then the rate of unemployment at any moment in time will instead be given by $u_t = [(a+\tau) - r_t + (1-\phi)(\pi_c - \pi_{h,t})]/b - (\phi/b)(\pi_{h,t} - \pi_{h,t}^e)$. This implies that unexpected inflation at any moment in time, $\pi_{h,t} - \pi_{h,t}^e > 0$, will reduce the unemployment rate below the 'no conflict' level currently prevailing. In doing so, it will redistribute income away from workers and towards domestic firms. Given the failure of inflation to redistribute income, we may alternatively think of the unemployment rate in the model as always being what Carlin and Soskice (1990, see especially p. 136) refer to as a 'competing claims equilibrium'.
10. The definition is an approximate one. It is derived from differentiating the exact definition $u_t = 1 - (E_t/N_t)$ where E_t denotes the level of employment in period t and N_t the size of the labour force in period t.
11. Equation (5.10) may be recognized as Kaldor's reformulation of Verdoorn's Law (Kaldor, 1966, p. 12). Also, the rate of employment growth in this equation should be thought of as a net rate, underlying which will be considerable microeconomic turbulence.
12. This equation is taken from Thirlwall (1980, p. 424; see also McCombie and Thirlwall, 1994, p. 480).
13. Equally, reductions in perceived employment opportunities are likely to induce falls in labour-force participation through such mechanisms as early retirement.
14. Balassa (1963, p. 763) suggested that Beckerman's model (Beckerman, 1962), which is a close relation of the standard Kaldorian model, be reformulated to include a (standard) Phillips curve. Not only this, but Balassa hinted that Beckerman's model also be extended to include a labour-force supply function such as that in equation (5.11). Potentially, therefore, Balassa was very close to constructing a model similar in spirit to that presented here. Beckerman (1962, p. 620) also noted the possibility that 'rising prices in a slow-growing economy might be "imported", via wages, into the faster-growing economy (and *vice versa*)' and furthermore states that 'in particular, small countries with less diversified economies, and hence more dependence on trade, are likely to import overseas inflation fairly rapidly'. These possibilities are captured in equations (5.6) and (5.7).
15. Indeed, Dixon and Thirlwall (1975, p. 207) introduce transitional dynamics into the standard Kaldorian model by introducing a one-period lag into equation (5.2).
16. Other candidates for the inclusion of lags are equations (5.4), and therefore also equations (5.10) and (5.11). However, including lags in these equations,

as well as equation (5.2), would only complicate the analysis without bringing much in the way of additional insight.
17. The $\Delta y_t = 0$ and $\Delta u_t = 0$ schedules derive from the system of two linear non-homogeneous difference equations, one for y_t and one for u_t, that follow from substituting and rearranging equations (5.1)–(5.4), (5.6)–(5.7) and (5.9)–(5.11). Both this system and the equations for the $\Delta y_t = 0$ and $\Delta u_t = 0$ schedules are provided in the mathematical appendix of Roberts (2002). Also provided in this appendix is an explicit discussion of the model's stability properties.
18. By the same token, $1/b$ can be thought of as reflecting workers' degree of real wage growth rigidity.
19. This equilibrium solution is the particular solution to the linear non-homogeneous system of first-order difference equations presented in the mathematical appendix of Roberts (2002).
20. These variations have been, and remain, very large. Thus, for example, whilst in the mid-1990s Switzerland's unemployment rate was around 4.0 per cent, Spain's was more than 20 per cent (Blanchard and Wolfers, 2000, p. C1).
21. Another interesting point is that if $\rho = v = 0$ then $y^* = (n_e + r_e)/(1 - \lambda)$ and $u^* = [(\delta + \eta)(1 - \phi)\pi_c + (1 - \phi)\varepsilon y_c - \eta(r_e + a - \tau)]/\eta b - [(1 - \phi + \gamma\eta\lambda)/\gamma\eta b][(r_e + n_e)/(1 - \lambda)]$. This corresponds to the case of the pure labour-constrained economy. It is this case that Kaldor believed to be applicable to the UK economy at the time of his 1966 inaugural lecture before subsequently changing his mind (Targetti and Thirlwall, 1989, p. 11).
22. This is because it is reasonable to postulate r_e in Verdoorn's Law as being an increasing function of knowledge spillovers from trading-partners, human capital accumulation and government expenditure on R&D. In particular, specification of r_e as dependent upon knowledge spillovers is consistent with attempts made in the empirical literature on Verdoorn's Law to control for spatial interdependence (Bernat, 1996; Fingleton and McCombie, 1998). Meanwhile, *if* the correct underlying specification of Verdoorn's Law is a Cobb–Douglas production function and human capital enters into this production function the law will be misspecified unless the accumulation of such capital is included in it or unless such accumulation has been orthogonal to output growth. Finally, De Benedictis (1998, p. 255) hypothesizes that R&D should enter Verdoorn's Law as a determinant of r_e. It is possible that such reforms could also affect other parameters in the model. Thus, for example, an increase in government expenditure on training, especially on the training of the unemployed, that increases the quantity and quality of human capital accumulation may also, from the standard unemployment literature, be expected to increase b. This is because an increase in such spending can be expected to increase the effective supply of labour, thereby reducing union bargaining power (Carlin and Soskice, 1990, p. 170; Layard *et al.*, 1991). To the extent that this is the case any long-run growth-unemployment trade-off arising from an increase in r_e, the possibility of which is discussed below, will be offset and perhaps even reversed.
23. It is only actually true that an increase in r_e or λ increases y^* if $v(1 - \phi + \gamma\eta\lambda) - \gamma\eta b(1 - \rho)(1 - v) > 0$ holds. To assume that this condition holds seems reasonable on both empirical grounds and on the grounds that

only if $(1 - \phi + \gamma\eta\lambda) > 0$ does the model have any chance of being globally stable (see the mathematical appendix of Roberts, 2002).
24. Analysing the consequences of an increase in λ using phase diagrams is more difficult. This is because changes in λ affect not only the intercepts of the $\Delta y_t = 0$ and $\Delta u_t = 0$ schedules, but also their slopes (see the mathematical appendix of Roberts, 2002). However, the intuition as to why the new equilibrium may involve a higher u^* is the same as for an increase in r_e.
25. From note 9 it follows that the creation of unexpected inflation has the potential to ease or even overcome this dilemma. Another exogenous variable in the model that, if it changes, creates the possibility of a long-run and/or short-run trade-off between growth and unemployment is n_e. In particular, assuming $v(1 - \phi + \gamma\eta\lambda) - \gamma\eta b(1 - \rho)(1 - v) > 0$ (which, from note 23 is reasonable), an increase in n_e will definitely result in an increase in y^*, but will only also result in a decline in u^* if $(1 - \phi + \gamma\eta\lambda) < 0$ holds. Note that this is true even when $\rho = 1$.
26. The absence of a long-run trade-off when $\rho = 1$ is also evident from equation (5.14). Had a lagged reaction of labour-force growth to relative employment growth been allowed for in equation (5.11) then a short-run trade-off would still exist even with $\rho = 1$.
27. Note that, when $\rho \leq 1$, in the course of moving from one equilibrium to another, the natural rate of growth is changing in the model. This is because the natural rate of growth is endogenous to the actual rate of growth of real output. This is consistent with the evidence presented by León-Ledesma and Thirlwall (2002) that the natural rate of growth has been responsive to changes in the actual rate of growth in a sample of 15 OECD countries over the period 1961–95.
28. This is because changes in the rate of real output growth produce, via Verdoorn's Law, changes in the rate of labour productivity growth.
29. Blanchard and Katz (1997, pp. 56–7) do note that the theoretical result that the long-run NAIRU is invariant to changes in the rate of labour productivity growth assumes that the productivity growth has been the result of 'a very rarefied form of technological progress, one that affected productivity but did not affect the organization of production in any other way'. However, as is clear from the quote from Blanchard and Wolfers (2000) in note 32 below, the main text provides a fair reflection of Blanchard's, if not necessarily Katz's, actual stance. The dependence of u^* in equation (5.13) on n_e and π_c is also contrary to the conventional wisdom of the unemployment literature (see Layard, et al., 1991, p. 31; Rowthorn, 1999, p. 414).
30. Thus, if y_t, and, hence, r_t, is perturbed upwards from the equilibrium value y^* in Figure 5.1, the equilibrium unemployment rate remains fixed at u^*.
31. During 1960–64 and the mid-1990s the overall unemployment rate in OECD Europe increased from 1.7 per cent to 11.0 per cent (Blanchard and Wolfers, 2000, p. C1).
32. To quote Blanchard and Wolfers (2000, pp. C4–C6) on this point: 'There is no question that a slowdown in TFP [total factor productivity] growth can lead to a higher equilibrium unemployment rate for some time ... Can the effects of such a slowdown on unemployment be permanent? Theory suggests that the answer, to a first approximation, is no ... There lies the first puzzle of European unemployment. The initial shock is clearly identified.

But, after more than twenty years, it is hard to believe that its effects are not largely gone' (see also Blanchard and Katz, 1997, p. 66, on this point). Interestingly, part of the reason Blanchard and Wolfers may find it a puzzle is that they argue that a slowdown in productivity growth affects the unemployment rate by leading to real wage growth in excess of productivity growth. Eventually, workers and firms realize that such excess real wage growth is unsustainable. This leads to real wage growth being reduced to bring it into line with productivity growth. Once this happens, the effect of the productivity slowdown on unemployment disappears. However, in the model, it is evident from equation (5.5) that, provided the reasonable assumption that $\tau = 0$ is made, the PDWI, and, hence, the actual rate of growth of the real product wage, always tracks productivity growth. This being the case, there is never any need for expectations to adjust. The use of the adjective 'direct' is important. This is because the standard unemployment literature does see the productivity slowdown as having had an important *in*direct role in explaining the time-series evolution of OECD unemployment.

33. Rowthorn (1999) and Daveri and Tabellini (2000) have also questioned the conventional wisdom that changes in the equilibrium unemployment rate have not been associated with changes in the rate of labour productivity growth.

References

Balassa, B. (1963) 'Some Observations on Mr Beckerman's "Export-Propelled" Growth Model', *Economic Journal* 62: 781–5.

Beckerman, W. (1962) 'Projecting Europe's Growth', *Economic Journal* 61: 912–25.

Bernat, G. A. J. Jr (1996) 'Does Manufacturing Matter? A Spatial Econometric View of Kaldor's Laws', *Journal of Regional Science* 36: 463–77.

Blanchard, O. J. and L. F. Katz (1997) 'What We Know and Do Not Know About the Natural Rate of Unemployment', *Journal of Economic Perspectives* 11: 51–72.

Blanchard, O. J. and J. Wolfers (2000) 'The Role of Shocks and Institutions in the Rise of European Unemployment: The Aggregate Evidence', *Economic Journal* 110: C1–C33.

Carlin, W. and D. Soskice (1990) *Macroeconomics and the Wage Bargain: A Modern Approach to Employment, Inflation and the Exchange Rate*, Oxford: Oxford University Press.

Daveri, F. and G. Tabellini (2000) 'Unemployment and Taxes: Do Taxes Affect the Rate of Unemployment?', *Economic Policy* 15: 47–104.

De Benedictis, L. (1998) 'Cumulative Causation, Harrod's Trade Multiplier and Kaldor's Paradox: The Foundations of Post-Keynesian Theory of Growth Differentials', in G. Rampa, S. Stella and A. P. Thirlwall (eds), *Economic Dynamics, Trade and Growth: Essays on Harrodian Themes*, London: Macmillan.

Dixon, R. and A. P. Thirlwall (1975) 'A Model of Regional Growth Rate Differences on Kaldorian Lines', *Oxford Economic Papers* 27: 201–14.

Fingleton, B. and J. S. L. McCombie (1998) 'Increasing Returns and Economic Growth: Some Evidence for Manufacturing from the European Union Regions', *Oxford Economic Papers* 50: 89–105.

Grubb, D. (1986) 'Topics in the OECD Phillips Curve', *Economic Journal* 96: 55–79.

Hooper, P. and J. Marquez (1995) 'Exchange Rates, Prices and External Adjustment in the United States and Japan', in P. B. Kenen (ed.), *Understanding Interdependence: The Macroeconomics of the Open Economy*, Princeton: Princeton University Press.

Kaldor, N. (1966) *Causes of the Slow Rate of Economic Growth of the United Kingdom*, Cambridge: Cambridge University Press.

Krugman, P. (1989) 'Differences in Income Elasticities and Trends in Real Exchange Rates', *European Economic Review* 33: 1031–54.

Landesmann, M. and A. Snell (1989) 'The Consequences of Mrs Thatcher for UK Manufacturing Exports', *Economic Journal* 99: 1–27.

Layard, R., S. J. Nickell and R. Jackman (1991) *Unemployment: Macroeconomic Performance and the Labour Market*, Oxford: Oxford University Press.

León-Ledesma, M. and A. P. Thirlwall (2002) 'The Endogeneity of the Natural Rate of Growth', *Cambridge Journal of Economics* 26: 441–60.

McCombie, J. S. L. (1998) 'Harrod, Economic Growth and International Trade', in G. Rampa, S. Stella and A. P. Thirlwall (eds), *Economic Dynamics, Trade and Growth: Essays on Harrodian Themes*, London: Macmillan.

McCombie, J. S. L. and A. P. Thirlwall (1994) *Economic Growth and the Balance-of-Payments Constraint*, London: Macmillan.

Petit, P. (1999) 'Integration and Convergence in the European Union', in M. Setterfield (ed.), *Growth, Employment and Inflation*, London: Macmillan.

Pugno, M. (1998) 'The Stability of Thirlwall's Model of Economic Growth and the Balance-of-Payments Constraint', *Journal of Post Keynesian Economics*, 20: 559–81.

Roberts, M. (2002) 'Cumulative Causation and Unemployment', in J. S. L. McCombie, M. Pugno and B. Soro (eds), *Productivity Growth and Economic Performance: Essays on Verdoorn's Law*, London: Palgrave.

Rowthorn, R. E. (1977) 'Conflict, Inflation and Money', *Cambridge Journal of Economics* 1: 215–39.

Rowthorn, R. E. (1999) 'Unemployment, Wage Bargaining and Capital-Labour Substitution', *Cambridge Journal of Economics* 23: 413–25.

Targetti, F. and A. P. Thirlwall (1989) *The Essential Kaldor*, London: Duckworth.

Thirlwall, A. P. (1980) 'Regional Problems are "Balance-of-Payments" Problems', *Regional Studies* 14: 419–25.

Young, A. (1928) 'Increasing Returns and Economic Progress', *Economic Journal* 38: 527–42.

6
A Post Keynesian Macroeconomic Policy Mix as an Alternative to the New Consensus Approach
Eckhard Hein and Engelbert Stockhammer

Introduction

Nowadays, mainstream macroeconomics is dominated by New Consensus Models (NCMs).[1] In these models there is again an impact of aggregate demand on output and employment, but only in the short run. Due to nominal and real rigidities the short-run Phillips curve is downward sloping. In the long run, however, there is no effect of aggregate demand on the 'Non Accelerating Inflation Rate of Unemployment' (NAIRU), which is determined by structural characteristics of the labour market, the wage bargaining institutions and the social benefit system.[2] Therefore, the long-run Phillips curve becomes vertical. In these models, monetary policy applying the interest rate tool is able to stabilize output and employment in the short run, but in the long run it is neutral and only affects inflation (Fontana and Palacio-Vera, 2007). Fiscal policy is downgraded and is restricted to support monetary policies in achieving price stability (Arestis and Sawyer, 2003).

Post Keynesians (PKs) have criticized these NCMs for a variety of reasons. Broadly summarized, the critique is related to the assumption of a stable long-run equilibrium NAIRU determined exclusively by supply-side factors to which actual unemployment can be adjusted by means of monetary policy interventions, on the one hand, and to the assumption of the independence of this NAIRU from the development of actual unemployment, and hence from effective demand and monetary as well as fiscal policies, on the other hand.

Already Sawyer (2002) had argued that the NAIRU should not be considered a strong attractor for actual unemployment. Stability of the NAIRU has been examined closer by Stockhammer (2004) including the effects of redistribution between profits and wages on effective demand which occur when actual unemployment deviates from the NAIRU. Hein (2006a) has focussed on the effects of redistribution between capitalists and rentiers on aggregate demand, triggered by accelerating or decelerating inflation. Both authors conclude that the NAIRU is not generally stable, but that a specific demand regime is required for stability. Considering the NCM recommendation of inflation targeting monetary policies in order to adjust actual unemployment to the NAIRU, Arestis and Sawyer (2004a, 2004b, 2005, 2006), Hein (2004, 2006a), Palacio-Vera (2005) and Fontana and Palacio-Vera (2007) have argued that monetary policy interventions will not be able to constrain instability in some cases for several reasons. Finally, long-run endogeneity of the NAIRU with respect to actual unemployment, and hence to macroeconomic and monetary policies, has been related to different channels. New Keynesian authors had already related it to labour market hysteresis (Blanchard and Summers, 1987, 1988; Ball, 1999). PKs have added further channels: capital stock and productivity growth effects of investment (Rowthorn, 1995, 1999; Sawyer, 2002; Arestis and Sawyer, 2004a, pp. 73–99, 2005), adaptive wage and profit aspirations (Setterfield and Lovejoy, 2006; Stockhammer, 2008), and distribution effects of interest rate variations (Hein, 2006a).

Because of the deficiencies and the problems of NCMs, PKs have started to amend these models and have proposed alternatives. First, the inflation generation and the income generation processes have been reformulated. Some PK authors have assumed away the existence of a short-run inflation barrier and hence the NAIRU (Setterfield, 2004, 2006a, 2006b; Atesoglu and Smithin, 2006), whereas others have accepted that there is such a short-run inflation barrier, which, however, is endogenous in the medium to long run through different channels (Lavoie, 2004, 2006; Hein, 2006a; Stockhammer, 2008). Some authors have accepted the interest rate inverse IS-curve from the NCM (Lavoie, 2004, 2006; Setterfield, 2004, 2006a; Atesoglu and Smithin, 2006; Rochon and Setterfield, 2007–8), whereas others have replaced it by a more elaborated PK/Kaleckian approach to effective demand allowing for real debt and different distribution effects (Hein, 2006a; Setterfield, 2006b; Stockhammer, 2008).

Second, different economic policy conclusions, in particular with respect to monetary policies, have been drawn. Whereas some authors have argued that central banks' inflation targeting is generally compatible with PK analysis (Palley, 2006; Setterfield, 2006a; Fontana and Palacio-Vera, 2007), but have demanded a higher emphasis on real stabilization and more adequate inflation targets, others have rejected any fine tuning by means of interest rate policies and have rather been in favour of stabilizing the interest rate at some growth and employment conducive level (Lavoie, 1996a; Smithin, 2004; Setterfield, 2006b; Gnos and Rochon, 2007; Rochon and Setterfield, 2007–8; Wray, 2007). From this perspective it follows that nominal stabilization should be delegated to wage or incomes policies (Arestis, 1996; Hein, 2002, 2004, 2006a; Davidson, 2006; Kriesler and Lavoie, 2007), and that fiscal policies should be in charge of real stabilization in the short and in the medium to long run (Arestis and Sawyer, 2003, 2004a, 2004c; Gnos and Rochon, 2007).

What is lacking in the PK discussion so far is a basic but general PK synthesis model, which allows for a short-run inflation barrier, which captures the major causes for the short-run instability of the inflation barrier and hence the NAIRU, into which the major channels of medium- to long-run endogeneity of the NAIRU can be integrated, and which allows for the derivation of a complete PK macroeconomic policy-mix of monetary, fiscal and wage policies. This chapter is intended to contribute to bridging this gap. Due to lack of space, however, we will not be able to integrate all the long-run endogeneity channels mentioned above.[3]

A basic Post Keynesian model

Production, finance, distribution and the inflation generation process

Production, finance and rentiers' income

We assume a closed economy with only rudimentary economic activity of the state. There will be no taxes and no state employment in the model, but only deficit financed government demand. Under given conditions of production, there is just one type of commodity produced with a constant coefficient technology. Assuming away overhead labour, the labour–output ratio and hence labour productivity (y) are constant up to full capacity output given by the capital stock. The capital–potential output ratio (v), which is the relation between the capital stock (K) and potential output (Y^v), is also constant. The capital stock is assumed not to depreciate. The rate of capacity utilization (z) is given by the relation between actual and potential output. Given these assumptions, the supply constraint can be written with the aid of the definition of the rate of profit, relating gross capital income (Π) to the capital stock. The rate of profit is decomposed into the profit share (h), the rate of capacity utilization and the inverse of the capital–potential output ratio:

$$r = \frac{\Pi}{pK} = \frac{\Pi}{pY}\frac{Y}{Y^v}\frac{Y^v}{K} = hz\frac{1}{v} \tag{6.1}$$

The supply constraint is only reached by accident and the economy usually operates below maximum capacity given by the capital stock, i.e. usually: $z < 1$.

The pace of accumulation is determined by entrepreneurs' decisions to invest, independently of prior savings because firms have access to credit generated by a developed banking sector ('initial finance'). We assume that long-term investment finance ('final finance') is supplied by firms' retained earnings or by long-term credit of rentiers' households (directly or through banks) (Hein, 2008, ch. 10). Introducing interest payments into the model, capital income or gross profits splits into (net) profit of enterprise (Π_F) and rentiers' income (R):

$$\Pi = \Pi_F + R \tag{6.2}$$

With respect to interest rate and credit, we follow the PK 'horizontalist' monetary view developed by Kaldor (1970, 1982, 1985), Lavoie (1984, 1992, pp. 149–216, 1996b) and Moore (1989) and assume that the interest rate is an exogenous variable for the production and accumulation process, whereas the quantities of credit and money are determined endogenously by economic activity. The central bank controls the base rate of interest, commercial banks mark-up the base rate and then supply the credit demand they consider creditworthy at this interest rate. In what follows we consider just one interest rate as representative for the whole structure of interest rates.

Writing i_n for the nominal rate of interest, we can define the real interest rate for given inflation expectations ($\hat{p}^e$), the 'ex ante' real interest rate (i^e), as.

$$i^e = i_n - \hat{p}^e \tag{6.3}$$

The 'ex post' real interest rate, i, becomes endogenous to unexpected inflation ($\hat{p}^u$):

$$i = i_n - (\hat{p}^e + \hat{p}^u) = i^e - \hat{p}^u \tag{6.4}$$

Firms' payments to rentiers are given by the stock of debt (B) at issue prices and the nominal rate of interest. Expected rentiers' interest income (R^e) can be decomposed into a part compensating for the expected inflationary devaluation of the stock of nominal assets held by rentiers ($\hat{p}^e B$), and into expected real net income determined by the *ex ante* real rate of interest ($i^e B$). Repayment of debt is not considered explicitly:

$$R^e = i_n B = (i^e + \hat{p}^e)B = i^e B + \hat{p}^e B \tag{6.5}$$

Firms' 'real' interest payments and rentiers' 'real' gross income (R) are affected whenever unexpected inflation occurs:

$$R = (i_n - \hat{p}^u)B = (i^e + \hat{p}^e - \hat{p}^u)B \tag{6.6}$$

The debt–capital ratio relates the stock of debt at issue prices to the capital stock at production prices and is hence given by:

$$\lambda = \frac{B}{pK} \tag{6.7}$$

Since real debt effects caused by unexpected inflation are delegated to the real income flows between firms and rentiers, the debt–capital ratio can be taken as a constant for the following analysis.

Conflicting claims, employment, unexpected inflation and distribution[4]

Unexpected inflation in our model is systematically generated by inconsistent income claims of rentiers, firms and workers.[5] The target gross profit share of firms (h_F^T), which has to cover retained earnings and interest payments to rentiers, is given by mark-up pricing on unit labour costs in incompletely competitive goods markets. In the short run, we assume the target mark-up to be constant up to full capacity output:

$$h_F^T = h_0, \quad 0 < h_0 \leq 1 \tag{6.8}$$

If unexpected inflation arises, the realized profit share becomes:

$$h = h_0 - h_2 \hat{p}^u, \quad 0 < h_0 \leq 1 \tag{6.9}$$

with h_2 denoting the effect of unexpected inflation on the realized profit share. The higher h_2, the less effective are firms in protecting the profit share against unexpected inflation caused by external shocks or workers' wage aspirations.

The target wage share of workers $[W_W^T = (1-h)_W^T]$ depends on the rate of employment (e), respectively unemployment (u), because unemployment has the function to contain distribution claims of labourers

(Kalecki, 1971, pp. 156–64). At this stage we assume that workers and labour unions do not consider the inflationary macroeconomic effects of their nominal wage demands and the potentially restrictive monetary policy reactions. There is neither coordination between unions in different firms or industries, nor between wage bargaining parties and monetary policy, with an eye to avoiding macroeconomic externalities of wage bargaining:

$$(1-h)_W^T = W_0 + W_1 e, \quad 0 < W_0 \leq 1, \quad 0 \leq W_1 \qquad (6.10)$$

We do not assume full utilization of productive capacities given by the capital stock to be necessarily accompanied by full employment. Therefore, the employment rate is a positive function of the rate of capacity utilization, but these two rates are not necessarily equal:

$$e = xz, \quad 0 < x \leq 1 \qquad (6.11)$$

Whenever there is unexpected inflation, the realized wage share becomes:

$$(1-h) = W_0 + W_1 e - W_2 \hat{p}^u, \quad 0 < W_0 \leq 1, \quad 0 \leq W_1, W_2 \qquad (6.12)$$

with W_2 denoting the effect of unexpected inflation on the realized wage share. The higher W_2, the less effective are workers in protecting the wage share against unexpected inflation caused by external shocks or firms' profit aspirations.

With adaptive expectations ($\hat{p}_t^e = \hat{p}_{t-1}$), we obtain the following short-run Phillips curve from equations (6.9) and (6.12):

$$\hat{p}_t^u = \Delta \hat{p}_t = \hat{p}_t - \hat{p}_{t-1} = \frac{W_0 + W_1 e + h_0 - 1}{W_2 + h_2} \qquad (6.13)$$

or

$$\hat{p}_t = \hat{p}_{t-1} + \frac{W_0 + W_1 e + h_0 - 1}{W_2 + h_2} \qquad (6.13a)$$

In our model we have, at each point in time, a short-run inflation barrier which is similar to the NAIRU in the NCMs. With consistent income claims $(1-h)_W^T + h_F^T = 1$, we obtain from equations (6.8) and (6.10) for the stable inflation rate of employment (e^N) and the NAIRU $u^N = 1 - e^N$:

$$e^N = \frac{1 - W_0 - h_0}{W_1} \qquad (6.14)$$

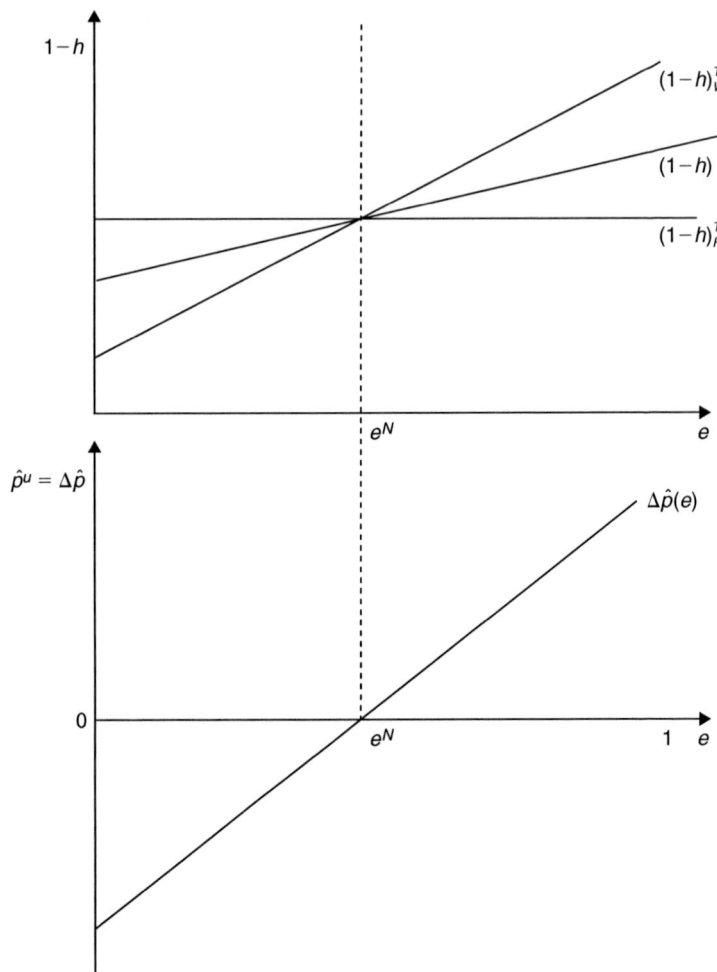

Figure 6.1 Conflicting claims, inflation and distribution

Whenever unemployment falls short of the NAIRU, inflation will accelerate because the sum of the income claims exceeds output, and unexpected inflation will arise, fuelling future inflation expectations. Whenever unemployment exceeds the NAIRU, inflation will decelerate.

Figure 6.1 shows the target wage shares of workers and firms as well as the realized wage share as a function of employment in the upper part, and the related unexpected inflation in the lower part.

Taking into account equation (6.11) for the relationship between the employment rate and the rate of capacity utilization, we obtain the following stable inflation rate of capacity utilization (z^N):

$$z^N = \frac{e^N}{x} = \frac{1 - W_0 - h_0}{xW_1} \qquad (6.15)$$

The income generation process[6]

Economic activity, and hence capacity utilization and unemployment in our model, is determined by effective demand. For the analysis of saving and investment and the related goods market equilibrium, we also assume that firms, rentiers and labourers form adaptive expectations. We assume a classical saving hypothesis, i.e. labourers do not save. The part of profits retained is completely saved, by definition. The part of profits distributed to rentiers' households, i.e. the interest payments, is used by those households according to their propensity to save (s_R). Therefore, total expected saving (S) comprises expected retained profits ($\Pi - i_n B$) and saving out of expected interest income (S_R). Taking equations (6.1), (6.2), (6.5) and (6.7) into account, we get the private saving rate (σ) which relates total saving to the capital stock:

$$\sigma = \frac{S}{pK} = \frac{\Pi - i_n B + S_R}{K} = h\frac{z}{v} - i_n\lambda(1 - s_R), \quad 0 < s_R \leq 1 \qquad (6.16)$$

For the accumulation rate (g), relating net investment (I) to the capital stock, we follow the arguments in Kalecki (1954) and assume that investment decisions are positively affected both by expected sales and by expected retained earnings. Expected sales are determined by the rate of capacity utilization. Retained earnings, in relation to the capital stock, are given by the difference between expected profits and expected payments to rentiers normalized by the capital stock, and hence by the nominal rate of interest and the debt–capital ratio. Taking into account equations (6.1), (6.2), (6.5) and (6.7) again, we obtain:

$$g = \frac{I}{pK} = g_0 + g_1 z + g_2\left[h\frac{z}{v} - i_n\lambda\right], \quad g_0, g_1, g_2 > 0, \ g_2 < 1 \qquad (6.17)$$

We also include deficit-financed demand by the government (D) in relation to the capital stock ($d = D/pK$). Government demand in real terms is exogenous for the purposes of our model:

$$d = \frac{D}{pK} = \bar{d} \qquad (6.18)$$

The goods market equilibrium is given by:

$$g + d = \sigma \qquad (6.19)$$

and the stability condition by:

$$\frac{\partial \sigma}{\partial z} - \frac{\partial g}{\partial z} - \frac{\partial d}{\partial z} > 0 \Rightarrow (1 - g_2)\frac{h}{v} - g_1 > 0 \qquad (6.20)$$

From equations (6.16)–(6.19), the equilibrium rate of capacity utilization can be calculated:

$$z^e = \frac{i_n \lambda (1 - s_R - g_2) + g_0 + d}{\frac{h}{v}(1 - g_2) - g_1} \qquad (6.21)$$

Since equation (6.21) is based on behavioural equations which by definition can only include expected inflation, the z^e equilibrium derived from these equations is a planned, or an *ex ante* equilibrium. Taking into account the relationship between the employment rate and the rate of capacity utilization from equation (6.11), we obtain the following rate of employment determined by the *ex ante* goods market equilibrium:

$$e^e = \frac{x[i_n \lambda (1 - s_R - g_2) + g_0 + d]}{\frac{h}{v}(1 - g_2) - g_1} \qquad (6.22)$$

Is the NAIRU a strong attractor in the short run and exogenous in the long run?

The *ex ante* goods market equilibrium rate of employment in equation (6.22) may deviate from the stable inflation rate of employment determined in equation (6.14). Such a deviation will trigger unexpected inflation which will change distribution between total profits and wages, on the one hand, and between retained profits and rentiers' income, on the other hand. The interesting question is now whether unexpected inflation will adjust the goods market equilibrium towards the NAIRU or not. If there is no endogenous convergence towards the NAIRU, the next question is then whether an inflation targeting central bank can stabilize the system. This will be analysed in a second step. In the third step the medium- to long-run effects of variations in the interest rate triggered by central bank interventions will be briefly addressed.

In order to be able to calculate the effects of changes in the inflation rate on the employment rate, the distribution effects of unexpected inflation from equations (6.6) and (6.9) have to be included into the goods market equilibrium (6.22):

$$e = \frac{x[(i_n - \hat{p}^u)\lambda(1 - s_R - g_2) + g_0 + d]}{\frac{1}{v}(h_0 - h_2\hat{p}^u)(1 - g_2) - g_1} \quad (6.23)$$

Since unexpected inflation causes a deviation from the *ex ante* goods market equilibrium employment rate in equation (6.22), equation (6.23) does not define an equilibrium in the behavioural sense, with expectations fulfilled. It is rather a temporary *ex post* goods market equilibrium caused by unexpected inflation. Since there is no positive or negative excess demand in the goods market, economic agents will not change the activity level defined in equation (6.23), but adjust inflation expectations in the next period. However, unless the employment rate determined by the *ex post* goods market equilibrium matches the stable inflation rate of employment, unexpected inflation will occur again, causing once more a deviation of the *ex post* from the *ex ante* goods market equilibrium and so on.

The NAIRU as a strong short-run attractor without central bank interventions?

From equation (6.23), the effect of unexpected inflation on the goods market equilibrium rate of employment can be derived as follows:

$$\frac{\partial e}{\partial \hat{p}^u} = \frac{\frac{h_2}{v}(1 - g_2)e - x\lambda(1 - s_R - g_2)}{\frac{1}{v}(h_0 - h_2\hat{p}^u)(1 - g_2) - g_1} \quad (6.23a)$$

First, there is redistribution between gross profits and wages affecting the goods market equilibrium, with unexpected inflation (disinflation) reducing (raising) the profit share and increasing (reducing) the wage share. Through this channel unexpected inflation (disinflation) has a positive (negative) effect on economic activity and employment, as can be seen in the first term in the numerator. Therefore, our model is unambiguously wage-led, as far as the effects of redistribution between capital and labour on capacity utilization and employment are concerned. Taken alone, this causes a further deviation of actual unemployment from the NAIRU.

Second, there is redistribution among gross profits, with unexpected inflation (disinflation) reducing (raising) the share of rentiers' income in gross profits. The effect of redistribution between firms and rentiers on economic activity through this channel is not clear in advance, but depends on the values of the rentiers' propensity to consume and the elasticity of firms' investment with respect to internal funds. If the former exceeds the latter $(1 - s_R > g_2)$, unexpected inflation and redistribution at the expense of rentiers has a dampening effect on economic activity (the 'puzzling case'). However, if the effect on firms' investment is stronger than the one on rentiers' consumption $(g_2 > 1 - s_R)$, unexpected inflation will have a stimulating effect on economic activity and capacity utilization (the 'normal case').[7]

For the total effect of unexpected inflation on the *ex post* employment rate determined by the goods market, we therefore obtain:

$$\frac{\partial e}{\partial \hat{p}^u} < 0, \text{ if: } 1 - s_R > \frac{h_2}{v}\frac{e}{x\lambda}(1 - g_2) + g_2 \qquad (6.23a')$$

The requirements for a negative effect of unexpected inflation on the goods market equilibrium rate of employment driving it towards the NAIRU are quite restrictive. We do not only need the conditions for the 'puzzling case' with respect to the macroeconomic effects of redistribution between firms and rentiers $(1 - s_R > g_2)$, but also very weak demand effects of redistribution between capital and labour caused by unexpected inflation or disinflation.

If the effect of unexpected inflation on the *ex post* goods market equilibrium is positive:

$$\frac{\partial e}{\partial \hat{p}^u} > 0, \text{ if: } \frac{h_2}{v}\frac{e}{x\lambda}(1 - g_2) + g_2 > 1 - s_R \qquad (6.23a'')$$

unexpected inflation will move the *ex post* goods market equilibrium farther away from the distribution equilibrium. This is shown in Figure 6.2: The initial *ex ante* goods market equilibrium rate of employment (e_1^e) exceeds the short-run stable inflation rate of employment (e^N) which triggers unexpected inflation. Since unexpected inflation has a positive effect on the *ex post* goods market equilibrium rate of employment, this will move the goods market equilibrium even farther away from the distribution equilibrium. With adaptive expectations economic agents will make the current inflation rate the expected rate in the next period, the *ex ante* goods market equilibrium will move to (e_2^e), and the *ex post* goods

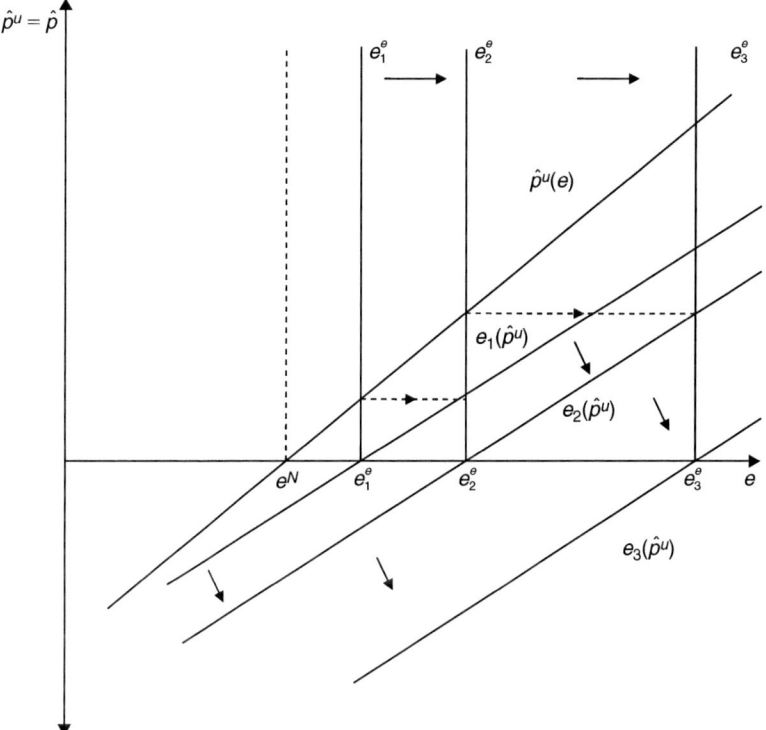

Figure 6.2 The NAIRU as a non-attractor

market equilibrium function in employment-unexpected inflation space will shift accordingly. Unexpected inflation will be triggered again and, as a result, the goods market equilibrium will diverge monotonically from the stable inflation rate of employment.

A negative relationship between unexpected inflation and the *ex post* goods market equilibrium rate of employment, as in equation (6.23a′), is, however, only a necessary but not yet a sufficient condition for the NAIRU to be a strong attractor. In order to make the goods market equilibrium rate of employment converge towards the stable inflation rate, the absolute value of the slope of the *ex post* goods market equilibrium employment curve has to exceed the slope of the short-run Phillips curve, as is shown in Figure 6.3.[8]

Therefore, for the NAIRU to be a strong attractor for the actual unemployment rate, the following condition derived from equations (6.13)

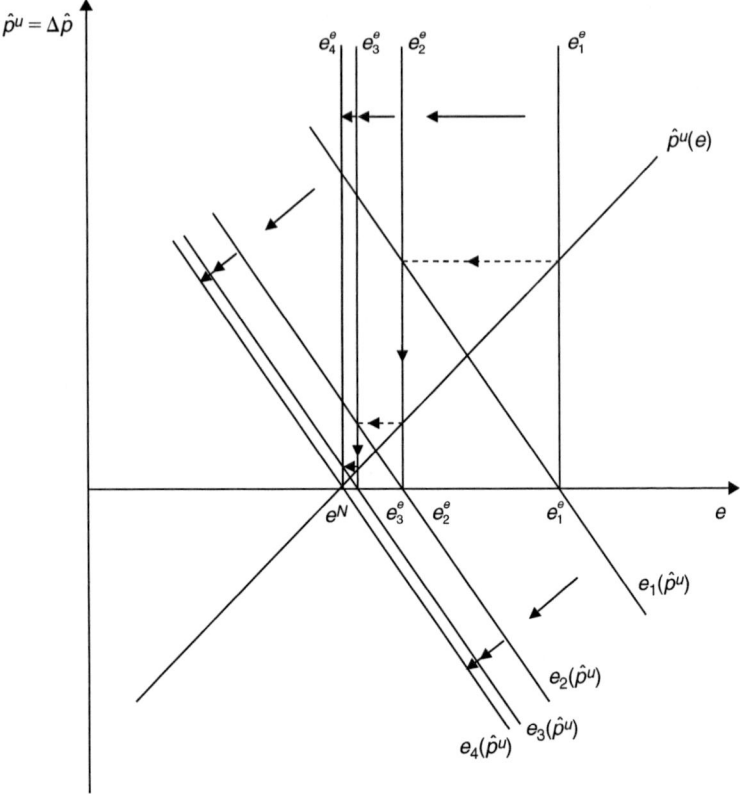

Figure 6.3 The NAIRU as an attractor

and (6.23) has to be valid:

$$\frac{\frac{1}{v}(h_0 - h_2\hat{p}^u)(1-g_2) - g_1}{\frac{h_2}{v}(1-g_2)e - x\lambda(1-s_R-g_2)} < -\frac{W_1}{W_2+h_2} \quad (6.24)$$

To sum up, the stability of the NAIRU requires a very low propensity to save out of rentiers' income, a very low elasticity of investment with respect to internal funds, weak redistribution effects of unexpected inflation on labour income and effective demand, and a very flat short-run Phillips curve. Since there is no economic mechanism in our model which will guarantee this very special constellation to hold, we next have to discuss the role of the central bank as a stabilizer of the NAIRU.

An inflation targeting central bank and the NAIRU as a short-run attractor?

Applying the NCM idea of inflation targeting by the central bank, we have to bear in mind that the central bank controls the nominal rate of interest in our model. Therefore this is the instrument an inflation targeting central bank can apply in order to achieve some target rate of inflation ($\hat{p}^T$). Here it is sufficient to assume that the central bank's inflation target equals expected inflation ($\hat{p}^T = \hat{p}^e$) and that the only aim of the central bank is to erase unexpected inflation from the system. Therefore the central bank reaction function becomes:

$$i_n = i_0^e + \hat{p}^e + \hat{p}^u + i_1(\hat{p} - \hat{p}^T) = i_0^e + \hat{p}^e + \hat{p}^u + i_1(\hat{p} - \hat{p}^e)$$
$$= i_0^e + \hat{p}^e + (1 + i_1)\hat{p}^u, \quad 0 \le i_0^e, \ 0 < i_1 \qquad (6.25)$$

with i_0^e being the central bank's estimation of the 'equilibrium real interest rate' and i_1 the reaction parameter with respect to unexpected inflation. From equation (6.23) we obtain the following effect of a change in the nominal interest rate on employment determined by the goods market:

$$\frac{\partial e^{cb}}{\partial i_n} = \frac{x\lambda(1 - s_R - g_2)}{\frac{1}{v}(h_0 - h_2\hat{p}^u)(1 - g_2) - g_1} \qquad (6.23b)$$

Changing the nominal interest rate will be positively related to capacity utilization and employment, if the 'puzzling case' with respect to the demand effects of redistribution between firms and rentiers prevails:

$$\frac{\partial e^{cb}}{\partial i_n} > 0, \text{ if: } 1 - s_R > g_2 \qquad (6.23b')$$

Inflation targeting monetary policy interventions following equation (6.25) will hence move employment farther away from the stable inflation level. Note that the condition in equation (6.23b'), indicating the inappropriateness of inflation targeting monetary policies, is not equivalent with the NAIRU being a strong attractor from equation (6.24). Therefore, if (6.23b') is valid, but (6.24) is not, neither is the NAIRU self-stabilizing in the face of accelerating (decelerating) inflation, nor is monetary policy able to adjust actual unemployment to the

NAIRU by means of raising (lowering) interest rates. In order to stabilize the NAIRU in this case, monetary policies would have to do just the opposite from what is suggested by equation (6.25), namely lowering (raising) the interest rate in the face of accelerating (decelerating) inflation.

If the 'normal case' with respect to the demand effects of redistribution between firms and rentiers prevails, inflation targeting monetary policies will have the required effects on economic activity and employment:

$$\frac{\partial e^{cb}}{\partial i_n} < 0, \text{ if: } g_2 > 1 - s_R \qquad (6.23b'')$$

If unexpected inflation caused by a deviation of unemployment from the NAIRU is not self-correcting, and the condition in equation (6.23b'') is fulfilled, the NAIRU may therefore be turned into an attractor by inflation targeting monetary policies following the monetary policy rule in equation (6.25). In this case, the effects of changes in the nominal interest rate have to over-compensate the effects of unexpected inflation on capacity utilization and employment. This does not seem to be a problem with unemployment falling short of the NAIRU and positive unexpected inflation. The central bank can always increase its instrument variable, the nominal interest rate according to equation (6.25), and wipe out unexpected inflation by means of erasing 'excess employment' from the system. This is shown in Figure 6.4.

For a stable adjustment it is again required that the absolute value of the slope of the (*ex post*) goods market equilibrium employment curve incorporating monetary policy responses (e^{cb}) has to exceed the slope of the short-run Phillips curve in employment-unexpected inflation space. Therefore central banks have to be careful in their responses in order to avoid excessive over- and undershooting which would destabilize the system.

There are further limitations for monetary policies adjusting actual employment to the stable inflation level, if unemployment exceeds the NAIRU and unexpected inflation is negative, in particular, in a climate of low inflation and hence low nominal interest rates. With unexpected disinflation or even deflation, a negative nominal interest rate according to equation (6.25) might be required in order to stabilize the system, which central banks cannot achieve due to the zero lower bound of its instrument variable. Therefore, central banks' capacities to adjust actual unemployment towards the NAIRU may be asymmetric.[9]

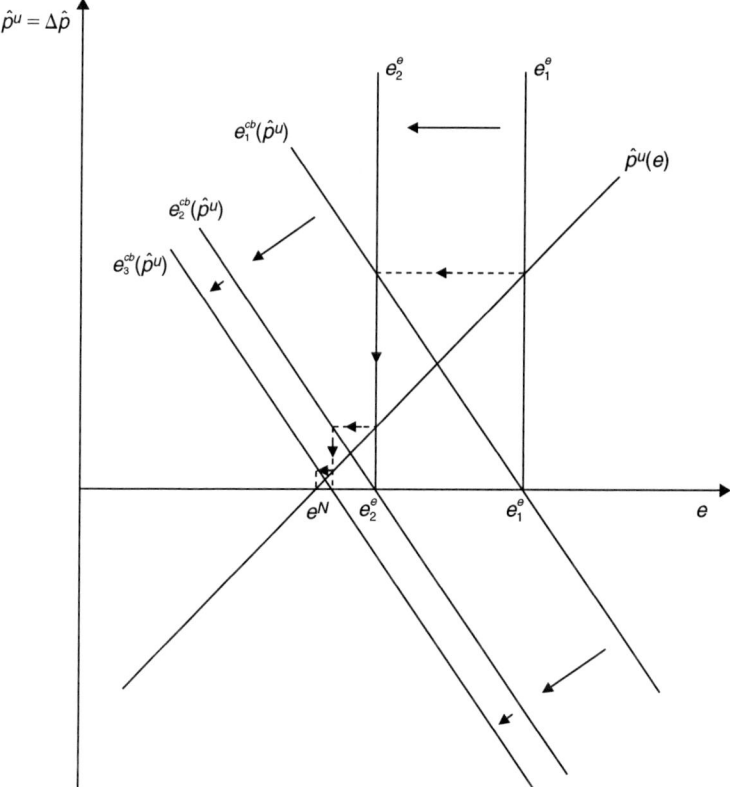

Figure 6.4 An inflation targeting central bank stabilizing the NAIRU

Medium-run endogeneity of the NAIRU through monetary policy

So far it has been shown that inflation targeting monetary policies, as the main stabilization tool proposed by the New Consensus Model (NCM), in the short run are only adequate for certain values of the model parameters, but are either unnecessary, counterproductive or limited in their effectiveness for other parameter values. In this section we integrate the medium-run effects of changes in the *ex ante* real interest rate associated with inflation targeting monetary policies.[10] We only discuss the effects of changing interest rates on the distribution equilibrium in the medium run and ignore the associated effects on the goods market equilibrium, which may give rise to complex interacting dynamics of these two equilibria.[11]

In Hein (2006a) it has been argued that persistent changes in the *ex ante* real interest rate affect firms' target profit share in the medium to long run.[12] Since interest payments are costs from the perspective of the firm which have to be covered by the mark-up on unit labour costs, persistent changes in the *ex ante* real interest rate will cause medium-run changes in the firms' target mark-up. The firms' target profit share from equation (6.8) has therefore to be expanded with h_1 denoting the medium-run interest rate effect on the target profit share:

$$h_F^T = h_0 + h_1 i^e, \quad 0 < h_0 \leq 1, \quad 0 \leq h_1 \tag{6.26}$$

Taking into account the workers' target wage share from equation (6.12), we obtain the following stable inflation rate of employment:

$$e^N = \frac{1 - W_0 - h_0 - h_1 i^e}{W_1} \tag{6.27}$$

A persistent change in the *ex ante* real interest rate will have an inverse effect on the stable inflation rate of employment:

$$\frac{\partial e^N}{\partial i^e} = -\frac{h_1}{W_1} < 0 \tag{6.27a}$$

Applying the inflation targeting interest rate rule (equation 6.25) may therefore stabilize inflation in the short run, but in the medium run the effects on the firms' target profit share may undermine the short-run stabilization effects and may create unexpected inflation again, triggering further central bank intervention, as is shown in Figure 6.5.

A Post Keynesian macroeconomic policy assignment

From our results so far it follows that the NCM policy assignment has to be completely revised in order to achieve a high and stable medium-run employment rate with stable inflation (expectations). Following our model, we restrict our discussion to a closed economy.

From the criticism of inflation targeting monetary policies developed above, different implications for more adequate monetary policies can be drawn. Applying the distinction made by Rochon and Setterfield (2007–8), either an 'activist' position or a 'parking-it' approach for the central bank applying the interest rate tool has been proposed by PKs. The proponents of the 'activist' position confirm the central bank's responsibility

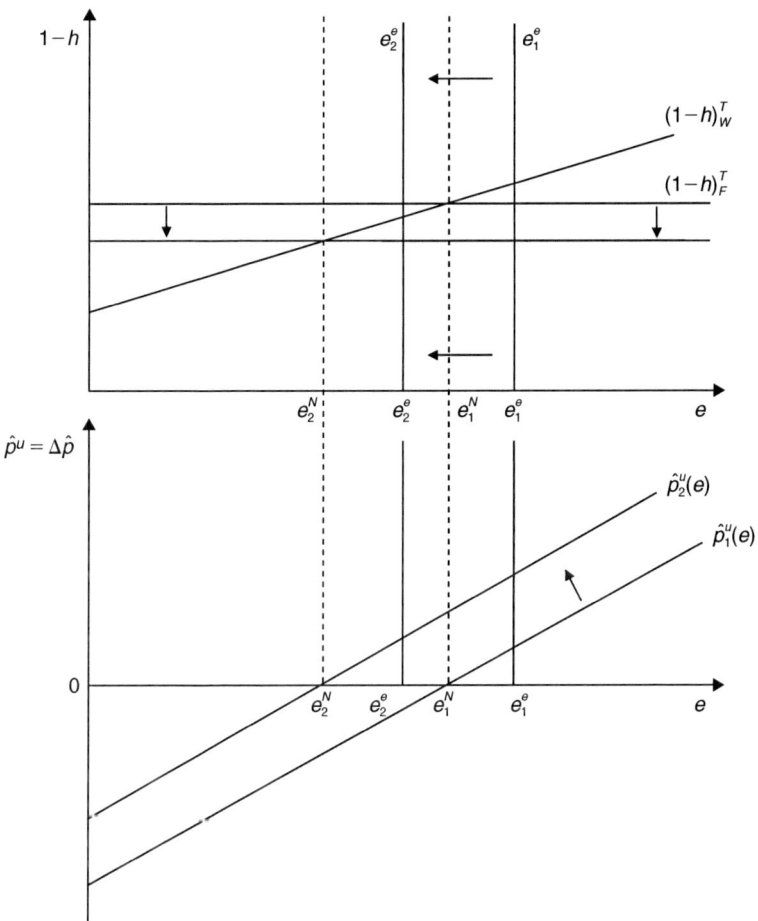

Figure 6.5 Persistent change in the *ex ante* real rate of interest and the NAIRU

for stable inflation and regard the interest rate as an appropriate tool to achieve this goal. Therefore, PK monetary economics is held to be generally consistent with inflation targeting by central banks and with the application of an interest rate operation procedure (Palley, 2006; Setterfield, 2006a; Fontana and Palacio-Vera, 2007). Contrary to NCMs, however, they demand more careful counter-cyclical stabilization by means of interest rate policies, taking into account the short- and medium-run real effects, as well as more reasonable, that is higher, inflation targets.

The 'parking-it' position, however, refrains from recommending fine tuning the economy by means of interest rate policies, but focuses on the long-run distribution effects of the central bank setting the interest rate, which we have highlighted above, and recommends stabilizing the long-term rate of interest at a certain level. Different targets have been proposed. Smithin (2004), for example, suggests that the real interest rate should be set to zero, or as close to zero as possible, allowing rentiers to maintain their stock of real wealth but not to participate in real growth. Lavoie (1996a) and Setterfield (2006b) are in favour of setting the real rate of interest equal to productivity growth, which allows rentiers to participate in real growth and keeps distribution between rentiers, on the one hand, and firms and labourers, on the other hand, constant (Pasinetti's (1981) 'fair rate of interest').[13] Since we have abstracted from productivity growth in our model, these two rules are essentially the same. Therefore we obtain the following monetary policy rule:

$$i_n = i_0^e + \hat{p}^e + \hat{p}^u \qquad (6.28)$$

with i_0^e being given by medium-run productivity growth. Central banks will have to adjust their policy instrument, the nominal interest rate, so that a constant expected real rate of interest equal to medium-run productivity growth emerges. This implies adjusting the nominal interest rate to unexpected inflation at the end of each period.

Note that monetary policies in this approach should neither pursue an inflation target nor make any attempts at adjusting the employment rate to some target. Of course, monetary policies remain responsible for the orderly working of the monetary and financial system, the definition of credit standards for refinance operations with commercial banks (credit controls), the implementation of compulsory minimum reserves of different types to be held with the central bank, the role of a 'lender of last resort' in the case of systemic crises, and so on.[14]

The NCM view on the role of wage formation and wage bargaining, demanding nominal and real wage flexibility by means of structural reforms in the labour market and decentralization of wage bargaining in order to accelerate the adjustment towards the NAIRU and in order to reduce the NAIRU itself, cannot be sustained on the basis of our model. Nominal wage flexibility generates unexpected inflation whenever unemployment deviates from the NAIRU. This affects distribution between firms and rentiers, on the one hand, and between capital and labour, on the other hand, and is hence associated with real wage flexibility. With realistic parameters, nominal wage flexibility makes actual unemployment diverge further from the NAIRU in our model, as we have shown above.

In order to avoid the destabilizing effects of nominal and real wage flexibility, PKs advocate rigid nominal wages and allocate the role of nominal stabilization to incomes or wage policies.[15] Therefore, nominal unit labour costs should grow at a rate similar to the country's inflation target, which means that nominal wage growth should equal the sum of medium-run growth of labour productivity ($\hat{w}_0$) and the target inflation rate:

$$\hat{w} = \hat{w}_0 + \hat{p}^T \tag{6.29}$$

Following this wage formula will also keep income shares constant, provided that the mark-up in firms' pricing remains constant and that imported material costs in an open economy grow in line with domestic unit labour costs (Kalecki, 1954, pp. 28–30). Under these conditions, the destabilizing effects of real wage flexibility in wage-led economies will be avoided, too.

The optimal way to achieve nominal stabilization is to make the target wage shares of workers and firms compatible for a relevant range of employment rates. In the context of our model this requires a reformulation of the workers target wage share from equation (6.10):

$$(1 - h)_W^T = W_0 + W_1 e, \text{ if: } e < e_1^N \text{ or } e_2^N < e \tag{6.30}$$

and

$$(1 - h)_W^T = (1 - h)_F^T = h_0, \text{ if: } e_1^N < e < e_2^N$$

The stable inflation rate of employment and hence the NAIRU becomes a corridor and the Phillips curve from equation (6.13) becomes a horizontal line between e_1^N and e_2^N (see Figure 6.6):

$$\hat{p}_t^u = \frac{W_0 + W_1 e + h_0 - 1}{W_2 + h_2}, \text{ if: } e < e_1^N \text{ or } e_2^N < e \tag{6.31}$$

and

$$\hat{p}_t^u = 0, \text{ if: } e_1^N < e < e_2^N$$

Variations in the employment rate between e_1^N and e_2^N do not trigger any unexpected inflation and hence no cumulative processes will set in. In this case, demand management is free to choose a high level of employment close to e_2^N without violating stable inflation rates. PKs argue that in particular a high degree of wage bargaining coordination at the national level, strong labour unions and employer organizations, and hence organized labour markets should be particularly suitable for pursuing this nominal stabilization role of wage bargaining.[16]

Because of the limitations associated with real and nominal stabilization by means of monetary policies, the complete neglect of discretionary fiscal policies in the NCM turns out to be a major problem (see in particular Arestis and Sawyer 2003, 2004a, 2004c).[17] Therefore PKs have argued in favour of real stabilization by means of fiscal policies. This has again two dimensions. Since an adjustment of actual unemployment to NAIRU cannot generally be expected, neither from market forces nor from monetary policies, fiscal policies are required for short-run real stabilization. And since the NAIRU is endogenous to actual unemployment and hence to effective demand in the medium to long run, fiscal policies do not only have short-run real effects but also affect the long-run development of the economy.

Arestis and Sawyer (2003) demonstrate that the major arguments put forward against a use of discretionary fiscal policies, 'crowding out' (through higher inflation and associated real balance effects or higher real interest rates) and the 'Ricardian equivalence theorem', are unconvincing, both on theoretical and empirical grounds. Both arguments have to assume that the economy operates at full employment equilibrium level. But if there is already full employment, there is no need to implement expansionary fiscal policies in order to achieve full employment and hence there is no need to think about 'crowding out' or 'Ricardian equivalence'! Making use of government deficit spending for stabilizing effective demand in the short and in the medium to long run, in the sense of 'functional finance', that is compensating private sector full (or stable inflation rate of) employment saving by government deficit spending,[18] however, requires that central banks do not interfere with expansionary fiscal policies and stick to a policy of low interest rates.

In the context of our model real stabilization should therefore be delegated to fiscal policies and equation (6.18) can be extended in the following way:

$$d = d_0 + d_1(e^T - e), \quad 0 < d_1 \qquad (6.32)$$

with d_0 as permanent government deficit or surplus, which is required if employment is at target (e^T), and d_1 as the reaction in the case of short-run deviations of employment from target. The employment target is the

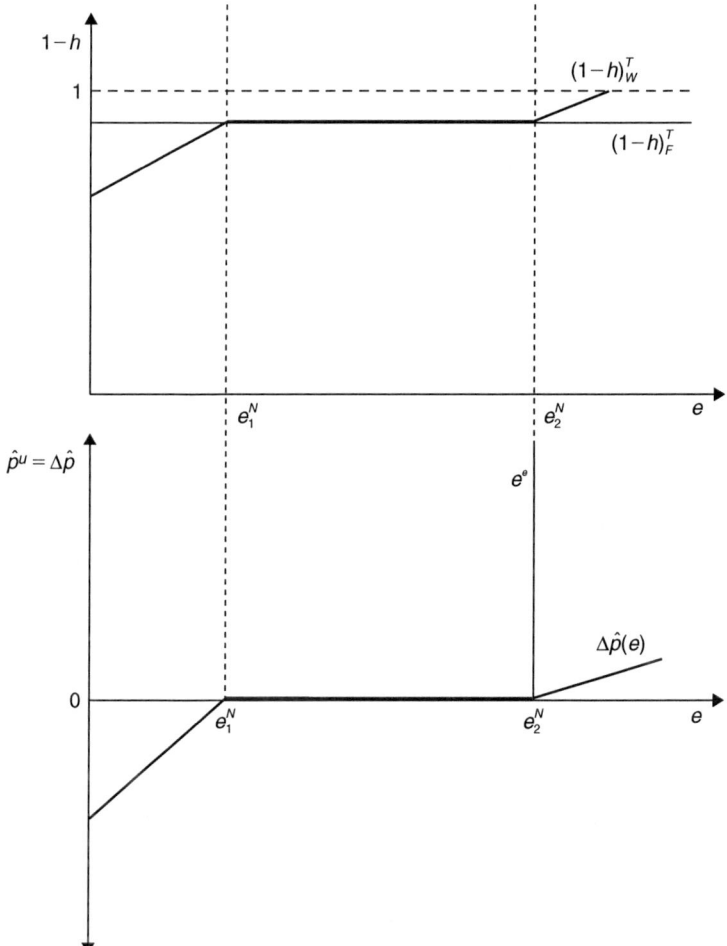

Figure 6.6 A Post Keynesian policy mix

maximum employment rate achievable without triggering unexpected inflation.

The PK assignment or policy-mix and its effects can finally be seen in Figure 6.6. Wage policies, and hence wage bargaining parties, are mainly responsible for stable inflation rates, and hence for nominal stabilization. Fiscal policies are responsible for the management of demand, maintaining effective demand at high employment levels, and hence for real stabilization in the short and in the long run. Monetary policies by the central bank should neither aim at fine tuning the economy in real nor in nominal terms, and should thus not interfere with the tasks of wage and fiscal policies, but should rather focus on low real interest rate stable distribution between rentiers, on the one hand, and firms and labourers, on the other hand. Coordination of macroeconomic policies along these lines will be more promising for high employment and stable inflation rates than the NCM economic policy approach.

Summary and conclusions

We have shown that, depending on the model parameters, inflation targeting monetary policies as the main stabilization tool in the NCM may be either unnecessary, counterproductive or limited in their effectiveness in the short run of our model. Taking into account the medium-run cost and distribution effects of interest rate variations renders monetary policies completely inappropriate as an economic stabilizer. Based on these results we have argued that the NCM macroeconomic policy assignment should therefore be replaced by a PK assignment. Enhancing employment without increasing inflation will be possible if macroeconomic policies are coordinated along the following lines. The central bank targets distribution between rentiers, on the hand, and firms and labourers, on the other hand, and it sets low real interest rates; wage bargaining parties target inflation; and fiscal policies are applied for short- and medium-run real stabilization purposes.

Notes

1. See Clarida et al. (1999), Meyer (2001) and Carlin and Soskice (2006, 27, p. −172) for NCMs.
2. See Layard et al. (1991, p. 96), Blanchard and Katz (1997), Mankiw (2001) and Ball and Mankiw (2002) for concepts of a NAIRU.
3. For a more extensive treatment, see Hein and Stockhammer (2007).
4. This part is developed on the basis of Stockhammer (2008) and extends the model presented there. For PK conflicting claims models of inflation, see also Lavoie (1992, pp. 391–421, 2002), Rowthorn (1977), Sawyer (2002), Arestis and Sawyer (2004a, pp. 73–87, 2005), and Hein (2006a).
5. Of course, there may also be exogenous shocks generating unexpected inflation.
6. The 'income generation process' in this paper is based on Hein (2006a, 2006b) and extends the models developed there. Rochon and Setterfield (2007–8b), Setterfield (2006b) and Stockhammer (2008) have also introduced a more elaborated income generation process than the one in the NCMs. However, they do not take fully into account the distribution effects of unexpected

7. See Lavoie (1995) and Hein (2006b, 2008, pp. 61–127) for a discussion of 'puzzling' and 'normal' cases in Kaleckian distribution and growth models.
8. We may also have converging oscillations which are not shown graphically.
9. Another reason for asymmetric effects of central bank policies, not explicitly discussed in our model with only one interest rate, arises from the interaction of the central bank with the commercial banking sector. Whereas the central bank can always force commercial banks to increase market rates by means of increasing the base rate, commercial banks might not follow the central bank decreasing interest rates, in particular in a recession with increasing uncertainty and risk assessments.
10. Further medium- to long-run endogeneity channels of the NAIRU with respect to actual unemployment, i.e. labour market persistence mechanisms, endogenous wage and profit aspirations, and the effects of capital stock growth, cannot be treated in this chapter due to a lack of space. Their integration into the present model structure is indicated in Hein and Stockhammer (2007).
11. For a discussion of the related dynamics associated with a persistent change in the real interest rate in a somewhat simpler model, see Hein (2006a).
12. The idea that lasting variations in interest rates may affect functional income distribution and hence the share of wages and gross profits in total income goes back to Sraffa (1960, p. 33) and has been proposed, in particular, by Neo-Ricardian authors (see for example Pivetti (1991)), but it can also be found in earlier PK work (Pasinetti, 1974, pp. 139–41; Kaldor, 1982, p. 63).
13. Wray (2007) proposes a zero nominal interest rate in order to get rid of the rentiers' class. However, this seems to imply overcoming the main characteristics of a monetary production economy, the advancement of credit in order to get production started. Obviously, with a zero nominal interest rate in a single interest rate model there is no incentive for banks/rentiers to grant credit for initial finance of production or final finance of the capital stock.
14. This view is shared by the PK proponents of the 'activist' position (see for example Palley (2006)) and of the 'parking-it' position (see for instance Lavoie (1996a)). A detailed discussion of central bank reactions towards financial market instabilities is outside the scope of the present chapter.
15. See, for example, Arestis (1996), Davidson (2006) and Setterfield (2006a).
16. See Hein (2006a) and Kriesler and Lavoie (2007) for the implementation of coordinated wage bargaining into PK models. See Hein (2002, 2004) for reviews of the related literature.
17. For the inappropriateness of this view, also within an NCM framework, see Setterfield (2007), who shows that there is good reason to conclude that 'fiscal policy is at least as, if not, *more* potent as an instrument of stabilization policy than is monetary policy' (p. 417, italics in the original).
18. The 'functional finance' view, pioneered by Lerner (1943), recommends government deficits, the difference between government spending (G) and taxes (T), to mop up the excess of private sector planned saving (S) over planned investment (I), plus the difference between imports (M) and exports (X), at a desired (full employment) level of economic activity: $G - T = S - I + M - X$ (see Arestis and Sawyer, 2004c). Applying government deficit spending in the

'functional finance' way assures that there is always enough saving to fund government deficits by means of issuing bonds and/or increasing the central bank's money supply, buying government bonds through open market operations.

References

Arestis, P. (1996) 'Post-Keynesian Economics: Towards Coherence', *Cambridge Journal of Economics* 20: 111–35.
Arestis, P. and M. Sawyer (2003) 'Reinventing Fiscal Policy', *Journal of Post Keynesian Economics* 26: 3–25.
Arestis, P. and M. Sawyer (2004a) *Re-examining Monetary and Fiscal Policy for the 21st Century*, Cheltenham: Edward Elgar.
Arestis, P. and M. Sawyer (2004b) 'Monetary Policy when Money is Endogenous: Going beyond the "New Consensus"', in M. Lavoie and M. Seccareccia (eds), *Central Banking in the Modern World. Alternative Perspectives*, Cheltenham: Edward Elgar.
Arestis, P. and M. Sawyer (2004c) 'On Fiscal Policy and Budget Deficits', *Intervention. Journal of Economics* 1 (2): 61–74.
Arestis, P. and M. Sawyer (2005) 'Aggregate Demand, Conflict and Capacity in the Inflationary Process', *Cambridge Journal of Economics* 29: 959–74.
Arestis, P. and M. Sawyer (2006) 'The Nature and the Role of Monetary Policy when Money is Endogenous', *Cambridge Journal of Economics* 30: 847–60.
Atesoglu, H. S. and J. Smithin (2006) 'Inflation Targeting in a Simple Macroeconomic Model', *Journal of Post Keynesian Economics* 28: 673–88.
Ball, L. (1999) 'Aggregate Demand and Long-run Unemployment', *Brooking Papers on Economic Activity* 2: 189–251.
Ball, L. and N. G. Mankiw (2002) 'The NAIRU in Theory and Practice', *Journal of Economic Perspectives* 16 (4): 115–36.
Blanchard, O. J. and L. F. Katz (1997) 'What We Know and Do Not Know about the Natural Rate of Unemployment', *Journal of Economic Perspectives* 11 (1): 51–72.
Blanchard, O. J. and L. H. Summers (1987) 'Hysteresis in Unemployment', *European Economic Review* 31: 288–95.
Blanchard, O. J. and L. H. Summers (1988) 'Beyond the Natural Rate Hypothesis', *American Economic Review* 78 (2): 182–7.
Carlin, W. and D. Soskice (2006) *Macroeconomics. Imperfections, Institutions and Policies*, Oxford: Oxford University Press.
Clarida, R., J. Galí and M. Gertler (1999) 'The Science of Monetary Policy: A New Keynesian Perspective', *Journal of Economic Literature* 37: 1661–707.
Davidson, P. (2006) 'Can, or Should, a Central Bank Target Inflation?', *Journal of Post Keynesian Economics* 28: 689–703.
Fontana, G. and A. Palacio-Vera (2007) 'Are Long-run Price Stability and Short-run Output Stabilization all that Monetary Policy Can Aim for?', *Metroeconomica* 58: 269–98.
Gnos, C. and L.-P. Rochon (2007) 'The New Consensus and Post-Keynesian Interest Rate Policy', *Review of Political Economy* 19: 369–86.

Hein, E. (2002) 'Monetary Policy and Wage Bargaining in the EMU: Restrictive ECB Policies, High Unemployment, Nominal Wage Restraint and Inflation above the Target', *Banca Nazionale del Lavoro Quarterly Review* 55: 299–337.

Hein, E. (2004) 'Die NAIRU – eine post-keynesianische Interpretation, *Intervention Zeitschrift für Ökonomie* 1: 43–66.

Hein, E. (2006a) 'Wage Bargaining and Monetary Policy in a Kaleckian Monetary Distribution and Growth Model: Trying to Make Sense of the NAIRU, *Intervention Journal of Economics* 3: 305–29.

Hein, E. (2006b) 'Interest, Debt and Capital Accumulation – A Kaleckian Approach', *International Review of Applied Economics* 2006: 337–52.

Hein, E. (2008) *Money, Distribution Conflict and Capital Accumulation. Contributions to 'Monetary Analysis'*, Basingstoke: Palgrave Macmillan.

Hein, E. and E. Stockhammmer (2007) 'Macroeconomic Policy Mix, Employment and Inflation in a Post-Keynesian Alternative to the New Consensus Model', Department of Economics Working Paper 108, Vienna University of Economics and Business Administration.

Kaldor, N. (1970) 'The New Monetarism', *Lloyds Bank Review* 97: 1–17.

Kaldor, N. (1982) *The Scourge of Monetarism*, Oxford: Oxford University Press.

Kaldor, N. (1985) 'How Monetarism Failed', *Challenge* 28 (2): 4–13.

Kalecki, M. (1954) *Theory of Economic Dynamics*, London: George Allen

Kalecki, M. (1971) *Selected Essays on the Dynamics of the Capitalist Economy, 1933–70*, Cambridge: Cambridge University Press.

Kriesler, P. and M Lavoie (2007) 'The New Consensus on Monetary Policy and its Post-Keynesian Critique', *Review of Political Economy*, 19: 387–404.

Lavoie, M. (1984) 'The Endogenous Flow of Credit and the Post Keynesian Theory of Money', *Journal of Economic Issues* 18: 771–97.

Lavoie, M. (1992) *Foundations of Post Keynesian Economic Analysis*, Aldershot: Edward Elgar.

Lavoie, M. (1995) 'Interest Rates in Post-Keynesian Models of Growth and Distribution', *Metroeconomica* 46: 146–77.

Lavoie, M. (1996a) 'Monetary Policy in an Economy with Endogenous Credit Money', in G. Deleplace and E. Nell (eds), *Money in Motion*, Basingstoke: Macmillan.

Lavoie, M. (1996b) 'Horizontalism, Structuralism, Liquidity Preference and the Principle of Increasing Risk', *Scottish Journal of Political Economy* 43: 275–300.

Lavoie, M. (2002) 'The Kaleckian Growth Model with Target Return Pricing and Conflict Inflation', in M. Setterfield (ed.), *The Economics of Demand-led Growth*, Cheltenham: Edward Elgar.

Lavoie, M. (2004) 'The New Consensus on Monetary Policy Seen from a Post-Keynesian Perspective', in M. Lavoie and M. Seccareccia (eds), *Central Banking in the Modern World. Alternative Perspectives*, Cheltenham: Edward Elgar.

Lavoie, M. (2006) 'A Post-Keynesian Amendment to the New Consensus on Monetary Policy', *Metroeconomica* 57: 165–92.

Layard, R., S. Nickell and R. Jackman (1991) *Unemployment. Macroeconomic Performance and the Labour Market*, Oxford: Oxford University Press.

Lerner, A. (1943) 'Functional Finance and Federal Debt', *Social Research* 10: 38–51.

Mankiw, N. G. (2001) 'The Inexorable and Mysterious Tradeoff between Inflation and Unemployment', *The Economic Journal* 111: C45–C61.

Meyer, L. H. (2001) 'Does Money Matter?', *Federal Reserve Bank of St. Louis Review* 83 (5): 1–15.
Moore, B. J. (1989) 'The Endogeneity of Credit Money', *Review of Political Economy* 1: 65–93.
Palacio-Vera, A. (2005) 'The "Modern" View of Macroeconomics: Some Critical Reflections', *Cambridge Journal of Economics* 29: 747–67.
Palley, T. (2006) 'A Post-Keynesian Framework for Monetary Policy: Why Interest Rate Operating Procedures are not Enough', in C. Gnos and L.-P. Rochon (eds), *Post-Keynesian Principles of Economic Policy*, Cheltenham: Edward Elgar.
Pasinetti, L. (1974) *Growth and Income Distribution*, Cambridge: Cambridge University Press.
Pasinetti, L. (1981) *Structural Change and Economic Growth*, Cambridge: Cambridge University Press.
Pivetti, M. (1991) *An Essay on Money and Distribution*, Basingstoke: Macmillan.
Rochon, L.-P. and M. Setterfield (2007–8) 'Interest Rates, Income Distribution and Monetary Dominance: Post-Keynesians and the "Fair Rate" of Interest', *Journal of Post Keynesian Economics*, 30: 13-42.
Rowthorn, R. E. (1977) 'Conflict, Inflation and Money', *Cambridge Journal of Economics* 1: 215–39.
Rowthorn, R. E. (1995) 'Capital Formation and Unemployment', *Oxford Review of Economic Policy* 11 (1): 26–39.
Rowthorn, R. E. (1999) 'Unemployment, Wage Bargaining and Capital-labour Substitution', *Cambridge Journal of Economics* 23: 413–25.
Sawyer, M. (2002) 'The NAIRU, Aggregate Demand and Investment', *Metroeconomica* 53: 66–94.
Setterfield, M. (2004) 'Central Banking, Stability and Macroeconomic Outcomes: A Comparison of New Consensus and Post-Keynesian Monetary Macroeconomics', in M. Lavoie and M. Seccareccia (eds), *Central Banking in the Modern World. Alternative Perspectives*, Cheltenham: Edward Elgar.
Setterfield, M. (2006a) 'Is Inflation Targeting Compatible with Post Keynesian Economics?', *Journal of Post Keynesian Economics* 28: 653–71.
Setterfield, M. (2006b) 'Macroeconomics without the LM Curve: An Alternative View', paper presented at the 9th Post Keynesian Conference, Kansas City.
Setterfield, M. (2007) 'Is there a Stabilizing Role for Fiscal Policy in the New Consensus?', *Review of Political Economy* 19: 405–18.
Setterfield, M. and T. Lovejoy (2006) 'Aspiration, Bargaining Power, and Macroeconomic Performance', *Journal of Post Keynesian Economics* 26: 117–48.
Smithin, J. (2004) 'Interest Rate Operating Procedures and Income Distribution', in M. Lavoie and M. Seccareccia (eds), *Central Banking in the Modern World: Alternative Perspectives*, Cheltenham: Edward Elgar: 57–69.
Sraffa, P. (1960) *Production of Commodities by Means of Commodities*, Cambridge: Cambridge University Press.
Stockhammer, E. (2004) 'Is there an Equilibrium Rate of Unemployment in the Long Run?', *Review of Political Economy* 16: 59–77.
Stockhammer, E. (2008) 'Is the NAIRU a Monetarist, New Keynesian, Post Keynesian or Marxist Theory?', *Metroeconomica* 59:479–510.
Wray, R. (2007) 'A Post-Keynesian View of Central Bank Independence, Policy Targets, and the Rules-versus-Discretion Debate', Working Paper 510, The Levy Economics Institute of Bard College.

7
The 'Unemployment Bias' of the New Consensus View of Macroeconomics
Giuseppe Fontana

Introduction

The last couple of decades have seen an unprecedented convergence in the theory and practice of monetary policy (Meyer, 2001; Goodhart, 2007). This process of convergence has quickly spread to the entire macroeconomics field. After decades of fierce debates between Keynesians and monetarists, there is indeed a degree of consensus in macroeconomics, which is unprecedented since the Keynesian 'Golden Age' of the 1960s. It is now safe to refer to the New Consensus view in macroeconomics without any risk of misunderstanding.

The purpose of this chapter is to review the major reasons for this success, before highlighting some problems with the New Consensus view, including the replacement of fiscal policy with monetary policy as the main stabilization tool, as well as the exclusive short-run view of the role of aggregate demand. More importantly, drawing on records of the Federal Open Market Committee (FOMC) meetings at the Federal Reserve System, I will discuss the 'unemployment bias' of the conventional policy strategy of the New Consensus view, namely the persistent tendency to keep the unemployment rate above the NAIRU, as long as the economy is not at price stability.

I shall go on to discuss a recently proposed amendment of the conventional or deliberate policy strategy of the New Consensus view, the so-called 'opportunistic' strategy. This alternative policy strategy was originally discussed during FOMC meetings in the 1990s. It contains two original features, namely path dependency and a zone of discretion. These two features have the potential to eliminate or at least contain the 'unemployment bias' of the conventional or deliberate policy strategy of the New Consensus view. For this reason, I will closely scrutinize the

The New Consensus view in macroeconomics

A 2005 UK Treasury-sponsored conference gathered well known economists and practitioners around the theme of 'Is There a New Consensus in Macroeconomics?' The book, which collects most of the contributions of the conference, and which bears the same title, does not leave space for any misunderstanding: 'There is indeed a degree of consensus in macroeconomics unprecedented since the Keynesian "Golden Age" from the late 1950s to the early 1970s. From a polemical "schools of thought" debate, the focus has now moved on to synthesis' (Arestis and Ross, 2007, p. 20). This New Consensus in macroeconomics is indeed so popular that it is slowly, but increasingly, being used to replace the iconic *IS-LM* model in undergraduate macroeconomic textbooks (e.g. Carlin and Soskice, 2006, ch. 3). This success is related to a combination of theoretical and practical arguments.

Starting with the theoretical arguments, the New Consensus model marks a significant progress over previous monetary models. It represents a dramatic shift from the quantity-theoretic framework, defended by monetarists and neo-classical synthesis Keynesians alike, toward a non-quantity theoretic framework in the spirit of the monetary contributions of Wicksell and Keynes (Fontana, 2007). This non-quantity theoretic framework has also shown remarkable flexibility, being able to encompass recent theoretical notions, including the natural rate hypothesis and the expectations-augmented or inertia Phillips curve. It has also absorbed the rational expectation hypothesis and built on the insights and methodology of the real business cycle theory.

The practical arguments in favour of the New Consensus view are not less powerful and innovative. Most central banks around the world, including the Bank of England and the Federal Reserve, have all rejected the monetarist credo and its policy prescriptions. Central banks do not control a (any) monetary aggregate, but the short-run nominal interest rate. The stock of money is thus a residual, an endogenous rather than an exogenous, element of the economic process. The old causal relationship between money and price is untenable. Similarly, any recommended cure for inflation based on a monetary targeting rule is considered impracticable. The void left by the monetarist credo and its policy implications has been replaced by new analyses and policies, which are consistent with the New Consensus view. Central banks now use the short-run nominal interest rate to achieve a particular combination of current and potential levels of output, the so-called output gap, which delivers the desired rate of inflation.[1]

Several authors have explored in detail the building blocks of the New Consensus model and its assumptions (e.g. Arestis and Sawyer, 2006; Fontana and Palacio-Vera, 2007). For the purposes of this chapter, it will suffice to recall the main features of the model, before considering in the next section the 'unemployment bias' implicit in its transmission mechanism. The core of the New Consensus view is based on a simple 3-equations model made of an expectations-augmented Phillips curve, an *IS*-type curve, and a monetary policy rule (Clarida *et al.*, 1999). The expectations-augmented Phillips curve represents the short-run aggregate supply-side of the model, where the *IS*-type curve and the monetary policy rule provide a reduced form account of the short-run aggregate demand-side of the model.

The three equations of the New Consensus model are all derived from explicit optimizing behaviour of individual agents in the presence of market failures, including imperfect competition, incomplete markets and asymmetric information. These market failures generate price and wage stickiness in the short run, which in turn gives support to the view that the central bank is able, via changes in the short-run nominal interest rate (i), to affect the short-run real interest rate (r), and hence to alter components of the *IS* curve, such as consumption (C) and investments (I). In this way, the central bank can modify the aggregate demand, and hence the current level of output (Y) and unemployment (UN) in the country.[2]

As far as the aggregate supply-side of the model is concerned, the Phillips curve shows that movements of the output gap ($Y - Y^*$) have an impact on the rate of change of the inflation rate (π). Therefore, the central bank via changes in the short-run nominal interest rate is able to alter the output gap, and hence to achieve the desired level of inflation in the country. The transmission mechanism described above can be represented by the process illustrated in Figure 7.1.

$$\Delta i \Rightarrow \Delta r \Rightarrow \Delta C \,\&\, \Delta I \Rightarrow \Delta AD \Rightarrow \Delta Y \,\&\, \Delta UN \Rightarrow \Delta(Y - Y^*) \Rightarrow \Delta \pi$$

Figure 7.1 The transmission mechanism of monetary policy in the New Consensus view

From a Post Keynesian perspective there are several problems with the New Consensus view and its policy implications.[3] To start with, the New Consensus model limits the role of aggregate demand to the short run. Aggregate demand affects the current level of output (Y), but never the potential level (Y^*), in the so-called output gap ($Y - Y^*$). Aggregate demand and therefore stabilization policies are neutral in the long run (Fontana, 2007). In fact, this long-run neutrality of aggregate demand raises an interesting conundrum for modern central bankers:

> Given the central bank claim that, in the medium and longer run, their influence is solely on nominal variables, e.g. inflation, and *not at all* on real variables, such as output and unemployment, it is somewhat difficult and sensitive to explain that, at much *higher* frequencies, up to two or so years out, their influence on inflation is via the transmission mechanism of bringing about changes to exactly such real variables, i.e. output and unemployment. Moreover, given the long lags involved before inflation responds to monetary policy ... an attempt to drive a deviation of inflation from target *rapidly* back to that target could only be done by enforcing an (undesirably) large change in output, especially if that deviation emanated from an initial supply shock. (Goodhart, 2007, pp. 64–5)

Another thorny issue is related to the different weight assigned to stabilization policies in the New Consensus model. The monetary authority has the role of achieving the desired inflation target, and, subject to that, it must deliver as much output stabilization as possible in the short run. By contrast, fiscal authorities are either ignored or asked to concentrate on the control and sustainability of public finances. In other words, the New Consensus view downplays the role of fiscal policy at the advantage of monetary policy. However, there is nothing intrinsically monetary in the nature of stabilization policy in the New Consensus model (Fontana, 2008). There may be reasonable practical arguments for doubting the effectiveness of fiscal policy. For instance, it is undeniable that fiscal policy has potentially long inside lags compared to monetary policy. These practical or political lags may shift the balance in favour of monetary policy, though the latter does have its own practical problems too (Arestis and Sawyer, 2006). Nevertheless, theoretically there is little or nothing to justify the current marginal role of fiscal policy in modern macroeconomics.

Interestingly, in the last couple years, some mainstream Keynesian economists like Allsopp and Vines (2005) and Blinder (2006) have shown dissatisfaction with the role of fiscal policy in the New Consensus. Whereas they have not challenged the pre-eminent position that monetary policy now holds in modern macroeconomics, they have maintained that there are circumstances under which monetary policy alone is a weak instrument of stabilization, and a combined monetary-fiscal strategy is needed. Indeed, in the case of the lower bound problem on the short-run interest rate (Krugman, 2005), or country-specific shocks in monetary unions (Kirsanova et al., 2007), some economists have gone so far as to claim that fiscal policy must reclaim a dominant position as a stabilization policy tool (Symposium, 2005).

In a similar way, some policy-makers have also argued that there are circumstances when a combined fiscal and monetary stimulus provides broader support for the economy than monetary policy actions alone. For instance, this is the view of the chairman of the Federal Reserve, who advocates the boosting of the US economy and the minimizing of the risk of a prolonged recession in response to the poor developments in financial markets and a fragile outlook for the real economy.

> Monetary policy (that is, the management of the short-term interest rate) is the Fed's best tool for pursuing our macroeconomic objectives, namely to promote maximum sustainable employment and price stability ... Monetary policy has responded proactively to evolving conditions ... However, in light of recent changes in the outlook for and the risks to growth, additional policy easing may well be necessary ... Based on that evaluation, and consistent with our dual mandate, we stand ready to take substantive additional action as needed to support growth and to provide adequate insurance against downside risks ... Fiscal Policy actions might usefully complement monetary policy in supporting economic growth over the next year or so. I agree that fiscal action could be helpful in principle, as fiscal and monetary stimulus together may provide broader support for the economy than monetary policy actions alone. (Bernanke, 2008)

Unfortunately, with some noteworthy exceptions (Arestis and Sawyer, 2003, 2006; Setterfield, 2007), this revival of fiscal policy in mainstream Keynesian economics has been completely ignored by Post Keynesian economists and heterodox economists, more generally. A young scholar looking for a Post Keynesian view on this revival of interest for fiscal policy in mainstream economics will look in vain for relevant works.[4]

The 'unemployment bias' in the New Consensus view of monetary policy

In the previous section I have argued that there is now a New Consensus in macroeconomics, which draws on modern theoretical notions, like the natural rate hypothesis and the expectations-augmented or inertia Phillips curve, and which has now been adopted implicitly or explicitly by central bankers around the world. Notwithstanding the theoretical and practical success, I have also discussed two problems of the modern New Consensus in macroeconomics.

Firstly, in the New Consensus there is no role for aggregate demand in the long run. This is in contrast to the important role that the latter must play in the short run, in order for the central bank to have any impact on the real economy (and hence on the inflation rate). Secondly, the New Consensus downplays the role of fiscal policy to the advantage of monetary policy. All that seems to matter in the New Consensus view is the role of the central bank in achieving price stability. These are serious issues, and in fact there is now an increasingly large literature discussing them. However, there is another major problem with the New Consensus view, which has surprisingly escaped critics of modern macroeconomics. It is its 'unemployment bias'. Some indirect evidence for the existence of this bias can be derived form a rather unsuspected source.

In late 1995, members of the FOMC at the Federal Reserve Board discussed alternative interest rate strategies in order to achieve the long-run aim of price stability. Since the different views about these strategies seemed to converge toward two main policy strategies, namely the conventional or 'deliberate' strategy, and the alternative or 'opportunistic' strategy (e.g. Federal Reserve Board, 1989), Donald L. Kohn, the current vice chairman of the Board of Governors of the Federal Reserve System was asked to prepare an FOMC briefing discussing similarities and differences between these strategies. In December 1995 Kohn circulated his report:

> Both strategies [i.e. the 'deliberate' and the 'opportunistic' strategies] start from the premise that price stability is the appropriate primary long-term goal of policy. The deliberate policy seeks to make steady progress toward this goal. The only way to ensure such progress is to keep some slack in the economy so as to put downward pressure on inflation in labor and product markets. Hence, the deliberate strategy would be earmarked by a persistent tendency for the unemployment rate to exceed NAIRU so long as the economy was not at price stability,

albeit by varying degrees depending on the amount of inflation and the Committee's desired trajectory to price stability. A Taylor Rule is an example of a deliberate disinflation strategy. (Federal Reserve Board, 1995, Appendix, p. 2)

It is important to note that Kohn opens his FOMC briefing report by making clear that the 'deliberate' and the 'opportunistic' monetary policy strategies share the same commitment to price stability in the long term. In other words, the 'deliberate' and the 'opportunistic' strategies are both fully consistent with the main tenet of the New Consensus view, namely that there is no long-run trade-off between inflation and unemployment. For this reason, in the long run the only appropriate policy aim for the monetary authority is price stability.

Leaving any discussion of the 'opportunistic' strategy to the next section, it is worthwhile elaborating on the suggestion that the 'deliberate' strategy seems to have an 'unemployment bias' built-in to its transmission mechanism: as long as inflation remains above its long-run target, the monetary authority must engineer a disinflationary process in order to open a gap between the actual and potential level of output, and hence between the current and NAIRU levels of unemployment, with the purpose of bringing inflation down. In other words, no matter whether inflation is high or low, as long as it is above its desired level, the monetary authority must trigger a disinflationary process in the economy by raising the nominal interest rate in order to curb, via the transmission mechanism described in the previous section, aggregate demand and current output (see Figure 7.1). The deliberate strategy, that is the conventional New Consensus policy strategy for central banks, is thus built on the assumption that the central bank must maintain the unemployment rate above the NAIRU level, when the economy is not at price stability.

Interestingly, members of the FOMC also discussed the nature of the inflation shocks to the economy. This is another important issue. I have argued that the central bank can only affect the real economy via short-run changes in aggregate demand. Implicitly, the New Consensus view thus assumes that the source of changes in the inflation rate is not important. Putting it differently, the New Consensus view assumes that the source of inflation is on the demand-side, or at least that any rise in inflation can be addressed through the demand-side. What it counts then is the current level of inflation rate compared to its targeted or desired level:

> What exactly does the term NAIRU mean? It means the level of unemployment we have to attain to stop inflation from accelerating. An oil

shock produces a lot of inflationary impetus in the economic system. To prevent an acceleration of inflation, the unemployment rate has to rise sharply and put downward pressure on wages to overcome the oil shock and hold inflation in place. The lesson is that the NAIRU is variable, but changes in it due to supply shocks are temporary. The NAIRU in history came back down again after the oil shock ended. (David E. Lindsey, in Federal Reserve Board, 1996, p. 88)

Lindsey offered this argument in an attempt to explain that the NAIRU is invariant to aggregate demand and monetary policy alike. The argument is also offered in the standard New Consensus framework, where there are one-off output costs and permanent benefits from price stability. Accepting all these assumptions, a supply-driven inflation shock (e.g. an increase in the price of oil) must then be compensated by a demand-driven inflation move of equal size but opposite sign, triggered by the central bank. This means that whatever the nature of the inflation shocks to the economy, i.e. whether the rise in the current or expected inflation rate is due to an increase in the price of imported inputs or to an excess demand for good and services, the central bank must adopt the same policy: it has to increase the nominal interest rate in order to depress the economy and bring the unemployment rate above the NAIRU rate. The excess of the former over the latter will put downward pressure on wages in the labour market, which should then be amplified by price reduction in the goods market. In short, and independently of the nature of the inflation shocks, the central bank must fine-tune unemployment in order to bring inflation to its target level.

From a Post Keynesian perspective, there are a few problems with this 'unemployment bias' of the New Consensus view. Starting with the final point about the nature of the inflation shocks, it is not clear why aggregate demand should be curbed, when changes in the inflation rate (and inflation expectations) are due to aggregate supply shocks, rather than aggregate demand shocks. Secondly, the 'unemployment bias' in the deliberate monetary policy strategy defended by the New Consensus relies on the view that there are no hysteresis effects in the labour market, or indeed anywhere else. If the latter is the case, then it is difficult to maintain that it is always worthy to face some short-run output-stabilization costs against long-run price stability benefits. Hysteresis effects in the labour market could make the fine-tuning of unemployment policy of the central bank a difficult business. If the NAIRU responds to the current unemployment level, the central bank may get trapped in a vicious circle, where it must trigger increasing levels of unemployment in the economy in order to bring inflation down to the desired level. The reason for this vicious circle is that restrictive policies raise now both the current and the NAIRU levels of unemployment. Therefore, for any given targeted reduction in the level of inflation, the more unemployment is triggered now, the more it will be needed in future.

In short, the modern New Consensus view seems to suffer from several problems, including the absence of any distinction between demand and supply inflation shocks, and the absence of any consideration for hysteresis effects. These two problems define what I call in this chapter the 'unemployment bias' of the New Consensus view. Interestingly, these problems where discussed at several meetings of the FOMC in the 1990s, and proposals were put forward in order to contain some of the deleterious effects of this 'unemployment bias' of the New Consensus view. I will now discuss some of these proposals.

Monetary policy without the 'unemployment bias'? An 'opportunistic' approach

I have argued that the 'unemployment bias' in the New Consensus view of monetary policy was the object of great debate at the Fed in the middle 1990s. One reason for the debate was that in that period the US economy was experiencing low levels of unemployment married to low levels of inflation. Importantly, there were few signs of the economy heating up. This was in contrast to the traditional view, since the unemployment rate had approached, or on some measures had gone below, the NAIRU level. As Laurence H. Meyer had argued,

> the unemployment rate is admittedly below the staff estimate of NAIRU ... However, there is no broad-based evidence of a demand-induced acceleration of inflation despite the persistence of a low unemployment rate for nearly two years. Indeed, core measures of inflation for both the CPI and the PPI actually have moved lower this year. So for my part, if there is any surprise about inflation, it is how well contained it is rather than how high it is. (Federal Reserve Board, 1996, p. 39)

The actual behaviour of the inflation rate in the middle 1990s led some members of the FOMC to question the deliberate policy strategy of the New Consensus view, especially its 'unemployment bias'. The discussion at the Fed converged around the idea of maintaining the goal of price stability over the long run, but with lower unemployment costs. This idea originates from the fact that when inflation is high and well above the implicit or explicit long-run inflation target, the support of policy-makers and economists alike for anti-inflationary actions is very strong, despite the cost of lost output and rising unemployment. But, when inflation is only marginally above the long-run target, the support for restrictive monetary policy strategies is less robust. In other words, the benefits from reducing the inflation rate when it is already high, say 10 or 15 per cent, are large, and may justify the unemployment costs associated with disinflation. But, the benefits of reducing the inflation rate from say a modest rate of 3 per cent are very difficult to pin down, and hardly justify the costs of disinflation. For this reason, in the mid-1990s members of the FOMC intensified attempts to explore the possibility of moderating the effects of the 'unemployment bias' in the New Consensus view of monetary policy by using what came to be labelled an 'opportunistic' strategy.[5] In fact, in his 1995 FOMC report, after discussing the conventional 'deliberate' policy strategy, Kohn highlights the strengths and weaknesses of the 'opportunistic' strategy:

> Under the opportunistic strategy, the policy approach depends on the level of inflation. If inflation is high, an opportunistic strategy will induce some output loss, just as under a deliberate strategy, to bring inflation down ... The contrast between the two strategies arises in situations like the present, when inflation is low and steady but not at the Committee's long-run goal. Under these circumstances, the opportunistic strategy attempts to hold the line against any increases in inflation and may need to accept some output shortfall to do so in the case of adverse supply shocks. But otherwise the opportunistic strategy attempts to keep the economy producing at its potential. In effect, it waits for unanticipated developments to produce further disinflation, accepting the reductions in inflation such developments bring, but always attempting to keep the economy at, or return it to, its potential. (Federal Reserve Board, 1995, Appendix, p. 3)

Before explaining what these unanticipated developments are, it is important to discuss the main general features of the 'opportunistic' strategy. It was mentioned in the previous section that this strategy shares with the deliberate strategy the same commitment to long-run price stability. However, the former has two original features compared to the latter strategy, namely path dependency and a zone of discretion, which have the potential of moderating the unemployment costs of pursuing the long-run goal of price stability. These two features are particularly relevant when the current inflation rate is low and steady, but not at its long-run target level. In these circumstances, the dynamic interplay of path dependency and of the zone of discretion suggests a way to contain the 'unemployment bias' of the deliberate policy strategy of the New Consensus view.

Let us start with the path dependency feature. Path dependency is here used as a generic term to indicate that policy decisions are the product of the historical sequence of previous economic outcomes and policy responses. In practice, this means that the central bank does not assess the current inflation rate per se, but rather it evaluates it against the historical sequence of previous inflation rates. In other words, the central bank may consider the current inflation rate of say 3 per cent more favourably if in the previous month it was 4 per cent rather than 2 per cent. This path dependency or evolutionary perspective explains the behaviour of the central bank to resist an increase in the inflation rate, even though this increase would have been acceptable by previous standards. The 'opportunistic' central bank thus strives to 'hold the line' on the current level of inflation, and for this reason it is prepared to increase the nominal interest rate, and hence to accept some unemployment in the case of an aggregate supply-induced price increase. This path dependency feature of the 'opportunistic' strategy plays a vital role in maintaining the credibility of the central bank in pursuing price stability in the long run. It shows the commitment to achieve the inflation target, though through a gradual approach.

The second feature of the 'opportunistic' strategy is the notion of a zone of discretion. This is the most innovative aspect of this strategy, and possibly the one closest to the Post Keynesian research agenda (Fontana and Gerrard, 2006). The idea is that when inflation is low and steady, even though above (below) its target level, the central bank should not take anti-inflation (anti-deflation) actions. In these circumstances, the central bank should not thus increase (decrease) the interest rate, curbing (stimulating) aggregate demand and inducing the required additional unemployment (employment) and output shortfall (surplus) in order to bring inflation to its target level. Instead, the central bank should wait for unanticipated developments, like unforeseen recessions (boom) and deflationary (inflationary) supply shocks producing further disinflation (inflation). In this way, under the right circumstances, namely low and stable inflation, the economy can operate around full employment without inflationary pressures:

> The answer is that there is an asymmetry built into an 'opportunistic' strategy, and here is how it works. During good times, we only get up to full employment; we never go beyond it. During other times, the unemployment rate is always above the NAIRU. If the unemployment rate averages above the NAIRU we are disinflating on average. That is what the 'opportunistic' strategy does. What goes with that is that if you want to stop at 2 percent inflation, that has interesting implications. It means that once you get there, for every recession you treat yourself to a boom. You treat yourself to a little overheating because that is what it will take to keep the average inflation rate constant. (Meyer, in Federal Reserve Board, 1996, p. 58)

Figure 7.2 illustrates the particular circumstances that justify this 'opportunistic' approach by the central bank. It describes the relationship between the level of inflation and the behaviour of the central bank. When prices are rising rapidly, say the current inflation rate (π) is above the given threshold ($+\delta$), the central bank adopts a deliberate anti-inflationary strategy. In this case, therefore there is no difference between the deliberate and the 'opportunistic' strategies. However, when prices are rising and the current inflation rate (π) is nevertheless below the given threshold ($+\delta$), i.e. (π) is between the upper threshold ($+\delta$) and the lower threshold ($-\delta$), the central bank adopts an 'opportunistic' strategy. This means that it counteracts inflation shocks that will take the inflation rate above the upper threshold ($+\delta$); otherwise it will wait for unanticipated favourable developments, i.e. accommodating shocks that bring the inflation rate down. Conversely, when prices are falling rapidly, i.e. the inflation rate (π) is below the threshold ($-\delta$), the central bank adopts a deliberate anti-deflationary strategy, cutting the interest rate and inducing additional employment and output surplus. Otherwise, the central bank adopts an 'opportunistic' strategy, waiting for unanticipated favourable developments bringing the inflation rate up.

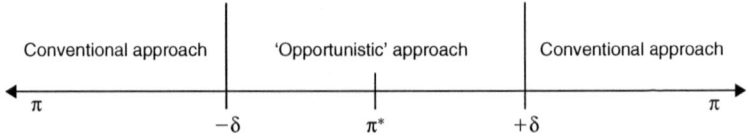

Figure 7.2 The zone of discretion of the 'opportunistic' strategy

The existence of a zone of discretion for the setting of monetary policy strategies has important implications. First, it means that the central bank assigns different weights to its policy objectives under different circumstances. When the current inflation rate (π) is between the upper threshold ($+\delta$) and the lower threshold ($-\delta$), the central bank concentrates on output stabilization rather than price stability. Outside the zone of discretion, the central bank reverses the order of its policy objectives. Now price stability takes first seat, and output stabilization is the subsidiary goal.

The second implication of the notion of a zone of discretion is that the central bank 'accommodates' recessions or booms – mild recessions and mild booms to be sure – for its own purpose of achieving its inflation target, rather than responding to them. Mild recessions or mild booms are the unanticipated developments that produce the required further disinflation or inflation. For instance, when the current inflation rate (π) is between the target rate of inflation (π^*) and the upper threshold ($+\delta$), as in Figure 7.2, the 'opportunistic' central bank will wait for the next unforeseen shortfall in aggregate demand, rather than inducing a reduction in aggregate demand by a rise in the interest rate. The unforeseen recession with the consequent shortfall in aggregate demand will automatically open up a gap between the NAIRU and the increasing unemployment rate, and hence put downward pressure on wages and prices. This means that as a result of the unforeseen shortfall in aggregate demand the current inflation rate (π) has now moved close to the target rate of inflation (π^*). The central bank can then wait for the next recession, until the inflation target is achieved. As Meyer said: 'when the next recession arrives, whatever the timing, inflation will ratchet down another notch. This strategy, gradually and at low cost, lowers inflation over time until price stability is achieved' (Meyer, 1996, p. 76). Alternatively, the central bank could wait for favourable aggregate supply shocks, like an unforeseen increase in productivity or an unexpected inflow of migrant workers (Mervyn King's 'Polish plumber' effect). In this case, it is the supply shock that opens a gap between a falling NAIRU and the current level of unemployment, with the result that the decline in prices and wages brings the current rate of inflation to, or close to, the target rate.

From a Post Keynesian perspective, the 'opportunistic' approach is a welcome attempt to amend the conventional or deliberate monetary policy strategy of the New Consensus view. The introduction into the conventional strategy of path dependency effects and of a zone of discretion is indeed a serious attempt to moderate the 'unemployment bias' of the deliberate strategy. For this reason, the 'opportunistic' approach should be the object of further analysis and investigations by post-Keynesian scholars, and more generally by all macroeconomists unsatisfied with the persistent tendency by conventional central banks to keep the unemployment rate above the NAIRU, at least as long as the economy is not at price stability.

Notwithstanding this positive view of the 'opportunistic' strategy, there are still serious limitations to this strategy. Most, if not all, of these limitations are due to the fact that the 'opportunistic' approach is still a policy strategy, a 'less-unemployment bias' strategy to be sure, of the modern New Consensus view, and as such it suffers from the same problems as the latter.

It is worth recalling some of the major problems of the modern New Consensus view discussed earlier. Firstly, like the conventional policy strategy of the New Consensus view, the 'opportunistic' approach does not distinguish demand-induced inflation shocks from supply-induced inflation shocks. It is not clear for instance why an 'opportunistic' central bank should 'hold the line' and hence curb aggregate demand, when changes in the inflation rate are due to supply-induced inflation shocks.[6] Secondly, and more importantly, whereas the 'opportunistic' approach acknowledges the possibility of hysteresis effects in the economy, a long-awaited advance compared to conventional policy strategies, it does not fully appreciate the policy implication of this theoretical advance. An 'opportunistic' central bank will not deliberately create slack in the economy when the current inflation rate is within the zone of discretion. It will wait and 'use' the next recession to bring the inflation rate at, or closer to, its target level. This means that an 'opportunistic' central bank will not induce further unemployment in the economy. Yet, it is not clear why in these circumstances an 'opportunistic' central bank should not try to trigger further employment through favourable hysteresis effects in the product and labour markets. In other words, in a low and stable inflation environment an 'opportunistic' central bank should try to reduce the real interest rate in order to stimulate aggregate demand and boost output and employment. Instead of waiting and using the next recession to bring the inflation rate at, or closer to, its target level, the central bank should treat the economy to a boom and bring the economy to, or closer to, full employment.

A word of clarification and caution should be added here. Hysteresis effects are a crucial way to introduce long-run effects of aggregate demand in the New Consensus view. Importantly, they are more than just another little assumption to add to the New Consensus model.

Hysteresis effects strike at the heart of modern macroeconomics. It is difficult to defend the view, like the advocates of the New Consensus do, that the central bank affects nominal variables in the long run, but not real variables, when these nominal effects are actually obtained via a transmission mechanism (see Figure 7.1), which works through changes of exactly these real variables.

However, be that as it may, hysteresis effects do not justify a 'boom and bust' type of policy strategy. They also do not lead to a 'hydraulic' view of monetary policy. In a low and stable inflation environment, an 'opportunistic' central bank should try to reduce the real interest rate in order to stimulate aggregate demand and boost output and employment, but it should do it with caution, and always with awareness of the potential inflationary costs of any policy easing. In other words, there are limitations to what a central bank can achieve. For this reason, this chapter has argued that the New Consensus view of stabilization policy is too biased toward monetary policy. Monetary policy should be complemented with fiscal policy (Fontana, 2008).

Concluding remarks

The last couple of decades have seen a convergence in the theory and practice of monetary policy, which has now widened to the entire macroeconomics field. This is true not only for the research field, but also in the teaching of our discipline. In this chapter I have reviewed the major reasons for the success of the New Consensus view, suggesting that this success is related to a combination of theoretical and practical arguments.

Notwithstanding this success, the paper has discussed several problems potentially affecting the modern New Consensus view in macroeconomics. Firstly, the New Consensus view downplays the role of fiscal policy at advantage of monetary policy. Secondly, in modern macroeconomics there is no role for aggregate demand in the long run. This is in contrast to the important role that the latter must play in the short run, in order for the central bank to have any impact on the real economy. More importantly, the paper has discussed another major problem with the New Consensus view, namely its 'unemployment bias'.

As argued by Donald L. Kohn, the current Vice Chairman of the Board of Governors of the Federal Reserve System, the long-run policy goal of the New Consensus view is price stability. The conventional policy strategy to achieve this goal is to keep some slack in the economy, in order to put downward pressure on inflation via the labour market and the product markets. Therefore, the main feature of the conventional policy strategy in the New Consensus view is a persistent tendency to keep the unemployment rate above the NAIRU, as long as the economy is not at price stability.

An amended version of the deliberate strategy of the New Consensus view is the so-called 'opportunistic' strategy. This original strategy created a great deal of interest at FOMC meetings of the Federal Reserve System, in the 1990s. Drawing on FOMC records, this paper has discussed two main features of the 'opportunistic' strategy, namely path dependency and the zone of discretion. The 'opportunistic' strategy is indeed a serious attempt to moderate the 'unemployment bias' of the deliberate strategy. For this reason, it should be object of further analysis and investigations. However, the 'opportunistic' strategy still suffers from two major vices of the New Consensus view (it could not have been differently since it was born out of this view). Firstly, the 'opportunistic' approach does not distinguish demand-induced inflation shocks from supply-induced inflation shocks. Secondly, and more importantly, the 'opportunistic' approach does not fully acknowledged the possibility of hysteresis effects in the economy. Instead of waiting and 'using' the next recession to bring the inflation rate at, or closer to, its target level, when inflation is low and stable, the central bank should treat the economy to a boom, and bring the economy at, or closer to, full employment.

Notes

1. Of course, strictly speaking what a zero output gap delivers is a constant rate of inflation, not necessarily the target rate. We finesse this issue as well as the distinction between achieving price stability or the target rate of inflation for the sake of simplicity.
2. There are two implicit assumptions here worthy of consideration. Firstly, there is a short-run trade off between unemployment and inflation, i.e. the Phillips curve is not vertical in the short run. Secondly, changes in the aggregate demand only modifies the current component of the output gap, namely the current level of output (Y), but not the aggregate supply-driven or potential level of output (Y^*).
3. There are also more general problems related to two issues. First, in the New Consensus view monetary policy is understood to work through changes in the output gap. However, the potential level of output is not observable, and for this reason the monetary authority may actually make some business cycle peaks endogenous to policy. Second, theoretical and empirical works on path dependency effects suggest that transitory changes in the level of aggregate demand may actually have permanent effects on output and employment. Fontana and Palacio Vera (2007) explore the implications of these two problems with the New Consensus view.

4. It is really astonishing that the *Cambridge Journal of Economics*, the *Journal of Economic Issues*, the *Journal of Post Keynesian Economics* and the *Review of Political Economy*, just to mention some of the typical outlets for nonmainstream economic papers, have nothing or very little on the role of discretionary fiscal policy in modern macroeconomics.
5. It should be added that in the last few years the mainstream interest for moderating the 'unemployment bias' of the modern New Consensus view has also affected other research areas in economics, including the now fashionable economics of happiness. For instance, in a recent NBER paper aptly titled 'Is Unemployment more Costly than Inflation?', David Blanchflower, a member of the Monetary Policy Committee at the Bank of England has concluded that 'across EU countries, a one percentage point increase in the unemployment rate lowers well being by at least one and a half times as much as a one percentage point increase in the inflation rate' (Blanchflower, 2007, p. 1).
6. More generally, some critics may even question the way supply shocks are presented in the New Consensus view, namely that supply shocks are random and average out at zero: if costs go up today, then they will come down at some point in the future.

References

Allsopp, C. and D. Vines (2005) 'Symposium on Fiscal Policy', *Oxford Review of Economic Policy* 21 (4): 485–635.
Allsopp, C. and D. Vines (2005) 'The Macroeconomic Role of Fiscal Policy', *Oxford Review of Economic Policy* 21 (4): 485–508.
Arestis, P. and A. Ross (2007) 'Introduction', in P. Arestis (ed.), *Is There a New Consensus in Macroeconomics?*, London: Palgrave Macmillan: 1–21.
Arestis, P. and M. Sawyer (2003) 'Reinventing Fiscal Policy', *Journal of Post Keynesian Economics* 26 (1): 3–25.
Arestis, P. and M. Sawyer (2006) 'Fiscal Policy Matters', *Public Finance/Finance Publiques* 54 (3–4): 133–5.
Bernanke, B. S. (2008) 'The Economic Outlook', Fed Chairman Testimony before the Committee on the Budget, US House of Representatives, 17 January, available at http://www.federalreserve.gov/newsevents/testimony/bernanke20080117a.htm.
Blanchflower, D. G. (2007) 'Is Unemployment more Costly than Inflation?', NBER working paper 13505, October.
Blinder, A. (2006) 'The Case against the Case against Discretionary Fiscal Policy', in R. W. Kopcke, G. M. B. Tootell and R. K. Triest (eds), *The Macroeconomics of Fiscal Policy*, London, MIT Press: 25–61.
Carlin, W. and D. Soskice (2006) *Macroeconomics: Imperfections, Institutions and Policies*, Oxford: Oxford University Press.
Clarida, R., J. Galí and M. Gertler (1999) 'The Science of Monetary Policy', *Journal of Economic Literature* 37 (4): 1661–707.
Federal Reserve Board (1989) 'Transcript of the Federal Open Market Committee Meeting, mimeo, December, available at http://federalreserve.gov/fomc/transcripts/transcripts_1989.htm.

Federal Reserve Board (1995) 'Transcript of the Federal Open Market Committee Meeting, mimeo, December, available at http://federalreserve.gov/fomc/transcripts/transcripts_1995.htm.

Federal Reserve Board (1996) 'Transcript of the Federal Open Market Committee Meeting, mimeo, July, available at http://federalreserve.gov/fomc/transcripts/transcripts_1996.htm.

Fontana, G. (2007) 'Why Money Matters: Wicksell, Keynes, and the New Consensus View on Monetary Policy', *Journal of Post Keynesian Economics* 30 (1): 43–60.

Fontana, G. (2008) 'Fiscal Policy in Today's Endogenous Money World', in J. Creel and M. Sawyer (eds), *Current Thinking on Fiscal Policy*, London: Palgrave.

Fontana, G. and B. Gerrard (2006) 'The Future of Post Keynesian Economics', *Banca Nazionale del Lavoro Quarterly Review* 59 (236): 49–80.

Fontana, G. and A. Palacio-Vera (2007) 'Are Long-run Price Stability and Short-run Output Stabilization all that Monetary Policy can Aim for?', *Metroeconomica* 58 (2): 269–98.

Goodhart, C. A. E. (2007) 'The Future of Central Banking', in P. Arestis (ed.), *Is There a New Consensus in Macroeconomics?*, London: Palgrave Macmillan: 61–81.

Kirsanova, T., M. Satchi, D. Vines and S. Wren-Lewis (2007) 'Optimal Fiscal Policy Rules in a Monetary Union', *Journal of Money, Credit and Banking* 39 (7): 1759–84.

Krugman, P. (2005) 'Is Fiscal Policy Poised for a Comeback?', *Oxford Review of Economic Policy* 21 (4): 515–23.

Meyer, L. H. (1996) 'Prepared Statement', in *Nominations of Alan Greenspan, Alice M. Rivlin and Lawrence H. Meyer*, Hearing Before the Committee on Banking, Housing, and Urban Affairs, US Senate, Washington DC: US Government Print Office.

Meyer, L. H. (2001) 'Does Money Matter?', *Federal Reserve Bank of St. Louis Review* 83 (5): 1–15.

Setterfield, M. (2007) 'Is There a Stabilizing Role for Fiscal Policy in the New Consensus?', *Review of Political Economy* 19 (3): 405–18.

8
Unemployment and the Natural Interest Rate in a Neo-Wicksellian Model

Philip Arestis and Elias Karakitsos

Introduction

Neo-Wicksellian or New Consensus Macroeconomic (NCM) models (see, for example, Arestis, 2007) suffer from an internal inconsistency in that the policy implications advocated therein are assumed rather than derived explicitly from such models.[1] In particular, the propositions that inflation is under the direct control of the central bank, while output and unemployment in the long run are not, are imposed on the model rather than demonstrated theoretically in a convincing manner. These propositions hold true in the case of transient shocks, which are only present for a few quarters, but not under long-lasting shocks, which last for several decades. The internal inconsistency of the Neo-Wicksellian models stems from the lack of sufficient equilibrating mechanisms; for such mechanisms may ensure that the system would always return to its original steady state, irrespective of whether the shocks are transient or long lasting. In these models the interest rate gap – the deviation of the real interest rate from its natural rate – is the only equilibrating mechanism. In particular, the entire path of expected future interest rate gaps is the only mechanism that determines current inflation and output. However, while output is affected in the short run by interest rate changes, in the long run it is exogenously given. In such models, fiscal policy has no effect on output and unemployment in the long run, by definition, given that output always converges to its exogenously given supply, and unemployment to its equally exogenously given NAIRU level.

In Neo-Wicksellian models the natural interest rate is also exogenous and the emphasis on this variable has shifted from its original insight as the reward to capital (the real profit rate) to a real interest rate that defines the stance of monetary policy as neutral, tight or easy. In this chapter we will endogenize the natural interest rate and the supply of (or potential) output in an otherwise Neo-Wicksellian model. We will show that in the presence of transient shocks the system returns to its initial steady state. However, under long-lasting shocks the system would converge to a different steady state. Thus, inflation, output and unemployment would converge to different long-run equilibrium values under long-lasting shocks. For example, in the case of a negative long-lasting demand shock, resulting, say, from globalization, inflation and output will be lower and therefore unemployment higher. We show that such a shock can be offset by economic policy, say fiscal policy. These results are different from the ones reached within the pure Neo-Wicksellian model. In the latter, although under conditions of transient shocks the system reverts to its exogenously determined output and unemployment to its NAIRU, no such mechanism prevails in the case of long-lasting shocks.

The following section is devoted to the concept of the natural interest rate, as advocated by Wicksell (1965 [1898]) and interpreted by Shackle (see Frowen, 1988). Its role in the determination of inflation and the policy implications of the model will be reviewed. We will then address the way Neo-Wicksellian models relate to the original model and whether they have been faithful to that tradition. We will present a reformulated Neo-Wicksellian model in which the natural interest rate and the supply of output are endogenized and its steady-state properties, as well as the conditions for stability, are analysed. We then discuss the dynamic adjustment of the economy to transient and long-lasting shocks and show how fiscal policy can be used to offset a long-lasting negative demand shock.

The natural interest rate

The idea of the 'natural rate of interest' was initiated and developed by Wicksell (1965 [1898]), and it played a key role in his explanation of inflation through his 'cumulative process'. As it is clear from Shackle's selected papers in Frowen (1988), Wicksell defined the natural rate of interest as the return on capital, i.e. the (real) profit rate, which is roughly equal to the marginal product of *new* capital.[2] Wicksell used the natural rate concept to explain the transmission mechanism of the quantity theory of money on the assumption that output is at its full employment level. He compared the profit rate with the cost of borrowing money – the interest rate gap – and argued that when the natural rate of interest is above the cost of borrowing money, entrepreneurs would borrow at the going money rate to buy capital (equipment and buildings), thereby increasing demand for all types of resources and their prices. Wicksell did not distinguish between nominal and real rates because under the gold standard of the time-sustained inflation was unlikely. Thus, the natural interest rate (the profit rate), as well as the money interest rate, should be viewed as real rates.

In Wicksell's framework, the supply of money is endogenous and it is the interest rate gap that explains how disequilibrium in the money market would spill over to disequilibrium in the goods market, thereby creating inflation. This was fundamental in his critique of Fisher's (1911) quantity theory of money. In the latter case, the supply of money is exogenous, and increases in it will lead to 'bidding wars' of commodities, as agents try to get rid of excess money holdings, thereby raising their prices. But, as Wicksell (1906) observed:

> A general rise in prices is therefore only conceivable on the supposition that the general demand has for some reason become, or is expected to become, greater than supply. This may seem paradoxical, because we have accustomed ourselves, with J. B. Say, to regard goods themselves as reciprocally constituting and limiting the demand for each other. And indeed *ultimately* they do so; here, however, we are concerned with precisely what occurs, *in the first place*, with the middle link... Any theory of money worthy of the name must be able to show how and why the monetary or pecuniary demand for goods exceeds or falls short of the supply of goods in given conditions. (pp. 159–60; emphasis in original)

Thus, Wicksell argued that Say's Law is incompatible with the quantity theory of money. We can easily see this by invoking Walras's Law:

$$(Y^d - Y^s) = (M^s - M^d)/P \text{ or } (I - S) = (M^s - M^d)/P$$

where Y^d and Y^s stand for demand for and supply of aggregate output, respectively, M^s and M^d for supply of and demand for money, and P for aggregate price level. According to Say's Law the left hand side is always equal to zero, thus implying the right hand side must also be zero at all times. Thus, Say's Law introduces a 'dichotomy' of the real from the monetary side of the economy. There is no way that disequilibrium in one market can spill over to the other. Therefore, as Wicksell (1906) pointed out Say's Law is incompatible with Fisher's (1911) 'bidding war' for goods as a result of an excess supply of money. Wicksell offered the interest rate gap as a way of explaining how disequilibrium in the money market can be created and spill over to the goods market, thereby producing inflation. The cumulative process describes precisely how an initial excess demand in the capital goods market would spread to other sectors of the economy and ultimately to consumer prices.

Wicksell (1906) makes investment independent of savings, thus rejecting Say's Law in the short, but not in the long, run. He further assumes that the natural interest rate can deviate from the money market interest rate, so that 'the normal rate rises or falls whilst the loan rate remains unchanged or only tardily follows it' (p. 205). Although money supply is endogenous, inflation is still a monetary phenomenon, irrespective of its nature, as it requires monetary validation. The endogeneity of money is the outcome of a credit-money economy where the excess demand for money is created by the discrepancy between the natural and money interest rate. This excess demand for money is met by a simultaneous increase in the supply of money through the 'loans create deposits' multiplier. For as long as the natural rate is above the money interest rate, prices would continue to increase. The process is not unbounded as two mechanisms would ensure the stability of the system. First, either by law or prudence, the expansion of the money supply is not infinite because of the limited supply of reserves. The loan rate would have to rise as the banks run out of reserves. This was the reason offered by Wicksell (1906) himself, but there was a second reason, which came about much later. In fact, the cumulative process would be brought to an end before the 'reserves constraint' is hit. The marginal product of capital (the natural rate) refers to *new* capital and, therefore, the rise in inflation would increase the 'cost' of new capital goods, thereby diminishing the attractiveness of investment. In other words, the MEI curve would shift downwards because of the rising supply price of capital. Thus, both the natural interest rate and the loan rate would adjust to ensure that inflation does not rise without limit. The natural rate would fall, as inflation increases, while the loan rate would increase. Stable inflation is achieved at the point where the natural rate is equal to the loan rate. This implies that the natural interest rate is defined as the rate at which inflation is stable (non-accelerating).

In addition, since equilibrium in the goods market implies that investment is equal to savings, the natural interest rate can also be defined as the rate that equilibrates savings and investment. Thus, there are three different ways of defining the natural rate: (1) as the reward of capital, i.e. the real profit rate, which is roughly equal to the marginal product of capital; (2) as the rate that equates savings and investment; and (3) as the rate that ensures stable inflation. Wicksell (1906) assumes that all three different definitions are consistent with each other, but he could not prove it. These different definitions – the 'Wicksellian muddle' as Laidler (1999, p. 57) calls it[3] – could be viewed as one of the reasons why early Swedish interpreters like Myrdal (1939) and Lindahl (1950) criticized the natural rate as non-operational and of little practical relevance.[4]

Wicksell's 1898 theory claims that an increase in the supply of money leads to the same proportional rise in the price level, but the original increase is *endogenous*, created by the relative conditions in the financial and real sectors. Moreover, the essence of the Wicksellian theory is that another pillar of the quantity theory of money holds true, namely that money is neutral in the long run. However, to establish this result the neoclassical dichotomy between the real and monetary sectors of the economy would have to be abandoned. Moreover, the neoclassical principles of the exogeneity of money, and Say's Law in the short run, break down.

Neo-Wicksellian models

The natural rate of interest has played a key role in theories of output and inflation determination in dynamic general equilibrium NCMs (see, for example, Rottemberg and Woodford, 1995; Arestis, 2007).[5] These models combine intertemporally optimizing agents from the real-business-cycle school with imperfect competition and nominal rigidities from traditional Keynesian models. These nominal rigidities, i.e. stickiness in prices and/or wages, imply that changes in the nominal short-term interest rate affect short-term *real* rates and, thus in turn, aggregate real activity and inflation. Woodford (1997) has described these models as 'Neo-Wicksellian', and, to repeat, we follow this tradition in this chapter. In these models the natural interest rate is defined as the equilibrium real interest rate that would prevail in a fictitious economy where there are no nominal rigidities, i e in an economy in which nominal adjustment is complete.

As the Neo-Wicksellian models are derived from intertemporal optimization, the emphasis is on the interdependency between current economic variables and expectations about their future realizations. Thus, current output and inflation depend on the entire path of expected future interest rates. This feature has immensely affected the theory and practice of monetary policy, as it assigns a major role to the management of private sector expectations and consequently to the credibility of the central bank as an important element in anchoring inflation expectations (see, for example, King, 2005; Arestis, 2007; Weber *et al.*, 2007).

Neo-Wicksellian models adopt all the principles of the original Wicksellian theory. Money is neutral in the long run, not because money is a 'veil', but because inflation is influenced by the interest rate gap, and not by the forces of demand for and supply of money. Say's Law does not hold in the short run; it does, though, hold in the long run. Consequently, disequilibrium in one market (money or goods) is transmitted to the other in the short run; but not so in the long run. Money is endogenous, although the word used to describe it is 'residual' (see, for example, Arestis, 2007).[6] The endogeneity of money implies that the traditional LM-curve is redundant and is replaced by a monetary rule that specifies how the central bank sets interest rates. In Neo-Wicksellian models the natural interest rate is defined as the rate that equilibrates aggregate demand with aggregate supply, namely at the intersection of the 'new' IS-curve with the fixed supply of goods. In accordance with this definition the natural interest rate plays a crucial role in modern monetary policy. In terms of monetary rules of the Taylor type, the real interest rate is equal to the natural interest rate at the long-run equilibrium. This provides a definition of the stance of monetary policy. When the real is equal to the natural rate of interest, monetary policy is neutral. A higher real interest rate than the natural implies tight policy and vice versa.[7]

In Neo-Wicksellian models the central bank controls the rate of inflation through changes in the rate of interest, which affects the output gap – the discrepancy between an endogenous demand for goods and an exogenous supply – with the latter affecting prices and price expectations in the short run. The assumption of an exogenous supply of goods and the requirement that in the long run the output gap should be zero implies that demand is always adjusting to supply and ensures the neutrality of monetary policy. Monetary policy can influence the rate of inflation, but not output (or the growth rate of the economy) and unemployment in the long run, i.e. the Phillips curve is vertical. The rate of growth is determined in the long run by supply considerations, such as multifactor productivity, the rate of growth of the labour force, market flexibility, especially in the labour market, etc., all of which are beyond the control of the monetary and fiscal authorities.[8] With output converging to its exogenously given supply unemployment will always converge to its exogenously given NAIRU.

What is stunning is that the original insight of the natural rate of interest as the reward of capital (the real profit rate) has been lost. In modern models it is simply a long-run equilibrium real interest rate. The attraction, therefore, has shifted from the original role of the real profit rate in determining inflation to a real interest rate that can define neutral monetary policy. The 'Wicksellian-muddle' may have significantly contributed to this diversion. Wicksell's insight is that as long as there is a positive divergence between the real profit rate and the loan rate, inflation will continue to rise. This may be self-evident, as any divergence between the two rates will affect demand in the economy, which, with a fixed supply, will lead to rising inflation. The natural interest rate should not be defined as the rate consistent with stable inflation and, therefore, the rate that equates demand and supply in the goods market. This is an equilibrium condition and not a definition. For example, according to the marginal productivity theory the real wage rate is equal to the marginal product of labour. This does not mean that the real wage rate is defined as the marginal product of labour. The loan interest rate is the rate at which households and business borrow money. The fact that with a constant real profit rate the interest rate equates savings and investment does not change the definition of the natural interest rate as the reward of capital.

Wicksell placed a lot of importance on distribution theory, although he did not explicitly connect it with inflation. As such the 'Wicksellian-muddle' may be due to the lack of integration of the distribution and inflation theories. So there is a missing equation in the Wicksellian theory: one that explains what determines the natural interest rate. In Neo-Wicksellian models the natural rate of interest is a constant. The real profit rate that plays such an important role in microeconomics is simply a constant in macroeconomics. It is about time to remove this anomaly and endogenize the profit rate. In doing so, other anomalies in macroeconomics, such as the counter-cyclical behaviour of the real wage rate, may also be remedied.

It is not the purpose of this chapter to reconstruct the macro-theory by introducing the missing equation of the profit rate and relate it to the theory of distribution. Instead, the agenda is much more limited. The purpose of this chapter is to show that Neo-Wicksellian models suffer from an internal inconsistency and do not support the policy implications they advocate. In particular, the models do not have the necessary equilibrating mechanisms to ensure that the system always returns to the initial steady state. This is only true in the case of transient shocks, which last for a relatively short period of time – a few quarters. But in the case of long-lasting shocks, which last for decades, such as deindustrialization, globalization or a long-lasting increase in the *rate of change* of the price of oil, the system will converge, but to a steady-state that is different from the initial one. This means that both inflation and output (the rate of growth of the economy) and consequently unemployment are not independent of long-lasting shocks. Long-lasting demand or supply shocks can cause inflation, output and unemployment to deviate from their original steady state. In such a case fiscal policy has a role to play in offsetting such long-lasting shocks. Thus, a negative long-lasting demand shock that otherwise would have led to lower output and higher unemployment can be offset by fiscal policy.

In this chapter we make some progress towards a consistent macro model by endogenizing the real profit rate in an otherwise typical Neo-Wicksellian model. The profit rate depends on the profit margin – the excess of the price of output over the variable cost of production, the unit labour cost. The profit margin therefore depends both on the pricing power of the corporate sector, which is affected by the market structure (perfectly competitive or monopolistic) and the variable costs of production, for example labour, and, thus, on the bargaining power of labour (Arestis and Karakitsos, 2004). The profit rate further depends on the volume of sales and thus on the level of demand for goods. We take one more step towards a consistent model in this chapter, and make the supply of output endogenous. In particular, we hypothesize that the supply of output depends on the productive capacity of the economy, as this is captured by a production function that portrays how capital and labour are combined with a given technology to produce the output in the economy. To avoid a full specification of the supply side of the economy we take a short cut and assume that the capital accumulation process depends on current and past profitability. High profitability would contribute to higher capital stock in the economy and vice versa. But the capital accumulation process would also affect the productivity of labour. Thus, the supply of output is a function of the entire history of the natural interest rate (the real profit rate) and multifactor productivity, but for simplicity we ignore the rate of growth of the labour force. The endogenization of the supply of output means that we reject Say's Law not only in the short run, as Neo-Wicksellian models do, but also in the long run, contrary to the latter models.

A reformulated Neo-Wicksellian model

$$D_t(=Y_t) = a_o(G-T) + a_1 Y_t + a_2 Y_{t-1} + a_3 E_t(Y_{t+1}) + a_4[R_t - E_t(P_{t+1}) - RR_t] + \varepsilon_{1t} \quad (8.1.1)$$

$$a_0, a_1, a_2, a_3 > 0; \quad a_4 < 0$$

$$Y_t^s = q + b_1 Y_t + b_2 RR_t + \varepsilon_{2t}^* \quad (8.1.2)$$

$$b_1, b_2 > 0$$

$$Y_t^g = Y_t - Y_t^s = \kappa; \quad \kappa = 0 \quad \text{or} \quad \kappa \neq 0 \quad (8.1.3)$$

$$w_t = q + E_t(P_{t+1}) + \eta(U_t - U^n) + \varepsilon_{3t} \quad (8.1.4a)$$

$$\eta < 0$$

$$U_t = U^n + \theta Y_t^g \quad (8.1.4b)$$

$$\theta < 0$$

$$w_t = q + E_t(P_{t+1}) + \delta Y_t^g + \varepsilon_{3t} \quad (8.1.4c)$$

$$\delta = \eta . \theta > 0$$

$$ulc_t = w_t - q \quad (8.1.5)$$

$$P_t = d_0 + d_1 ulc_t + d_2 Y_t^g + d_3 P_{t-1} + \varepsilon_{4t} \quad (8.1.6)$$

$$d_1, d_2, d_3 > 0$$

$$RR_t = f_1(P_t - ulc_t) + f_2 Y_t + f_3 R_t + \varepsilon_{5t} \quad (8.1.7)$$

$$f_1, f_2 > 0; \quad f_3 < 0$$

$$R_t = (1 - \gamma_0)[RR_t + E_t(P_{t+1}) + \gamma_1 Y_{t-1}^g + \gamma_2(P_{t-1} - P^T)] + \gamma_0 R_{t-1} \quad (8.1.8)$$

$$\gamma_0, \gamma_1, \gamma_2 > 0$$

$$E_t(X_{t+1}) = X_{t+1} + \varepsilon_{6t}; \quad \lim_{T \to \infty} X_T = X_{T-1} \quad (8.1.9)$$

All variables are expressed as rates of growth (log differences): Y is (the rate of growth of) output, which is equal to the rate of aggregate demand (D); Y^s is (the rate of growth of) the supply of output (potential output); Y^g is the output gap, the difference between the growth rates of current output and potential output; R is the nominal short-term interest rate; RR is the natural interest rate or real profit rate; w is (the rate of growth of) the nominal wage rate; q is (the rate of growth of) multifactor productivity; ulc is (the rate of growth of) unit labour cost; P is the inflation rate; P^T is the central bank target inflation rate; U is the unemployment rate as a per cent of the labour force; U^n is the non-accelerating inflation rate of unemployment (NAIRU); and $E_t(X_{t+1})$ is the expectation of variable X in period $t+1$, as with information at time t.

Equation (8.1.1) describes the demand for goods and services as a positive function of current, past and future output and a negative function of the discrepancy between the real interest rate and the natural interest rate. It is the 'new' IS-curve derived from the intertemporal optimization by households of current and future consumption subject to an estimate of the lifetime resources. The latter consist of labour income and accumulated wealth through savings and the valuation of assets (Rottenberg and Woodford, 1995, 1997; Wooford, 2003). Fiscal Policy has a role to play in aggregate demand in the form of a balanced budget (G −T). The coefficient a_0 can be equal to unity to reflect the short-run balanced budget multiplier, but in reality all that is required is that it is positive and less than unity. This term is not important, as the influence of fiscal policy can be operated through the stochastic process ε_{1t}. Consequently, output is demand determined in the short run; hence, $D = Y$ as in equation (8.1.1). As a result, equation (8.1.1) is an equilibrium condition in the goods market; it determines the equilibrium level of output at all times – demand is always equal to supply. This implies rejection of Say's Law in the short run and puts demand at the centre of the economy.

The explicit introduction of a long-run, as opposed to a short-run, supply function of output is recognition of the importance of the capital accumulation process in determining the potential productive capacity of the economy through savings and investment and in the role of the latter in affecting multifactor productivity. This implies a rejection of Say's Law not only in the short, but also in the long run – a feature that it is absent from the Neo-Wicksellian (NCM) type of models. Equation (8.1.2) is derived from the simultaneous decision of households on how much to consume and save and of firms on how much to invest. The intertemporal decision of firms on how much to invest depends on current profitability multiplied by the inverse of the discount rate (the marginal efficiency of capital) less the current estimate of the expected average rate of growth of profitability (see Appendix). Thus the coefficient b_2 in equation (8.1.2) is capturing the impact of the expected future profitability on current decisions. *Mutatis mutandis*, the intertemporal decision of households on how much to consume and save depends on the current level of income multiplied by the inverse of the discount rate (the elasticity of substitution between current and future consumption) less the current estimate of the expected average rate of growth of future income. Thus, the coefficient b_1 is capturing the impact of expected future income on current decisions. The two decisions (of the firms and households) are not independent of each other, since savings is equal to investment in equilibrium. This equilibrium is achieved by the simultaneous determination of income (output) growth and the rate of growth of profitability. These levels determine the rate of growth of potential output, which only affect the economy in the long run through the pricing of output and the factors of production. Hence, the long-run supply (or potential output), equation (8.1.2), is a positive function of output and of the profitability rate.[9] The potential capacity of the economy is also influenced by the rate of multifactor productivity, q, which in the context of this model is assumed to be an exogenous variable.

Output affects the level of demand faster than supply and this implies that the sum of $a_1 + a_2 + a_3$ exceeds b_1. In reality the capital accumulation process depends on the entire history of the profit rate. However, for the purposes of our analysis the current value is sufficient to capture the essence of the process, while avoiding an artificial hysteresis effect – see equation (8.1.2).

The importance of the long-run supply of (or potential) output lies in determining the output gap. The output gap, Y_t^g, is the difference between the level of output, Y, which is demand determined, and the level of the long-run supply (or potential) output, which is gradually adjusting to the level of demand and the capital accumulation process. The output gap is constant in the long run, which can be either zero or non-zero, as shown in equation (8.1.3). If the shocks to the economy are transient then the output gap is zero in the long run. But if the shocks are long lasting then the output gap is simply a constant, which can be positive or negative depending on the nature of the shock.

The output gap is important in the pricing of the supply of output and the factors of production. Wage inflation, equation (8.1.4a), is equal to productivity and expected inflation in the long run. This is the fair share of wages, which assumes a constant distribution of output between capital and labour. The fair share of wage inflation is also the rate associated with the NAIRU. But wage growth can be greater or lower than the fair share depending on whether unemployment is above or below the NAIRU level (Ball and Romer, 1990). But unemployment depends exclusively on the level of output through 'Okun's Law'. When the output gap is zero the level of unemployment is equal to the NAIRU level, see equation (8.1.4b). When the output gap is positive, the level of unemployment falls below the NAIRU and vice versa. In this simple model the NAIRU is simply a constant in-line with the NCM model. Elimination of the discrepancy of unemployment from NAIRU by the output gap results in equation (8.1.4c). On the assumption that productivity is exogenous, the unit labour cost follows wage inflation on a one-to-one basis – as in equation (8.1.5).

The price of output is a mark-up on the remuneration of the variable cost of production, which is labour. Hence, inflation is a mark-up on the rate of growth of unit labour cost, equation (8.1.6). The mark-up depends positively on the output gap, on the assumption that firms operate in monopolistic competition. Inflation depends on past inflation reflecting costs of adjustment in prices, such as *menu costs* (see, for example, Calvo, 1983).

Equation (8.1.7) is in-line with the true spirit of Wicksell, that the natural interest rate is the return on capital or the real profit rate.[10] This is a positive function of the profit margin, the excess of the price of output over unit labour cost, and the volume of output less the impact of the interest rate on capital stock. Homogeneity implies that $f_1 = f_2$; however, in general this condition need not apply. The impact of the interest rate on capital stock may be thought of as the mechanism through which monetary policy affects profits. An increase in the real rate of interest adversely affects business as well as consumer confidence by indicating willingness by the central bank to create a negative output gap for a period of time. A relevant example is when the central bank wishes to fight a cost-push inflation that emanates from the rest of the world, say from an increase in the price of oil.

Equation (8.1.7) relies heavily on the Wicksellian comparison between RR and R. In this context, RR is compared with the cost of borrowing money (R), so that when the two deviate from each other banks and entrepreneurs play an important role in investment and savings decisions. Two important implications of our endogenization of RR follow. The first relates to the assignment of an essential role to the difference between RR and R, the loan rate. This reinstates the significant role of commercial banks in the investment/savings process, which, unlike in Wicksell's 1898 original analysis, is completely missing from the Neo-Wicksellian approach (see also Goodhart, 2004; Fontana, 2006). The second implication relates to distributional effects. To illustrate, we may assume that due to negative output gap the rate of interest is reduced by the central bank, thereby initiating an expansionary monetary policy. The fall in R leads to an excess of investment over savings, which leads to higher prices. Higher profits emerge as a result of the ensuing inflation, which causes redistribution from wages to profits. This fills the gap between investment and savings, and RR converges to the lower level of real R. In other words, it is the redistribution of real income from wages to profits that causes RR to revert to the lower real R.

The central bank operates monetary policy via a simple feedback rule that relates the level of the nominal interest rate to the output gap and the deviation of observed inflation from its target (see equation (8.1.8)). Such simple feedback rules have been popularized in the literature by Taylor (1993) and Svensson (1999, 2003), although their appeal in conducting credible monetary policy that affects favourably inflation expectations and the optimal derivation of their parameters had already been demonstrated by Artis and Karakitsos (1983) and Karakitsos and Rustem (1984, 1985). In the long-run equilibrium, when inflation is equal to the central bank target and the output gap is zero, the nominal short-term interest rate is equal to the natural interest rate and expected inflation. The lagged interest rate in equation (8.1.8), often ignored in the literature, represents interest rate 'smoothing' undertaken by the monetary authorities (see, for example, Rottemberg and Woodford, 1997; Clarida *et al.*, 1998, 2000; Woodford, 1999). It actually reflects the willingness of the central bank to implement systematic and consistent changes in monetary policy – one direction – and avoid stop-go policies.

Expectations in this model are assumed to be formed rationally (see equation (8.1.9)). This entails that such expectations are on average correct, as the error over the forecast period is purely random with a zero mean and a constant standard deviation. Rational expectations require the imposition of a transversality condition. The most common such condition is that of stationarity, which implies that at the limit, as the forecast horizon tends to infinity, there is no material difference, and the expectation of a variable in successive periods is equal, beyond a remote point of time.

The stochastic processes in the model are essential in allowing the introduction of shocks in the economy. We distinguish between three different types of shocks. First, there are shocks that can be purely random with a zero mean and a constant standard deviation. However, random shocks do not require a change in monetary policy in a systematic way, as they cancel each other out in the course of time. The second category includes shocks that are persistent in nature (i.e. shocks that are auto-correlated). But persistent shocks can be transient or long lasting. Most shocks in the real world are persistent but transient, and induce deviation from long-run equilibrium. Such shocks can last for a few quarters, but their effect dies out in time and the long-run equilibrium remains unaffected. This second type of shock requires a change of monetary policy for a time. However, in spite of the auto-correlating nature of these shocks a stable economy would be able to weather them out. The systematic change of monetary policy simply helps the economy to move faster to its long-run equilibrium. Monetary policy plays an auxiliary role in an otherwise stable economy. Examples in this second category include a persistent hike in the price of oil, a bubble in asset prices (financial or housing), the pursuit of wage increases by militant trade unions, to name but a few. The third type of shock, persistent and long lasting in nature, refers to shocks that can last for several decades. Examples from the real world abound: deindustrialization, the discovery of oil or other natural resources that may lead to the 'Dutch disease', and globalization. Such long-lasting shocks affect the long-run equilibrium of the economy. Systematic monetary policy can offset such shocks but convergence would be achieved around a different, rather than the initial, long-run equilibrium.

The system of equations (8.1.1)–(8.1.8) can easily be reduced to five equations, (8.2.1)–(8.2.5), as follows:

$$Y_t = a_0(G - T) + a_1 Y_t + a_2 Y_{t-1} + a_3 E_t Y_{t+1} + a_4[R_t - E_t(P_{t+1}) - RR_t] + u_{1t} \tag{8.2.1}$$

Substitution of (8.1.1) and (8.1.2) into (8.1.3) yields the output gap:

$$Y_t^g = a_0(G - T) - q + (a_1 - b_1)Y_t + a_2 Y_{t-1} + a_3 E_t(Y_{t+1}) + a_4[R_t - E_t(P_{t+1})] \\ - (a_4 + b_2)RR_t + u_{2t} \tag{8.2.2}$$

Substitution of (8.1.4) and (8.1.5) into (8.1.6) yields the familiar Phillips curve relationship of the NCM model:

$$P_t = d_0 + d_1 E_t(P_{t+1}) + d_3 P_{t-1} + (d_4)Y_t^g + u_{3t} \tag{8.2.3}$$

where $d_4 = d_1\delta + d_2 > 0$. Substitution of (8.1.4) and (8.1.5) into (8.1.6) yields the reduced form equation for the rate of profit:

$$RR_t = q + f_1[P_t - E_t(P_{t+1})] + f_2 Y_t + f_3 R_t + f_4 Y_t^g + u_{4t} \tag{8.2.4}$$

where $f_4 = -f_1\delta < 0$.

$$R_t = (1 - \gamma_0)[R_t + E_t(P_{t+1}) + \gamma_1 Y_{t-1}^g + \gamma_2(P_{t-1} - P^T)] + \gamma_0 R_{t-1} + u_{5t} \tag{8.2.5}$$

The system of equations (8.2.1)–(8.2.5) determines the five endogenous variables: Y_t^g, Y_t, P_t, R_t and RR_t.

The similarities and differences with the NCM (or Neo-Wicksellian) models are now apparent. The NCM model is simply equations (8.2.2), (8.2.3) and (8.2.5) with the last two terms in (8.2.2) being omitted. In our reformulated model there are two more equations: equation (8.2.1), which determines the equilibrium level of output from the level of demand in the economy; and equation (8.2.4), which determines the rate of profit, which is treated as a constant in NCM models. Finally, our model is obtained by adding the last term in equation (8.2.2), which reflects the influence of the profit rate in determining the output gap through demand and the long-run supply of potential output.

Steady-state and stability of the system

In the long-run equilibrium (steady-state) the output gap is zero, or simply a constant, and inflation expectations are realized and equal to the target inflation rate (i.e. $E_t(P_{t+1}) = P_{t+1} = P^T$). Hence, the system is reduced to:

$$Y = \frac{1}{A}[a_0(G-T) - q + a_4(R - P^T) + B(RR)] \quad (8.3.1)$$

where $A = b_1 - a_1 - a_2 - a_3 < 0;\quad B = -a_4 - b_2 > 0$.

$$P^T = \frac{1}{C}[d_0 + d_4\kappa] \quad (8.3.2)$$

where $C = (1 - d_1 - d_3) > 0,\quad d_4 > 0$.

$$RR = q + f_2 Y + f_3 R \quad (8.3.3)$$

$$R = RR + P^T \quad (8.3.4)$$

Figure 8.1(a) shows the long-run equilibrium. The curve YG represents long-run equilibrium in the goods market, where the output gap is zero or simply a constant. In the (R, Y) space the curve is positively sloped, since an increase in the rate of growth of output increases demand more than supply. To restore equilibrium (i.e. zero output gap) the rate of interest must increase to reduce demand to the level of supply. This is a representation of equation (8.3.1). The difference between the YG curve and the NCM aggregate demand equals aggregate supply curve should be stressed, as it sounds counter-intuitive that the YG curve should have

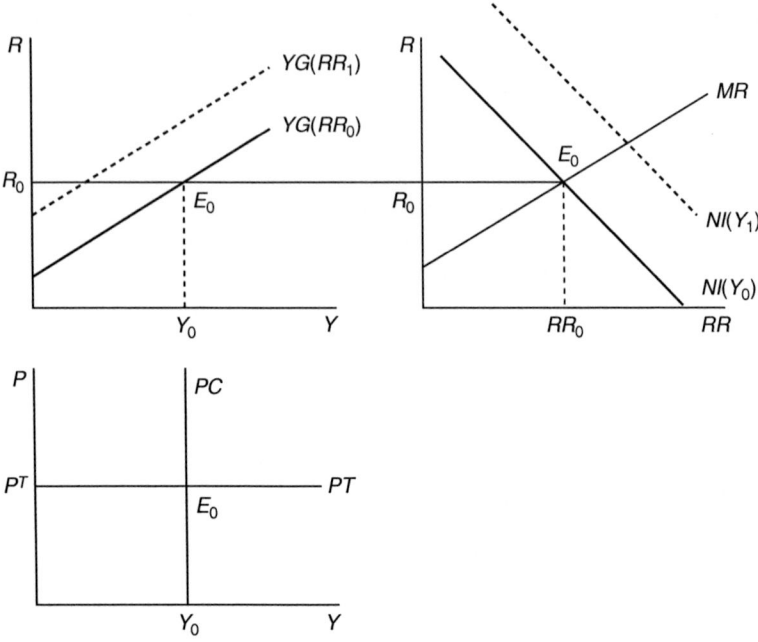

Figure 8.1a Steady state

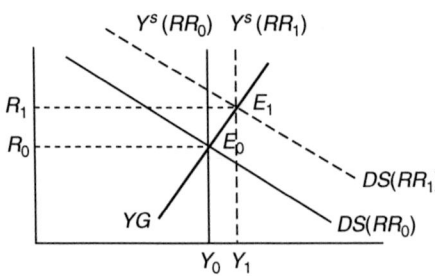

Figure 8.1b Derivation of the YG curve

a positive slope in the (R,Y) space. Figure 8.1(b) illustrates this point. The NCM demand equals supply curve, DS, is shown in Figure 8.1(b) as negatively sloped. This is a representation of equation (8.2.1) and is depicted as the DS curve in Figure 8.1(b). This curve shifts to the right by $-a_4$ as a result of an increase in the profit rate. The long-run supply (or potential) output is shown as a vertical curve, Y^s. An increase in the profit rate shifts the Y^s curve to the right by b_2 (see equation 8.1.2).[11] The initial long-run equilibrium, where the output gap is zero, is attained at E_0. As a result of an increase in the profit rate, final equilibrium is achieved at E_1, where the level of output and the rate of interest are higher. Consequently, we may derive the YG curve as the locus of equilibrium points between Y and R for each RR level. Hence, the YG curve is positively sloped.

An increase in the profit rate would increase both demand (see equation 8.2.1) and supply (see equation 8.1.2), but demand increases more than supply ($B > 0$ in (8.3.1)). To restore a zero output gap the interest rate would have to rise to reduce demand to the level of supply. Hence, the YG curve would shift to the left. Furthermore, an increase in the rate of growth of multifactor productivity will shift the YG curve to the right. In terms of Figure 8.1(b) the Y^s curve shifts to the right, whereas the DS curve remains unchanged. Hence, the rate of output increases, while the interest rate falls.

Equation (8.3.2) is portrayed in the (P, Y) space, where the $P^T PT$ line intersects the vertical axis at P^T. The PT curve is the central bank inflation target, which is independent of the rate of growth of output, as shown in equation (8.3.2). It intersects the vertical axis at the target inflation rate P^T.

We next deal with equation (8.3.3), which is plotted in the (R, RR) space as the NI curve. It represents equilibrium of the profit rate and is negatively sloped. An increase in the rate of interest reduces the profit rate by adversely affecting the business and consumer confidence. An increase in output or a rise in multifactor productivity shifts the NI curve to the right. The MR curve represents the central bank feedback rule, equation (8.3.4). It is positively sloped with a coefficient of unity. The nominal short-term interest rate is equal to the profit rate plus the target inflation rate. Long-run equilibrium is attained at E_0. The intersection of the NI curve with the MR curve determines the short-term interest rate, R_0, and the profit rate RR_0. Given the levels of the two variables, R_0 and RR_o, the YG curve determines the long-run equilibrium rate of growth of output, Y_0. The inflation rate is always equal to the target inflation rate at the intersection of the vertical Phillips curve. In the long run, wages are growing at the rate of productivity and the target inflation rate, while unemployment is equal to the NAIRU.

The stability of the system requires that $A < 0$ in equation (8.3.1). This requires that as demand and output increase, demand rises at a faster rate than supply (i.e. $a_1 + a_2 + a_3 > b_1$). If this condition is not satisfied, a negative demand shock that creates a recession will create a positive

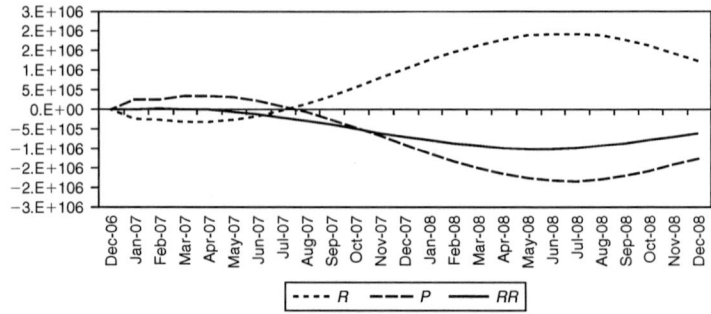

Figure 8.2 Unstable model ($A > 0, B < 0$): interest rate, inflation and natural interest rate

output gap and hence inflation will rise. If the coefficient b_1 is higher than $(a_1 + a_2 + a_3)$, the system would then become unstable in that as output declines, the output gap and inflation increase ad infinitum.

The stability of the system also requires that $B > 0$ in equation (8.3.1). This condition entails that the shift in the Y^s curve in Figure 8.1(b) is smaller than the shift in the DS curve (i.e. that $b_2 < -a_4$). Otherwise, the system is again unstable. A negative demand shock that creates a recession induces the central bank to lower the interest rate and the natural rate increases. This creates a positive output gap that increases inflation. If $b_2 > -a_4$ and, hence, $B < 0$, the system leads to increasingly lower output and higher output gap, and, thus, higher inflation.

If $A > 0$ and $B < 0$, then the system is unstable in an oscillatory manner. A negative demand shock leads to periods of lower output, higher output gap and rising inflation followed by the reverse pattern. The amplitude of the cycles is increasing through time (see Figure 8.2).

The dynamic adjustment of the economy

The dynamic adjustment of the economy to a persistent shock is studied by simulating a numerical analogue of the theoretical model. The parameter values that satisfy the inequality constraints of the underlying equations are given in Table 8.1. We have also simulated the original Neo-Wicksellian model (i.e. equations (8.3.2), (8.3.3) and (8.3.5)) in addition to simulating our reformulated model. The results for the Neo-Wicksellian model are very much as expected. Persistent shocks have no impact on NAIRU or Y^g.[12] In the case of our reformulated model, long-lasting shocks have a distinctly different impact as shown below. In

Table 8.1 Numerical model

	Y–EQ		
a(1)	a(2)	a(3)	a(4)
0.3	0.25	0.25	−0.4
	P–EQ		
D(1)	D(2)	D(3)	D(4)
0.3	0.1	0.3	0.16
	RR–EQ		
F(1)	F(2)	F(3)	F(4)
0.20	0.85	−0.25	−0.04
	R–EQ		
1-G(0)	G(1)	G(2)	G(0)
0.5	0.75	1.5	0.5
Y(S)–EQ			
B(1)	B(2)		
0.6	0.2		
W–EQ	D–EQ		
Delta	Theta		
0.2	−0.33		

what follows in the rest of this section we focus on the results obtained from the reformulated model.

Transient shocks

We assume that demand falls by 1 per cent of output for four consecutive quarters and then the shock disappears. Such a negative shock may be attributed to a recession abroad that lowers the demand for exports or to a temporary collapse of business and/or consumer confidence that reduces domestic demand. Figure 8.3(a) shows the dynamic response of the interest rate, profit rate and inflation to this transient drop in demand. The central bank reacts by lowering the interest rate immediately and aggressively to fend off the economy from this adverse demand shock. The profit rate falls more and faster than the interest rate as a result of the drop in demand that lowers the volume of sales.[13] But the profit rate is the first variable to bottom and to begin to recover. This is due to the cut in the interest rate by the central bank that lifts business and consumer confidence. The economy falls into recession as output growth and the output gap become negative (see Figure 8.3(b)), which exerts a downward pressure on inflation and wage growth as well as unit labour cost (see Figures 8.3(a) and 8.3(c)). Unemployment rises temporarily above

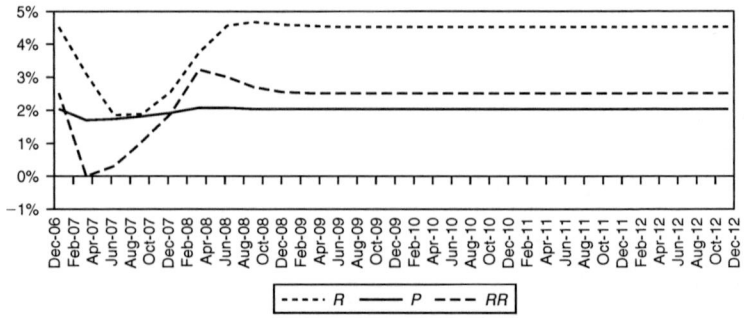

Figure 8.3a The dynamic adjustment of the interest rate, inflation and the natural interest rate to a temporary drop in demand

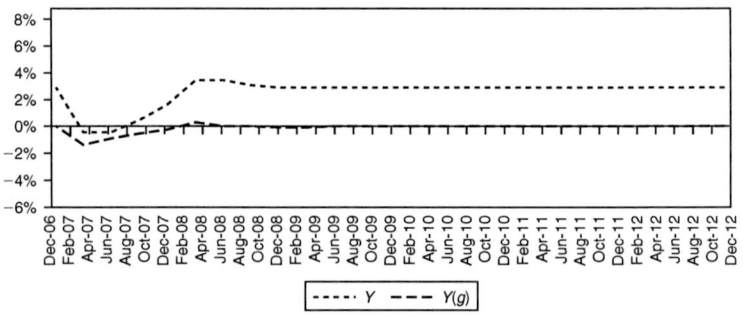

Figure 8.3b Dynamic adjustment of output to a transient drop in demand

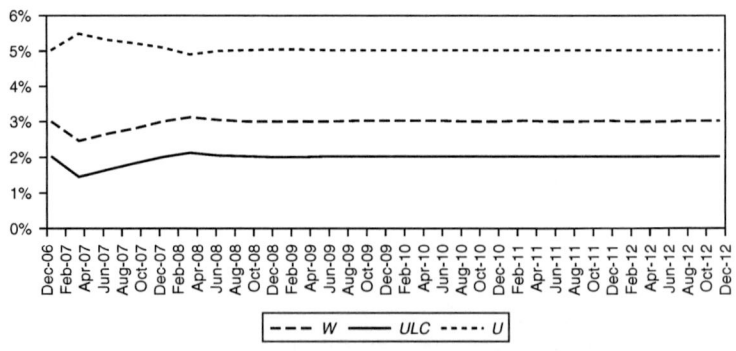

Figure 8.3c Wage inflation, *ULC* and unemployment response to a transient drop in demand

the NAIRU level, but returns to that level in the long run (see Figure 8.3(c)). The output gap bottoms before output, as the supply falls less than demand.[14] The central bank keeps the interest rate low until there are clear signs of a recovery and then begins to remove the accommodation bias. All variables overshoot their steady state during the recovery, but then gradually converge to the initial steady state.

Long-lasting shocks

As has been pointed out, long-lasting shocks prevail for a few decades and therefore remain active throughout the forecast horizon (i.e. they are long-lasting for the period of analysis). Over a much longer horizon the economy *might* be able to absorb even such shocks. But in the context of the New-Wicksellian macroeconomics tradition, there are no explicit mechanisms that would enable the adjustment to the initial steady state. In this sense, the new steady state may be more appropriately termed as interim equilibrium, which leaves open the issue of whether the economy might be able to return to its original steady state. The substantive point, which should be viewed as a criticism of this class of models, is that such models are incomplete in illustrating the necessary adjustments that should take place to restore the initial steady state, if that is at all possible.

Negative demand shock

For comparison purposes we assume that there is a long-lasting negative demand shock of 1 per cent, which may be attributed to deindustrialization or globalization that shifts production abroad to countries with

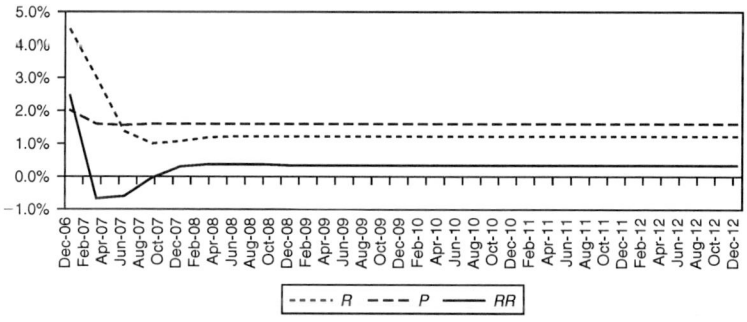

Figure 8.4a The dynamic adjustment of the interest rate, inflation and the natural interest rate to a permanent drop in demand

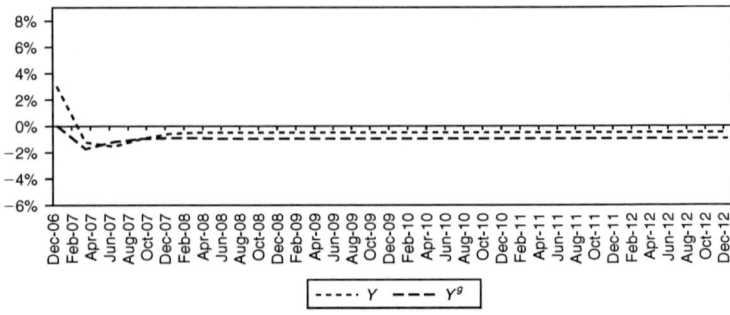

Figure 8.4b Dynamic adjustment of output to a permanent drop in demand

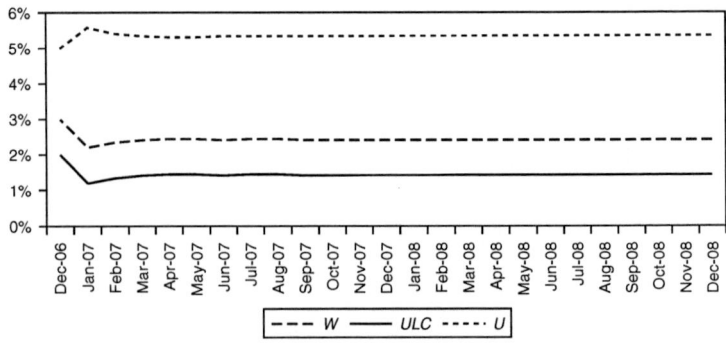

Figure 8.4c Wage inflation, ULC and unemployment: response to a permanent drop in demand

lower wages. Figures 8.4(a), 8.4(b) and 8.4(c) show the dynamic adjustment of all relevant variables to this long-lasting demand shock. The pattern is the same as in the case of the transient demand shock. Thus, the central bank lowers interest rates, the profit rate falls, the economy falls into recession with a negative output gap and unemployment rises above the NAIRU. Inflation, wage growth and the unit labour cost all decline. However, the substantive difference is that under a long-lasting shock the economy, with the equilibrating mechanisms now postulated, will converge to a new steady state, in which all relevant variables are lower than the initial one. Thus, the output gap will remain negative, but will assume a constant value; output growth will be lower; unemployment will rise above the NAIRU; inflation as well as wage growth and the unit labour cost will be lower; and the interest rate as well as the profit rate will be lower in the new steady state.

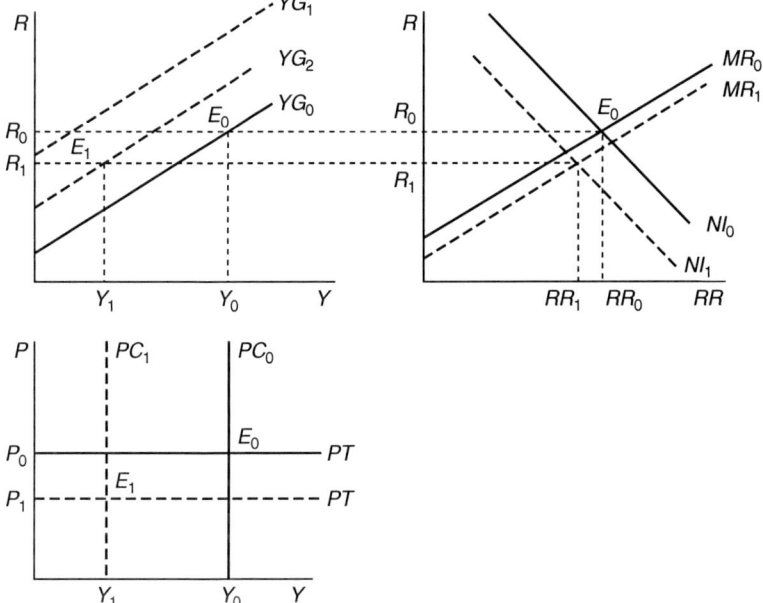

Figure 8.5 Negative demand shock

The long-run comparative statics are illustrated in Figure 8.5. Initial equilibrium is at E_0 with output growth Y_0, inflation P_0, interest rate R_0 and profit rate RR_0. The (long-lasting) negative demand shock shifts the YG curve to the left, becoming YG_1. The lower output growth shifts the NI curve to the left to NI_1 and the lower inflation rate shifts the MR curve to the right to MR_1, as the central bank lowers its inflation target. The lower profit rate shifts the YG curve to the right to YG_2. The new long-run equilibrium is attained at E_1. Output growth is lower at Y_1; the interest rate falls to R_1; the profit rate drops to RR_1. As the vertical long-run Phillips curve shifts to the left, i.e. P_0PT shifts down to P_1PT, inflation falls.

It is obvious from the previous analysis that a fiscal stimulus is the only possible policy that can offset such a long-lasting negative demand shock. An increase in government expenditure financed by a corresponding increase in taxes (balanced budget) can restore the initial steady state. Figures 8.6(a), 8.6(b) and 8.6(c) show that a fiscal stimulus introduced after a year from the initial shock of the order of 2.7 per cent of GDP

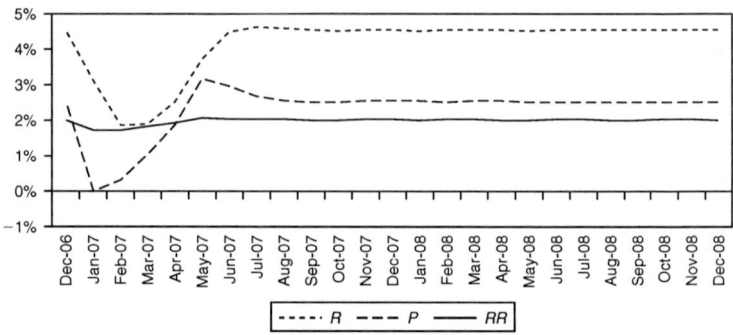

Figure 8.6a Action fiscal policy: interest rate, inflation and natural interest rate

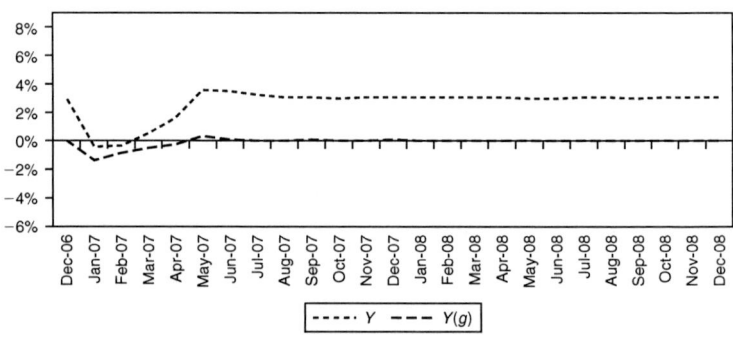

Figure 8.6b Active fiscal policy: output

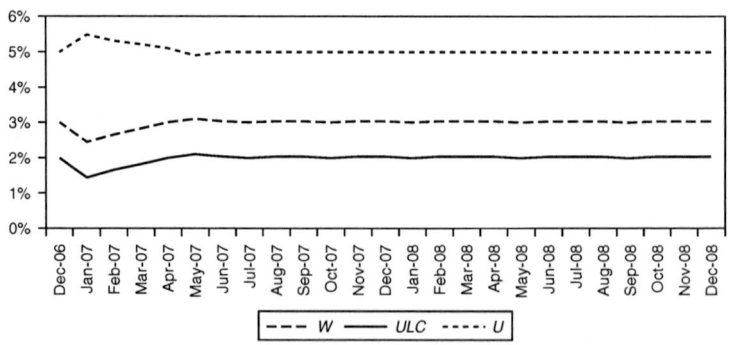

Figure 8.6c Active fiscal policy: wage inflation, *ULC* and unemployment

is sufficient to restore the initial steady state. Unemployment returns to the NAIRU.

Summary and conclusions

Wicksell defined the natural interest rate as the reward of capital, i.e. the real profit rate, and used it to explain inflation. Probably because of the 'Wicksellian muddle' the original insight of the natural rate was lost and in Neo-Wicksellian models the natural rate is simply a real interest rate that in comparison with the real short-term interest rate helps to define the stance of monetary policy as neutral, tight or easy. While in theoretical models the natural rate of interest is simply a constant, in the field of monetary policy there has been a quest to find empirical estimates of the natural rate. But such approaches have been fraught with difficulties, giving vastly diverse estimates of the natural interest rate (see, for example, Weber *et al.*, 2007). We believe that this is due to the wrong interpretation of the natural rate as a benchmark interest rate rather than the real equilibrium profit rate consistent with stable inflation.

Neo-Wicksellian models adopt the basic principles of the original model – the endogeneity of money, rejection of Say's Law in the short, but not in the long run, and use of the interest rate gap in the determination of output and inflation, albeit in a forward looking manner. They retain the policy implications of the original Wicksellian theory, namely that money is neutral in the long run, as its effect on output and unemployment is zero and inflation is a monetary phenomenon and under the control of the central bank. The cause of the increase in the supply of money, though, is due to a divergence between the real and monetary factors – the interest rate gap, namely the deviation of the real profit rate from the real interest rate.

However, Neo-Wicksellian models are inherently inconsistent, as their policy implications are derived from two assumptions, the natural interest rate and the long-run supply of (potential) output, which are fixed and exogenously determined. We have attempted in this chapter to remain faithful to the original concept of the natural interest rate as the reward of capital, and have integrated the real profit rate, which plays such a vital role in microeconomics and yet is treated as a constant in modern macroeconomics, within an otherwise Neo-Wicksellian model. The real profit rate should be allowed to adjust with respect to the main macrovariables, and in the long-run equilibrium it should be consistent with stable inflation, the basic insight of the original Wicksellian model.

For as long as the real profit rate is not in equilibrium, inflation would not reach a stable equilibrium, since companies will have an incentive to change prices. We do not pretend to have reconstructed modern macro theory by endogenizing the natural interest rate and the supply of output even in a rudimentary way. However, we hope to have demonstrated the internal inconsistency of the Neo-Wicksellian model, which claims to be the New Consensus Macroeconomics. This inconsistency is due to the lack of a sufficient number of equilibrating mechanisms – in fact there is only one, the interest rate gap, and as we have shown this is by far insufficient.

Our model shows that output, unemployment and inflation will return to the initial steady state in the face of transient, but not long-lasting, shocks. In the presence of the latter, there is scope for fiscal policy to offset them. In this model there are two equilibrating mechanisms, the interest rate gap and the supply of output. But this self-adjustment is not rich enough to allow for other equilibrating mechanisms, which operate in the real world. Even if self-adjustment may bring the system back to equilibrium, this would take time. In this respect, policy, both fiscal and monetary, would expedite this process. From this perspective the current model breaks ground with Neo-Wicksellian models that deny both fiscal and monetary policy any role in affecting output and unemployment in the long run.

Appendix

The supply of (or potential) output, equation (8.1.2), can be derived as follows. For simplicity, consider a Cobb-Douglas production function with constant returns to scale. Although this may seem a restrictive assumption, there is no loss of generality, while the arguments are more vivid:

$$Y(t) = Q(t) \, K^\alpha \, L^{1-\alpha} \qquad (8.1.2a)$$

where the symbols are as in the text. By totally differentiating the log of (8.1.2a) we obtain the determinants of the rate of growth of output in the long run, since output is demand determined in the short run, as in equation (8.1.2b):

$$\dot{Y} = \dot{q} + \alpha \, \dot{K} + (1-\alpha) \, \dot{L} \qquad (8.1.2b)$$

This equation shows that the long term determinants of potential output are the rate of growth of multifactor productivity ($\dot{q}$), capital ($\dot{K}$) and labour force ($\dot{L}$). The latter is exogenous in conventional economic analysis and, while it can account for secular growth, it can be considered as non-varying in business cycle analysis and therefore its role can be subsumed into a constant. But the role of the growth rate of the capital stock is more complicated as it is affected, on the one hand, by the decision of households on how much to consume and save through time and, on the other hand, by the decision of firms on how much to invest at any point in time. We begin with the investment decision of the firm.

Consider the definition of gross investment as the sum of net investment plus replacement investment. Assuming that depreciation is a constant fraction of the capital stock, net investment is defined as:

$$\dot{K}_t = I_t - \delta K_t \qquad (8.1.2c)$$

Using this definition of net investment, the capital stock is simply the accumulation of past gross investment, but at a rate, δ, that takes into account the decay of capital due to depreciation:

$$K_t = \int_{\infty}^{t} I(t) \, \exp\{-\delta(t-s)\} \, ds \qquad (8.1.2d)$$

Now assume that the flow of profit (profit out of current production or operating profit) follows a geometric Brownian motion:

$$d\pi = \alpha \pi \, dt + \sigma \pi \, dz \qquad (8.1.2e)$$

where dz is the increment of a Wiener process:

$$dz = \varepsilon_{2t} \sqrt{dt} \quad \varepsilon_{2t} \approx N(0, 1) \qquad (8.1.2f)$$

Equation (8.1.2e) implies that the current level of the flow of profit is known, but future values are log-normally distributed with a variance that grows linearly with the time horizon. Although information arrives over time the future value of the profit is always unknown.

If $\pi(0) = \pi_0$ denotes the current profit flow, the expected value and the variance of the geometric Brownian profit process are given by:

$$E[\pi(t)] = \pi_0 \, e^{\alpha t}; \quad V[\pi(t)] = \pi_0^2 \, e^{2\alpha t}(e^{\sigma^2 t} - 1) \qquad (8.1.2g)$$

This implies that the expected average profit grows through time at the rate α. Possible future realizations can be computed by drawing random values from a normal distribution; and confidence intervals can also be computed using, for example, one or two standard deviations from the variance of the profit in (8.1.2g).

The present value of the expected stream of future profits is given by:

$$V(t) = E \int_t^\infty \pi(s)\, e^{-\rho(s-t)} ds = \pi(t)/(\rho - \alpha), \quad \text{if } \rho > \alpha \qquad (8.1.2\text{h})$$

where ρ is the discount factor. This is obtained by substituting (8.1.2g) into the left-hand side of (8.1.2h). Hence, the present value of expected profits can simply be expressed in terms of the current profit, the current estimate of the expected average profit growth and the discount rate (or marginal efficiency of investment), i.e. all observable variables. The time derivative of the right-hand side of (8.1.2h) is simply the natural rate of interest, the period-by-period growth profit rate, and the coefficient b_2 in equation (8.1.2) in the main text should be thought of as $1/(\rho - \alpha)$. The natural rate oscillates randomly through time around the current estimate of its average value α.

The decision to invest is obtained from the maximization of (8.1.2h) subject to (8.1.2e). If investment is irreversible, then irrespective of whether there is uncertainty or not the firm would expand capacity up to the point where investment is equal to the present value of expected future profits less the *opportunity* or option to invest, $F[V(t)]$ (see, Dixit and Pindyck, 1994):

$$I(t) = V(t) - F[V(t)] \qquad (8.1.2\text{i})$$

The amount of investment is less than that implied by the Jorgensonian user cost of capital by the opportunity cost of waiting, which is equal to the price of a perpetual call option (see, ibid.).

The intertemporal decision of households between consumption and saving is similarly obtained by maximizing the expected value of the utility derived from current and future consumption, subject to the exhaustion of all future lifetime resources. Assuming that income follows a geometric Brownian motion its expected value is equal to the current level of output divided by the discount rate (the rate of substitution between current and future consumption) less the expected average rate of growth of income. Hence, by substituting the rates of growth of the present value of the expected stream of future profits and income into (8.1.2b) we obtain equation (8.1.2) in the main text.

Notes

1. We prefer the terminology 'Neo-Wicksellian' in this chapter, however, simply because we focus on the notion of the 'natural' rate of interest, an important factor within the New Consensus Macroeconomics (Weber *et al.*, 2008), but initially due to Wicksell (1898).
2. The definition of the natural rate as the profit rate is very clear in Wicksell (1901). Shackle emphasized that the natural interest rate 'in English would be more suitably called the rate of profit or rate of trading revenue' (Shackle, 1972, pp. 335-6). The profit rate, though, can be viewed as the *ex ante* return for the entire life of the extra unit of the capital stock. In this sense, it is equivalent to Keynes's concept of the marginal efficiency of capital, which Keynes defined as follows: 'I define the marginal efficiency of capital as being equal to the rate of discount which would make the present value of the series of annuities given by the returns expected from the capital asset during its life just equal its supply price' (Keynes, 1936, p. 135). This was more accurately rephrased by Lerner (1953) as the 'marginal efficiency of investment' (MEI). Fisher (1911) had long ago called the return of capital the 'rate of return over cost'. Shackle (1988) made a distinction of the two concepts, as the profit rate out of current production and as a discount rate. But as Shackle (1972, pp. 336-8) pointed out Wicksell (1901) oscillated between the two concepts, perhaps, because of the influence of the Austrian theory of capital, which he had studied. It is clear that Wicksell defined the profit rate (the natural rate) as a discount rate. But in other instances, as Shackle pointed out, 'Wicksell thinks of the natural rate as a datum to which the market rate must be adjusted, if businessmen are not to have an incentive to make investment exceed saving' (Shackle, 1988, p. 32).
3. Shackle (1967) attributes the 'Wicksellian muddle' to a misunderstanding by Myrdal (1939).
4. It is worthwhile noticing that in some of his works Wicksell rejected the proposition that the natural rate is equal to the marginal product of capital. In fact, he showed that the profit rate is greater than the marginal product of capital (Wicksell, 1906, p. 180). Moreover, Wicksell (ibid., p. 178) showed that the profit rate is equal to the rate of growth of output, the infamous 'Golden Rule' of growth theory, or what Wicksell (ibid.) called 'Jevons's well-known formula'. However, the most elegant definition of the natural interest rate as the marginal product of capital is found in Shackle's (1954) introduction to Frowen's 1954 translation of Wicksell's *Value, Capital and Rent*, where it is argued that 'It is a measure of the "worthwhileness" at any stage of the development of the economy's total assemblage of productive equipment, of adding one more unit to that equipment' (p. 10).
5. It is also true to say that Friedman's (1968) natural rate of unemployment, an important ingredient in the New Consensus Macroeconomics, was heavily influenced by Wicksell's 1898 natural rate of interest concept.
6. From a mathematical viewpoint there is a distinction between recursive and post-recursive variables. Recursive variables are the ones that are determined by the *minimum* reduced-form equations. For example, a system of, say, eight equations in eight unknowns can be reduced to three equations in three unknowns. The three endogenous variables are referred to as recursive

variables, the other five as post-recursive, as they are determined, *ex post*, after the recursive variables have been determined, as residuals.
7. A number of studies have tried to provide empirical estimates of the natural rate of interest (for a review of the literature, see Cuaresma *et al.*, 2004). Three methods have been used in the literature: (1) (univariate) filtering approaches; (2) structural econometric models with the natural rate as a latent variable; and (3) fully fledged equilibrium models with microeconomic foundations. Some of the problems encountered in these approaches can be found in Amato (2005) and Weber *et al.* (2008).
8. Clearly fiscal policy is ineffective within the NCM analysis. It may have temporary effects but none in the long run.
9. Equation (8.1.2) should, of course, contain the rate of growth of the labour force, as it is derived from a production function (see Appendix). This factor is more important than capital in explaining the secular growth of the economy. However, since in the current model we are interested in business cycles rather than in secular growth, we can safely omit the rate of growth of the labour force. Including it, provided it is exogenous, will not alter the results in any case.
10. In terms of the levels of the variables, rather than the growth rates, profit out of current production, including the remuneration of capital, is equal to $\pi = PL \cdot YL - W \cdot L$; where π is the profit rate plus the return of capital, PL is the price level, YL is the level of output, W is the wage rate, and L is the employment level. Unit profit, $UP = \pi/YL$, is thus defined as $UP = PL - W/Q$; where Q is productivity. Totally differentiating the log of the last expression, and defining the natural interest rate as the rate of growth of profit and R is the interest rate or the return of capital, we obtain $RR = (P - ulc) + Y - \lambda \cdot R$; where P is the rate of growth of the price level, ulc is the rate of growth of unit labour cost, Y is rate of growth of output. This implies that the rate of growth of profit is equal to the rate of growth of the profit margin *plus* the rate of growth of output less the impact of the interest rate on capital stock. In other words, homogeneity is imposed in the first two terms. However, companies because, say, of globalization, may shift part of the production abroad, for example to China. In this case the unit labour cost of the country concerned, say the US, ceases to be important, while that of China emerges as the important variable. In this case homogeneity should not be imposed and equation (8.1.7) is obtained.
11. Note that since $-a_4 > b_2$ the shift in the supply curve, Y^s, is smaller than the shift in the demand curve, YG.
12. We do not cite the simulation results in the case of the Neo-Wicksellian model but they can be obtained from the authors upon request.
13. This is consistent with the stylized facts. The profit rate falls more rapidly than the policy controlled interest rate. The profit rate is also the first to recover.
14. This is also consistent with the stylized facts, but in the real world this is due to some scrapping of capacity.

References

Amato, J. D. (2005) 'The Role of the Natural Rate of Interest in Monetary Policy', BIS working paper 171.

Arestis, P. (2007) 'What is the New Consensus in Macroeconomics?', in P. Arestis (ed.), *Is there a New Consensus in Macroeconomics?*, Houndmills, Basingstoke: Palgrave Macmillan.

Arestis, P. and E. Karakitsos (2004) *The Post–Bubble US Economy: Implications for Financial Markets*, London: Palgrave Macmillan.

Artis, M. J. and E. Karakitsos (1983) *Memorandum of Evidence on International Monetary Arrangements*, Fourth Report from the Treasury and Civil Service Committee on International Monetary Arrangements, London: H.M.S.O, HC 21-III, 142–206.

Ball, L. and D. Romer (1990) 'Real Rigidities and the Non-neutrality of Money', *Review of Economic Studies* 57 (1): 179–98.

Calvo, G. (1983) 'Staggered Prices in a Utility Maximising Framework', *Journal of Monetary Economics* 12 (2): 383–98.

Clarida, R., J. Galí and M. Gertler (1998) 'Monetary Policy Rules in Practice: Some International Evidence', *European Economic Review* 42 (2): 1033–68.

Clarida, R., J. Galí and M. Gertler (2000) 'Monetary Policy Rules and Macroeconomic Stability: Evidence and Some Theory', *Quarterly Journal of Economics* 115 (1): 147–80.

Cuaresma, C. J., E. Gnan and D. Ritzberger-Grünwald (2004) 'Searching for the Natural Rate of Interest: A Euro Area Perspective', *Empirica* 31: 183–204.

Dixit, A. K. and R. S. Pindyck (1994) *Investment under Uncertainty*, Princeton: Princeton University Press.

Fisher, I. (1911) *The Purchasing Power of Money*, New York: Macmillan.

Fontana, G. (2006) 'The "New Consensus" View of Monetary Policy: A New Wickselian Connection?', Levy Economics Institute working paper 476, New York: Levy Economics Institute of Bard College.

Friedman, M. (1968) 'The Role of Monetary Policy', *American Economic Review* 58 (1): 1–17.

Frowen, S. F. (ed.) (1988) *Business, Time and Thought, Selected Papers of G. S. L. Shackle*, London: Macmillan;

Goodhart, C. A. E. (2004) 'Review of *Interest and Prices* by M. Woodford', *Journal of Economics* 82 (2): 195–200.

Karakitsos, E. and B. Rustem (1984) 'Optimally Derived Fixed Rules and Indicators', *Journal of Economic Dynamics and Control* 8 (1): 33–64.

Karakitsos, E. and B. Rustem (1985) 'Optimal Fixed Rules and Simple Feedback Laws in the Design of Economic Policy', *Automatica* 21 (2): 169–80.

Keynes, J. M. (1936) *The General Theory of Employment, Interest and Money*, London: Macmillan.

King, M. (2005) 'Monetary Policy: Practice Ahead of Theory', Mais Lecture, Cass Business School, City University, London, 17 May.

Laidler, D. (1999) *Fabricating the Keynesian Revolution*, Cambridge: Cambridge University Press.

Lerner, A. (1953) 'On the Marginal Product of Capital and the Marginal Efficiency of Investment', *Journal of Political Economy* 61 (1): 147–68.

Lindahl, E. (1950) *Studies in the Theory of Money and Capital*, 2nd edition, London: Allen and Unwin.

Myrdal, G. (1939) *Monetary Equilibrium*, London: Hodge.

Rottemberg, J. J. and M. Woodford (1995) 'Dynamic General Equilibrium Models with Imperfectly Competitive Product Markets', in T. J. Cooley (ed.) *Frontiers of Business Cycle Research*, Princeton: Princeton University Press: 243–93.

Rottemberg, J. J. and M. Woodford (1997) 'An Optimization-Based Econometric Framework for the Evaluation of Monetary Policy', *NBER Macroeconomics Annual 1997*, Cambridge, MA: National Bureau of Economic Research: 297–346.

Shackle, G. L. S. (1954) Foreword to the English Translation by S. F. Frowen of Wicksell's *Uber Wert, Kapital und Rent*, first published in 1893.

Shackle, G. L. S. (1967) *The Years of High Theory: Invention and Tradition in Economic Thought 1926–1939*, Cambridge: Cambridge University Press.

Shackle, G. L. S. (1972) *Epistemics and Economics: A Critique of Economic Doctrines*, Cambridge: Cambridge University Press.

Shackle, G. L. S. (1988) *Business, Time and Thought*, Selected Papers by G. L. S. Shackle, ed. Stephen F. Frowen, Macmillan: Basingstoke.

Svensson, L. E. O. (1999) 'Inflation Targeting as Monetary Policy Rule', *Journal of Monetary Economics* 43 (4): 607–54.

Svensson, L. E. O. (2003) 'What is Wrong with Taylor Rules? Using Judgement in Monetary Policy through Targeting Rules', Journal of Economic Literature XLI (2): 426–77.

Taylor, J. B. (1993) 'Discretion Versus Policy Rules in Practice', *Carnegie-Rochester Conference Series on Public Policy*, December: 195–214.

Weber, A., W. Lemke and A. Worms (2008) 'How Useful is the Concept of the Natural Real Rate of Interest for Monetary Policy?', *Cambridge Journal of Economics* 32 (1): 49–63.

Wicksell, K. (1906) *Lectures on Political Economy*, vol. 2, New York: Kelley.

Wicksell, K. (1954) *Value, Capital and Rent*, tr. S. F. Frowen, London: George Allen Unwin; reprinted by Augustus Kelley, New York, 1970.

Wicksell, K. (1965 [1898]) *Geldzins und Güterpreise*, Frankfurt: Verlag Gustav Fischer; English translation in R. F. Kahn (1965) *Interest and Prices*, New York: Kelley.

Woodford, M. (1997) 'Doing without Money: Controlling Inflation in a Post-monetary World', mimeo, Princeton University.

Woodford, M. (1999) 'Optimal Monetary Policy Inertia', NBER working paper series, no. 7261, Cambridge, MA: National Bureau of Economic Research.

Woodford, M. (2003) *Interest and Prices*, Princeton: Princeton University Press.

9
Is Inflation Targeting Inimical to Employment?
Mark Setterfield

Introduction

Mainstream macroeconomic models portray capitalism as a 'real exchange' economy, in which real outcomes are supply-determined and money is neutral (at least in the long run). The inevitable upshot of these models is that inflation targeting is ultimately neutral with respect to real macroeconomic performance: *any* rate of inflation can be achieved consistent with the same (supply-determined) rate of employment.

According to the Post Keynesian tradition, however, capitalism is properly conceived as a 'monetary production' economy, in which real outcomes are demand-determined and money is non-neutral, even in the long run. The question addressed in this chapter is: does this fundamentally different characterization of the workings of the economy make inflation targeting inimical to employment? We will show that in the Post Keynesian approach, inflation targeting can be inimical to employment, neutral with respect to employment or can even enhance employment *depending on the architecture of macroeconomic policy*. The main conclusion we will draw is that policy activism contributes to the social construction of the economy. As such, *both* competing characterizations of the workings of the economy *and* the nature of macroeconomic policy interventions affect the propriety of controversial policies such as inflation targeting.

We will begin by outlining the processes responsible for generating inflation and employment outcomes. The resulting characterization of the economy makes the models utilized throughout this chapter identifiably Post Keynesian in spirit. We will then introduce a variety of policy interventions and examine the impact of these on inflation and employment when policy-makers are assumed to engage in inflation targeting.[1]

Characterizing the workings of the economy: the determination of inflation and employment[2]

The inflation process

Inflation is modelled as a conflicting-claims process.[3] Nominal wages and prices are set in reference to workers' and firms' target shares of total income or, in other words (taking the level of labour productivity as given in the short run), their target real wages. This conflicting-claims process can be described as follows:

$$w = \mu[(\omega_W - \omega) + p^e] \tag{9.1}$$

$$p = \varphi(\omega - \omega_F) + w \tag{9.2}$$

$$\mu = \mu_e e \tag{9.3}$$

where w denotes the rate of growth of the nominal wage, ω_W is the target wage share of workers, ω is the actual wage share, p^e and p denote the expected and actual rates of inflation, respectively, ω_F is the target wage share of firms (where $\omega_W > \omega_F$ by assumption), and e is the rate of employment. In equation (9.1), workers bargain for nominal wage increases in accordance with their inflation expectations and the difference between their preferred wage share and the actual wage share. Workers' ability to incorporate changes in these variables into nominal wage increases is limited by their incomplete bargaining power vis-à-vis firms – hence $\mu < 1$. In equation (9.2), meanwhile, firms increase prices in accordance with the rate of growth of unit labour costs, w,[4] and the difference between the actual and their preferred wage share. Firms' ability to increase prices in response to their distributional aims is again considered incomplete (this time depending on the prevailing state of competition in the goods market) – hence $\varphi < 1$. Finally, equation (9.3) makes the relative power of workers in the wage bargain dependent on the rate of employment, with $\mu_e > 0$.

Steady-state equilibrium requires that $p^e = p$ and $\omega = \bar{\omega}$, the second of these conditions implying, from the definition of the wage share, that $p = w$.[5] Using these equilibrium conditions to solve equations (9.1) and (9.2) for the equilibrium wage share and rate of inflation, we obtain:

$$\omega^* = \omega_F \tag{9.4}$$

$$p^* = \frac{\mu}{1-\mu}(\omega_W - \omega^*) \tag{9.5}$$

where an asterisk (*) denotes the equilibrium value of a variable. Finally, substituting equations (9.3) and (9.4) into (9.5), we obtain the following expression for the equilibrium rate of inflation:

$$p^* = \frac{\mu_e e}{1 - \mu_e e}(\omega_W - \omega_F) \qquad (9.6)$$

Note that equation (9.6) is essentially a long-run Phillips curve, in which increases in the employment rate (i.e. decreases in the unemployment rate) are associated with increases in the steady-state rate of inflation.[6] In other words, the long-run Phillips curve (in inflation, unemployment space) is negatively sloped.

The model of inflation outlined above and summarized in equation (9.6) exhibits a number of important Keynesian features. First, it involves nominal wage bargaining. This is consistent with the principle that the economy is an intrinsically monetary construct, in which reference to the money unit of account is a basic feature of economic behaviour. Exchange agreements are conducted in nominal terms, with variables such as the real wage or real rate of interest determined *ex post* by the values of nominal variables. Money is not simply a convenient medium of exchange that otherwise conceals the fact that the terms of trade are agreed in real terms.

None of this implies that decision-makers are unaware of the distinction between nominal and real values, in other words, that they suffer 'money illusion'. On the contrary, both workers and firms are described in equations (9.1) and (9.2) as aspiring to particular values of the real wage, and as seeking to protect their real incomes against the encroachments of price and wage inflation, respectively. This brings us to a second important Keynesian feature of the model outlined above: incomplete indexation ($\mu, \varphi < 1$). As intimated earlier, this is explained by incomplete bargaining power (of workers vis-à-vis firms in the wage bargain, and of firms vis-à-vis the goods market), *not* irrationality. The importance of incomplete indexation can be seen in equations (9.4) and (9.5). Were we to replace equation (9.3) with $\mu = 1$ (allowing workers fully to index inflation expectations into nominal wage growth), the equilibrium real wage would become:

$$\omega^* = \frac{\omega_W + \varphi \omega_F}{(1 + \varphi)} \qquad (9.4a)$$

and the equilibrium rate of inflation would become indeterminate. This last result is consistent with a vertical Phillips curve and an accompanying NAIRU, which can be seen by solving equations (9.1) and (9.2) under the assumptions that $\mu = 1$ and $\omega_W = \theta e$. This yields equation (9.4a) above and:

$$e^* = \frac{\omega_F}{\theta}$$

where $1 - e^*$ is the NAIRU (an equilibrium rate of unemployment determined independently of the aggregate demand for goods). Clearly, then, incomplete indexation by workers plays an important role in expunging from our model the notion of a supply-determined equilibrium rate of (un)employment that is invariant with respect to demand conditions.[7]

The final Keynesian feature of the model in equations (9.1)–(9.3) is that it describes a process of wage and price determination in which the real wage is set in the goods market independently of workers' efforts to influence the nominal wage. This is clearly demonstrated by the solution for the equilibrium real wage in equation (9.4) above, which is independent of either μ (workers' bargaining power) or ω_W (their real wage target). Indeed, it follows from (9.2) that at *any* point in time, the real wage is always set independently of μ and ω_W as $w - p = -\varphi(\omega - \omega_F)$. This feature of our model is consistent with Keynes's (1936) description of the real wage as a variable that is determined *after* nominal wages have been set, by the process of price setting in the goods market.[8]

The level of employment

Our description of the level of employment begins with a modified neo-Kaleckian model of the form:

$$g = \gamma + g_u u + g_r(r - i\lambda) \tag{9.7}$$

$$g^s = s_\pi r \tag{9.8}$$

$$r = \frac{(1 - \omega)u}{v} \tag{9.9}$$

where g is the rate of accumulation, u is the rate of capacity utilization, r is the rate of profit, i is the nominal interest rate, λ (which we assume to be fixed in the short run) is the ratio of corporate debt to the value of the capital stock, g^s is the rate of growth of savings, s_π is the propensity to save out of profits, and v is the (fixed) capital–output ratio. Equation (9.7) is a canonical neo-Kaleckian investment function which has been modified so that the rate of accumulation depends on the rate of 'enterprise' profits, $r_E = r - i\lambda$, rather than gross profits (r). In other words, investment is sensitive to variations in profit, net of firms' debt servicing commitments.[9] Equation (9.8) is the familiar Cambridge equation and equation (9.9) is true by definition.

Steady-state equilibrium is achieved when $g = g^s$. Using this equilibrium condition, recalling that $\omega^* = \omega_F$,[10] and solving (9.7)–(9.9) for u, we obtain:

$$u^* = \frac{(\gamma - g_r i^* \lambda)v}{(s_\pi - g_r)(1 - \omega_F) - g_u v} \tag{9.10}$$

Note that, by definition, the rate of employment, e can be written as:

$$e = \frac{a\kappa u}{v} \tag{9.11}$$

where a is the employment–output ratio (which is fixed by virtue of our assumption that there is no labour productivity growth) and κ is the ratio of the capital stock to the labour force. This latter ratio is also fixed since, as befits a short-run model, we assume that both the capital stock and the size of the labour force are given.[11] Combining equations (9.10) and (9.11), we can therefore write the equilibrium rate of employment as:

$$e^* = \frac{a\kappa(\gamma - g_r i^* \lambda)}{(s_\pi - g_r)(1 - \omega_F) - g_u v} \tag{9.12}$$

In what follows, we assume that:

$$s_\pi > g_r + \frac{g_u v}{(1 - \omega_F)} \tag{9.13}$$

and:

$$\gamma > g_r i^* \lambda \tag{9.14}$$

which makes the equilibrium solution in (9.12) both positive and stable.

The model of employment determination outlined above, like the model of inflation in the previous subsection, has several important Keynesian features. First, note that the equilibrium rate of employment in equation (9.12) derives from features of both the supply-side (a, κ and v) and the demand-side (ω, i and the various parameters of equations (9.7) and (9.8)). It is thus equivalent to the rate of employment that would be observed at a Keynesian point of effective demand.

Second, the model of employment developed above is consistent with the paradox of thrift: an increase in the savings rate will depress aggregate demand and hence the level of economic activity, as reflected in the rate of employment. Hence note that, given (9.14), it follows from (9.12) that:

$$\frac{\partial e^*}{\partial s_\pi} = \frac{-(1-\omega_F)a\kappa(\gamma - g_r i^*\lambda)}{[(s_\pi - g_r)(1-\omega_F) - g_u v]^2} < 0$$

Third, the model is consistent with the notion that, in the event of a balanced deflation (an equal proportional fall in all prices that leaves all relative prices – including the equilibrium real wage – unchanged), debt-deflation effects will dominate.[12] As a result, both aggregate demand and the rate of employment will decrease. To see this, recall that:

$$\lambda = \frac{D_R}{K} = \frac{D}{PK}$$

so that:

$$\frac{\partial \lambda}{\partial P} = \frac{-D}{P^2 K} < 0$$

It therefore follows, given (9.13), that:

$$\frac{\partial e^*}{\partial P} = \frac{\partial e^*}{\partial \lambda}\frac{\partial \lambda}{\partial P} = \frac{a\kappa g_r i^* D}{P^2 K[(s_\pi - g_r)(1-\omega_F) - g_u v]} > 0$$

This result follows from the negative impact of an increase in firms' real debt burden on their cash flow, and hence their ability to invest. Specifically, a drop in prices redistributes gross profit income away from enterprise profits (to which investment is sensitive) and towards rents.

The foregoing analysis is, however, incomplete, because it does not take into account the fact that a redistribution of real income away from firms and towards rentiers may affect aggregate consumption behaviour as well as aggregate investment. To see this, note that total saving in the economy is given by:

$$S = \Pi - i^*D + s_r i^*D = \Pi - (1-s_r)i^*D$$

where s_r is the propensity to save of rentiers, and we assume for simplicity that all enterprise profits ($\Pi - i^*D$) are retained by firms (i.e. there are no distributed earnings). It follows that:

$$\frac{S}{\Pi} = s_\pi = 1 - (1-s_r)\frac{i^*D}{\Pi}$$

which can be written as:

$$s_\pi = 1 - (1-s_r)\frac{i^*D_R}{\Pi_R}$$

Since a balanced deflation will leave Π_R unchanged but cause D_R to rise, it is evident from the expression above that, by increasing rentiers' share of real profit income, a balanced deflation will reduce the value of s_π. Intuitively, this is because some part of the gross profits that would previously have been saved as retained earnings will now be spent on consumption goods by rentier households. Only if $s_r = 1$ (in which case $s_\pi = 1$, so that s_π is rendered invariant with respect to the ratio D_R/Π_R) will this effect disappear. But in general (i.e. with $s_r \neq 1$) we will observe:

$$\frac{\partial e^*}{\partial P} = \frac{\partial e^*}{\partial \lambda}\frac{\partial \lambda}{\partial P} + \frac{\partial e^*}{\partial s_\pi}\frac{\partial s_\pi}{\partial D_R}\frac{\partial D_R}{\partial P}$$

$$\Rightarrow \frac{\partial e^*}{\partial P} = \frac{a\kappa g_r i^* D}{P^2 K[(s_\pi - g_r)(1 - \omega_F) - g_u v]}$$
$$+ \left(\frac{-(1-\omega_F)a\kappa(\gamma - g_r i^* \lambda)}{[(s_\pi - g_r)(1-\omega_F) - g_u v]^2}\right)\left(\frac{-(1-s_r)i^*}{\Pi_R}\right)\left(\frac{-D}{P^2}\right)$$

The sign of this expression is ambiguous since, given (9.13) and (9.14), the first term on the right-hand side is positive whilst the second term is negative. Nevertheless, a balanced deflation will reduce employment as long as its negative effect on debtors' spending outweighs its positive effect on creditors' spending. The general sentiment in Post Keynesian economics is that this is the case (see, for example, Palley, 1996).

A final important property of our model of employment is that, given (9.14), it follows from equation (9.12) that:

$$\frac{\partial e^*}{\partial (1-\omega_F)} = \frac{-a\kappa(\gamma - g_r i^* \lambda)(s_\pi - g_r)}{[(s_\pi - g_r)(1-\omega_F) - g_u v]^2} < 0 \qquad (9.15)$$

In other words, the economy is stagnationist: increases in the wage share of income will boost aggregate demand and thus raise the rate of employment. The significance of this last result for the macroeconomics of inflation targeting will become evident in due course.

The impact of policy interventions on macroeconomic outcomes: is inflation targeting inimical to employment?

So far we have outlined a model that consists of a Phillips curve (equation (9.6)) and an employment function (equation (9.12)). Both of these components of our model have been shown to display various important Keynesian features, indicative of their fidelity to the properties of a monetary production economy. But the model specified thus far is incomplete. This is evident from equation (9.12), in which the equilibrium rate of employment depends on the equilibrium value of the nominal interest rate. We must specify the determination of the nominal interest rate in order to close our model.[13] This brings us directly to the conduct of macroeconomic policy and thence to the impact of inflation targeting on employment, with which we are ultimately concerned.

Since our model demands, in the first instance, a description of how the nominal interest rate is determined, we will begin by characterizing macroeconomic policy regimes in terms of the conduct of monetary policy. As will become clear in what follows, however, monetary policy is not the only type of policy intervention that we will consider in this section.

Following the first principles of Post Keynesian monetary theory, we assume that the quantity of money in circulation is determined endogenously through the process of credit creation. Profit-seeking commercial banks create credit in response to the demands of credit-worthy borrowers, and the central bank accommodates this process by varying the size of the monetary base in response to private sector credit creation, in order to keep commercial banks liquid. As the monopoly supplier of base money, the central bank performs this last task at a price (i.e. nominal interest rate) of its own choosing. In short, we are dealing with a monetary environment in which the instrument of monetary policy is the nominal interest rate. Specifying the determination of the nominal interest rate in order to close our model therefore amounts to specifying the interest rate operating procedure (IROP) employed by the central bank.[14]

Suppose initially, then, that the central bank sets the nominal interest rate in accordance with the following IROP:

$$di = \alpha(p - p^T) \qquad (9.16)$$

where p^T is an inflation target set by the central bank. In equation (9.16), the central bank varies the interest rate in response to the difference between the actual rate of inflation and its preferred or target rate (with $\alpha > 0$). This is a simple example of what Rochon and Setterfield (2007) label 'activist' IROPs, the best known of which is the Taylor Rule.

Equilibrium in our model now requires that $di = 0$, which from (9.16), implies that:

$$p^* = p^T \qquad (9.17)$$

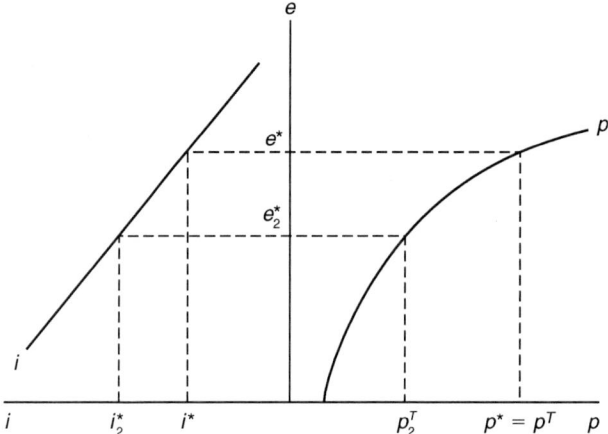

Figure 9.1 The adverse employment effects of inflation targeting

Together with equations (9.6) and (9.12), equation (9.17) gives us three equations in three unknowns, which we can solve for the general equilibrium configuration of the economy. This general equilibrium configuration is illustrated in Figure 9.1, which comprises the Phillips curve in equation (9.6) in the right-hand panel and the employment function in equation (9.12) in the left-hand panel. The result in equation (9.17) is then imposed on the diagram in order to derive the equilibrium rates of employment and interest.

As is clear from Figure 9.1, inflation targeting and monetary policy 'rule the roost' in this variant of our model. The central bank's inflation target determines both the equilibrium rate of employment necessary to achieve the inflation target and hence the equilibrium rate of interest. More importantly, inflation targeting is clearly inimical to employment. Hence if the central bank lowers its inflation target (from p^T to p_2^T in Figure 9.1) this will be associated with a rise in the equilibrium interest rate (from i^* to i_2^*) and a fall in the equilibrium level of employment (from e^* to e_2^*). The intuition for this sequence of events is straightforward. By lowering its inflation target, the central bank initially creates a situation where the actual rate of inflation exceeds the new target rate. This induces an increase in the nominal interest rate (as per equation (9.16)), which deflates the economy and reduces the rate of employment (as per equation (9.12)). Finally, by reducing the rate of employment, the central bank succeeds in reducing the relative bargaining power of workers, the rate of nominal wage growth, and hence the rate of price inflation (consistent with equation (9.6)). Interest rates will continue to rise (and employment and inflation rates will continue to fall) until inflation is equal to its new target level. In short, absent a supply-determined equilibrium rate of employment towards which the economy gravitates in equilibrium regardless of the rate of inflation, employment suffers as a result of inflation targeting. This is precisely the sequence of events feared by many Post Keynesian economists.[15]

However, inflation targeting need not have these adverse consequences. This is because the results above are as much a product of policy design as they are of the intrinsic workings of the economy, as modelled in the previous section. To see this, suppose that we replace the central bank IROP in (9.16) with:

$$i = \bar{i} \tag{9.18}$$

We are now assuming that the central bank fixes the nominal interest rate at a rate of its own choosing, independently of current macroeconomic conditions. Equation (9.18) is sometimes associated with horizontalists such as Moore (1988),[16] and is advocated by Wray (2004, 2007) and Mosler and Forstater (2004), who recommend that central banks set their overnight rates at (or close to) zero.

It follows directly from (9.18) that the equilibrium interest rate is now given by:

$$i^* = \bar{i} \tag{9.18a}$$

Substituting equation (9.18a) into equation (9.12), we obtain:

$$e^* = \frac{a\kappa(\gamma - g_r \bar{i} \lambda)}{(s_\pi - g_r)(1 - \omega_F) - g_u v} \tag{9.12a}$$

Equations (9.6) and (9.12a) now give us two equations in two unknowns, which we can solve for the general equilibrium configuration of the economy. This general equilibrium configuration is illustrated in Figure 9.2, which comprises the Phillips curve in equation (9.6) and the employment function in equation (9.12a). In Figure 9.2, the equilibrium interest rate determined by the central bank's exogenously given benchmark rate determines the equilibrium rate of employment which, in turn, determines the equilibrium rate of inflation.

Suppose, once again, that the policy-maker's only explicit policy objective is an inflation target. Suppose further that the initial equilibrium

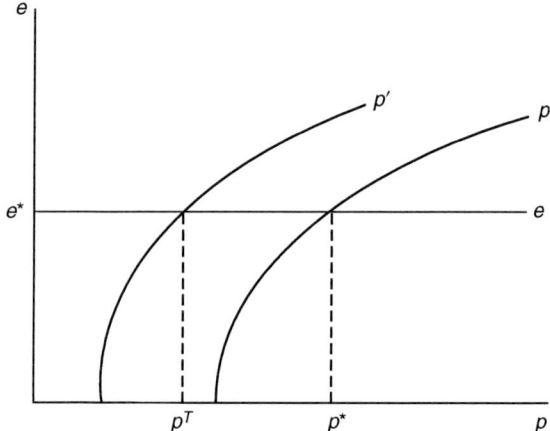

Figure 9.2 Inflation targeting with a fixed nominal interest rate

rate of inflation depicted in Figure 9.2 (p^*) lies above this target. Note, however, that because of our reformulation of monetary policy in equation (9.18), this will not provoke a response from the central bank. But this does not mean that policy-makers cannot pursue their inflation target. Inspection of equation (9.6) reveals that the steady-state rate of inflation depends not just on e, but also on the size of the 'aspiration gap' $\Omega = \omega_W - \omega_F$. Specifically:

$$\frac{\partial p^*}{\partial \Omega} = \frac{\mu_e e}{1 - \mu_e e} > 0$$

Policy-makers can therefore seek to reduce inflation towards their target rate by pursuing an incomes policy that reduces the size of the aspiration gap. In practical terms, this involves mediating workers' and firms' conflicting claims on total income in an effort to reconcile better these conflicting claims before they have undesirable inflationary consequences.[17] Formally, the type of policy intervention we are now contemplating can be written as:

$$\dot{\Omega} = -\beta(p - p^T) \qquad (9.19)$$

Given the definition of Ω, and recalling that we are dealing with a situation in which $p > p^T$ initially, it is clear that equation (9.19) might involve reducing ω_W, increasing ω_F, or both. Hence suppose initially that policy-makers' behaviour can be described as:

$$\dot{\omega}_W = -\beta(p - p^T) \tag{9.19a}$$

The effects of this policy intervention are illustrated in Figure 9.2. In accordance with the partial derivative of p^* with respect to Ω as stated above, reducing ω_W in response to $p > p^T$ will shift the Phillips curve to the left. This will decrease the rate of inflation without affecting the equilibrium rate of employment. The process of adjustment will continue until, as illustrated in Figure 9.2, the Phillips curve reaches the position p' where $p = p^T$ with e^* unchanged.

As in the previous case, inflation targeting still 'rules the roost' in the sense that inflation is the only variable with which policy-makers are explicitly concerned. Moreover, there has been no change in our specification of the intrinsic workings of the economy. Nevertheless, by changing the design of macroeconomic policy, we now have a case where inflation targeting is neutral with respect to employment.[18]

Finally, consider the situation where the central bank uses the IROP:

$$i = p \tag{9.20}$$

Equation (9.20) is a variant of the Pasinetti or 'fair' interest rate rule,[19] as a result of which the value (in wage units) of any initial outstanding stock of debt will remain constant over time. This interest rate ensures that the claims of rentiers on labour time are neither enhanced nor diminished by their rentier activity, and is thus distributionally neutral.[20]

It follows directly from (9.20) that the equilibrium interest rate is now given by:

$$i^* = p^* \tag{9.20a}$$

Substituting this expression into equation (9.12) yields:

$$e^* = \frac{a\kappa(\gamma - g_r p^* \lambda)}{(s_\pi - g_r)(1 - \omega_F) - g_u v} \tag{9.12b}$$

The general equilibrium rates of employment and inflation are now determined by the simultaneous interaction of equations (9.6) and (9.12b), with the equilibrium interest rate determined as a residual in equation (9.20a). This is illustrated in Figure 9.3 below, in which the Phillips curve and the employment function in the top panel determine

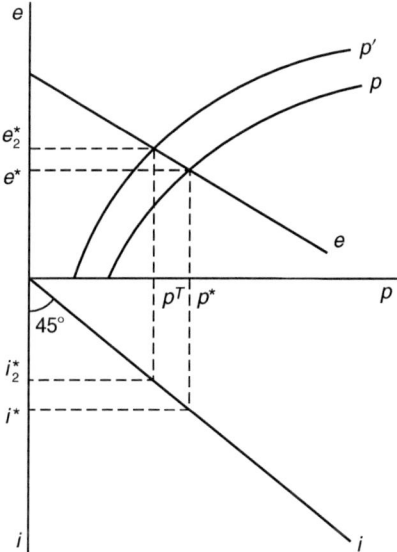

Figure 9.3 Inflation targeting under the Pasinetti rule

the equilibrium rates of employment and inflation, with the equilibrium interest rate determined in the bottom panel by the Pasinetti rule.

As in the previous case, suppose that the policy-maker's only explicit concern is with inflation and that the initial equilibrium rate of inflation, depicted in Figure 9.3 (p^*), lies above this target. As before, this latter situation will not provoke a response from the central bank, because the interest rate is set (in equation (9.20)) independently of policy-makers' inflation target. But as before, inflation targeting can be pursued by means of an incomes policy. Hence suppose that, once again, policy-makers' behaviour is described by equation (9.19a). The effects of this are illustrated in Figure 9.3. As before, reducing ω_W in response to $p > p^T$ will shift the Phillips curve to the left. But this time, as inflation falls, the rate of employment *rises* – and will continue rising until the Phillips curve reaches the position p' where $p = p^T$. The intuition for this result is straightforward. As inflation falls as a result of an incomes policy, the nominal interest rate falls (in equation (9.20a)) which raises the equilibrium rate of employment (in equation (9.12)). This series of events is captured by equation (9.12b), which shows that the lower is the equilibrium rate of inflation (i.e. the lower is the policy-makers' inflation target), the higher the equilibrium rate of employment will be. Note that, as in

194 *Is Inflation Targeting Inimical to Employment?*

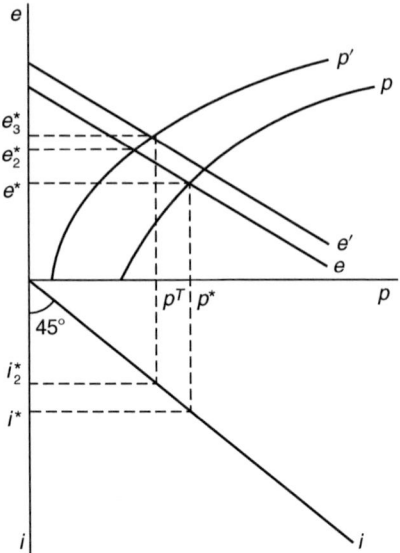

Figure 9.4 Inflation targeting and the 'stagnationist bonus'

the previous case, inflation is the sole concern of policy-makers and we have made no change to the intrinsic workings of the economy. Nevertheless, the precise design of macroeconomic policy now makes inflation targeting *beneficial* for the equilibrium rate of employment.

Indeed, it is possible that the situation depicted in Figure 9.3 *underestimates* the positive impact on employment that inflation targeting can have. Once again, it is the architecture of macroeconomic policy that is fundamental to this claim. Hence suppose that instead of (9.19a), policy-makers execute an incomes policy of the form:

$$\dot{\omega}_F = \gamma(p - p^T) \qquad (9.19b)$$

in the pursuit of an inflation target that is below the initial equilibrium rate of inflation. The effects of this policy are illustrated in Figure 9.4. The immediate effect of the incomes policy in (9.19b) will be to shift the Phillips curve to the left (to p'). As before, this will raise the rate of employment (to e_2^*) since lower inflation will result in a lower interest rate which will increase employment. But because the incomes policy in (9.19b) acts on the target wage share of firms (and hence, as per equation (9.4), the equilibrium wage share), and because the economy is stagnationist (equation (9.15)), there will be a second, direct effect on the real economy: a rise in the wage share will boost aggregate demand and hence raise the rate of employment. This is captured by the shift in the employment function in Figure 9.4 to e'. Ultimately, general equilibrium is restored at $p=p^T$ with the corresponding equilibrium rate of employment (e_3^*), higher than in the previous case thanks to the 'stagnationist bonus' described above. This 'stagnationist bonus' is created by the precise form of the incomes policy in (9.19b).[21]

Conclusion

The purpose of this chapter has been to investigate whether or not inflation targeting is inimical to employment in a monetary production economy, where real outcomes are demand-determined and money is non-neutral. The answer that has been provided is that inflation targeting may or may not be inimical to employment, depending on the conduct of macroeconomic policy. Determining the propriety of inflation targeting, then, depends not just on the innate workings of the economy (whether it is a real exchange or monetary production process), but also on the design of policy interventions.

The main conclusion to be drawn from this analysis is that policy activism contributes to the social construction of the economy and hence the type of outcomes the economy generates (on which, see Smithin, 2004). Ironically, this theme has recently received considerable (implicit) attention in the literature on the New Consensus. Hence critics such as Setterfield (2005) and Palacio-Vera (2005) argue that New Consensus models owe their stability to policy interventions, because the choice of monetary policy instrument in these models supplants the workings of internal stability mechanisms (such as the Pigou effect) that would otherwise be operative. Meanwhile, a well-known result within the New Consensus literature is that only certain types of monetary policy (that obey the 'Taylor principle') will yield stability.[22] The point here, however, is to make the contribution of policy to the social construction of the economy an *explicit* focus of attention. This is an important first step towards combating the 'fatalism' that has entered much contemporary (and, in particular, popular) policy discussion, in which the 'inevitabilities' of the 'free market' are seen as thwarting any effort to change economic outcomes.[23] Contrary to this fatalism, the analysis in this chapter suggests that with the appropriate mix of policy interventions, a monetary-production economy can, in principle, be socially constructed so that inflation targeting can be reconciled with improved real performance and even a more equitable distribution of income.

Notes

1. Following Setterfield (2006a, p. 653), inflation targeting is defined as 'the public announcement of inflation targets coupled with a credible and accountable commitment on the part of government policy authorities to the achievement of these targets'. Note that this definition is more general than that adopted by many inflation targeting advocates. For example, Mishkin (2002, p. 361) defines inflation targeting to include 'an institutional commitment [on the part of the central bank] to price stability as the primary goal of monetary policy, to which other goals are subordinated'. There is no doubt that these are prominent characteristics of inflation targeting as it has actually been practised to date. Nevertheless, the position adopted in this chapter is that neither the policy instrument used to pursue inflation targeting nor the relative importance of inflation targeting vis-à-vis other policy goals need or should be part of a definition of inflation targeting.
2. The description of inflation and employment outcomes in this section draws extensively on Setterfield (2006b), to which the reader is referred for further discussion of the underlying models.
3. See Rowthorn (1977), Lavoie (1992, ch. 7) and Burdekin and Burkett (1996) for further discussion of the conflicting claims approach to inflation.
4. Recall that there is no labour productivity growth – hence the rate of growth of unit labour costs is given by the rate of growth of the nominal wage.
5. Again, recall that there is no labour productivity growth.
6. The first derivative of (9.6) with respect to e is given by:

$$\frac{\partial p^*}{\partial e} = \frac{\mu_e(\omega_W - \omega_F)}{(1-\mu_e)^2} > 0$$

Intuitively, this is because an increase in the employment rate will raise the relative bargaining power of workers (equation (9.3)) and hence the rate of growth of nominal wages (equation (9.1)) and hence the rate of inflation. Note, however, that this does not mean that inflation is the fault of workers. If firms varied their mark-ups inversely with respect to the nominal wage, inflation could be avoided by allowing the real wage to rise. It is firms' resistance to this that translates wage growth into inflation. Hence we are reminded that it is the *interaction* of workers and firms in a conflicting-claims framework that generates inflation, not simply the behaviour of one of these parties.
7. Note that the NAIRU result derived above does require strictly *partial* endogeneity of the real wage targets ω_W and ω_F. If these targets were *fully* endogenous – for example, if $\omega_W = \theta e$ and $\omega_F = \eta e$ – then the value of e^* would be indeterminate. This is consistent with 'aspirational hysteresis' (see Skott, 1999), as can clearly be seen if we write:

$$e^* = \frac{\omega_F}{\theta}$$

and

$$\dot{\omega}_F = \tau(e - e^*)$$

These equations create a dynamic in which any departure of e from e^* – due, for example, to incorrect inflation expectations in the short run – will revise the value of ω_F and hence e^*, creating hysteresis in the NAIRU. Clearly, then, the non-existence of a unique NAIRU determined on the supply-side of the economy is not entirely dependent on the absence of complete indexation of inflation expectations by workers. But the 'hysteretic NAIRU' is not a fully satisfactory alternative to the negatively sloped Phillips curve in equation (9.6), because it does involve other non-Keynesian features. For example, we need only postulate what Flaschel et al. (1997) term myopic perfect foresight ($p^e = p$) on the part of workers and, recalling that $\mu = 1$, equation (9.1) can be written as $w - p = (\omega_W - \omega)$. This describes real wage bargaining by workers in the labour market – a behaviour that is typical of a real exchange economy but which is incompatible with the workings of a monetary production economy.

8. The expression in (9.4a) above reveals the part that incomplete indexation has to play in producing this last result: in the absence of incomplete indexation of inflation expectations by workers, the real wage depends on ω_W as well as φ and ω_F. Note, however, that incomplete indexation is *necessary* but not *sufficient* to ensure that the real wage is determined in the goods market, independently of workers' efforts to influence the nominal wage. Hence note that if we were to replace equation (9.2) with

$$p = \varphi[(\omega - \omega_F) + w] \tag{9.2a}$$

(in other words, if we were to assume that firms are unable to fully index increases in unit labour costs into prices), the equilibrium solution for ω^* resulting from (9.1) and (9.2a) would be:

$$\omega^* = \frac{\mu(1 - \varphi)\omega_W + \varphi(1 - \mu)\omega_F}{\mu(1 - \varphi) + \varphi(1 - \mu)} \tag{9.4b}$$

Even with incomplete indexation on the part of workers, then, it is possible for the equilibrium real wage to depend on the bargaining power and real wage aspirations of both workers and firms. See Setterfield (2007a) for further discussion of equation (9.2a) above.

9. See Setterfield (2006b) for further discussion of this specification. Note in particular that the specification of the rate of enterprise profits, r_E, described above is derived from the expression $\Pi_E = \Pi - iD$, where Π_E denotes nominal enterprise profits, Π denotes nominal gross profits and iD denotes debt-servicing payments to rentiers (the nominal interest rate, i, multiplied by the nominal stock of debt, D). Deflating by the price level, we arrive at $\Pi_{ER} = \Pi_R - iD_R$, where an R-subscript denotes the real value of a variable. Finally, dividing through by the capital stock, K, we get $r_E = r - i\lambda$. The 'rate of enterprise profits' so-derived is best thought of as the 'real cash flow rate'. The investment function in equation (9.7) is thus congruent with the empirical evidence of, *inter alia*, Fazzari et al. (1988), in which firms' real cash flow

is shown to influence the level of investment. I am grateful to Marc Lavoie of the University of Ottawa for drawing this interpretation of r_E to my attention.

10. It follows from (9.9) and the definition of r_E above that:

$$r_E = \frac{(1-\omega)u - i\lambda v}{v} \Rightarrow \omega = 1 - \frac{v(r_E + i\lambda)}{u}$$

If ω_F – the target wage share of firms – is designed to yield a target rate of enterprise profits (r_E^T) at what firms identify as the normal rates of interest (i_n) and capacity utilization (u_n), then the value of ω_F is now revealed as:

$$\omega_F = 1 - \frac{v(r_E^T + i_n\lambda)}{u_n}$$

Clearly, ω_F remains constant only as long as r_E^T, i_n and u_n remain constant. An implicit assumption of this model is, therefore, that r_E^T, i_n and u_n remain constant regardless of the values of r_E, i and u, an assumption that is likely plausible only in the short run.

11. Note that κ is *not* the capital–labour ratio in the process of production, which is instead given by the ratio of utilized capital to employed labour (and is also fixed, in accordance with the ratio v/a).

12. It should be noted that the dominance of the debt-deflation effect demonstrated in what follows arises, in part, because our model contains no explicit Pigou effect, whilst it is assumed that the equilibrium interest rate is invariant with respect to the price level – i.e. that there is no Keynes effect. As will become clear in the following section, this is perfectly consistent with the monetary foundations of the model, which are horizontalist: the total stock of money in circulation, including the stock of 'outside' (fiat) money, varies endogenously (and directly) with nominal income, with the nominal interest rate set exogenously by the central bank. The exogeneity of the interest rate precludes the existence of a Keynes effect. Meanwhile, if we assume that the monetary base varies in equal proportion to any change in nominal income, so that $M = \xi P Y_R$, where M is the monetary base, P is the price level, Y_R is real output and ξ is constant, it follows that real balances, B_R, are given by $B_R = \frac{M}{P} = \xi Y_R$. The substance of this result is that, given the current level of real income, real balances are constant. In other words, B_R is invariant with respect to the price level – there is no Pigou effect.

13. Note that this and the various other closures implicit in the model should be regarded as conditional rather than absolute, in keeping with the open-systems ontology of Post Keynesian economics and the fundamental uncertainty to which this gives rise. See Setterfield (2007b) on conditional closure.

14. We abstract, for simplicity, from the distinction between the central bank's overnight rate and the spectrum of commercial interest rates that are influenced by the former. In so doing, we overlook the possibility that commercial interest rates may vary independently of the interest rate set by the central bank, as emphasized by authors in the 'structuralist' tradition of Post Keynesian monetary theory (see, for example, Dow, 2007).

15. See, for example, various contributions to the symposium on inflation targeting in the *Journal of Post Keynesian Economics*, volume 28, number 4, 2006.

16. See, for example, Palley (1996).
17. This can be achieved in a variety of ways. In general, an incomes policy can be either cooperative or conflictual, depending on whether the objective is to reach a mutually satisfactory agreement as to the appropriate distribution of income, or to impose an outcome on either workers or firms (or both). For example, a cooperative incomes policy might involve greater centralization of the wage bargain resulting in a 'social bargain' of the type described by Cornwall (1990). A conflictual incomes policy might involve reducing the power of trade unions in order to decrease workers' target wage share, or using competition policy to reduce firms' target wage share via the target rate of return on their assets (see Setterfield, 2006b).
18. Note that the results illustrated in Figure 9.2 are brought about by a *combination* of policy interventions. Hence implicit in the figure (and subsequent figures) is some amount of cooperation between different macroeconomic policy authorities, who are required to coordinate their policy interventions. This, in turn, suggests that in a monetary production economy, central bank independence – one of the shibboleths of mainstream advocates of inflation targeting – may thwart rather than assist the reconciliation of low inflation with other (real) macroeconomic objectives.
19. In general the Pasinetti rule can be written as $i = p + q$, where q denotes the rate of growth of labour productivity. Since we are assuming that $q = 0$, however, the Pasinetti rule reduces to equation (9.20).
20. See, for example, Lavoie and Seccareccia (1999), Setterfield (2006b) and Rochon and Setterfield (2007) for further discussion of the distributional effects of the Pasinetti rule.
21. Note that the stability of equilibrium is not guaranteed in this final case. Intuitively, and using the events described in Figure 9.4 as an example, stability will only be observed if $\dot{\omega}_F > 0$ in response to $p < p^T$ in (9.18b) succeeds in moving p closer to p^T. This requires that the reduction in inflation resulting from the increase in ω_F must exceed the increase in inflation resulting from: (i) the increase in employment brought about by the fall in the nominal interest rate; and (ii) the increase in employment resulting from the increase in ω_F. As long as these conditions are observed, pursuing the incomes policy in (9.18b) will always yield a net reduction in inflation, thus propelling the economy towards equilibrium.
22. The Taylor principle requires $di/dp > 1$ in the central bank's IROP – in other words, that central banks change *real* interest rates in response to changes in inflation. See, for example, Clarida *et al.* (1999, p. 1701) and Woodford (2001).
23. See, for example, Palley (1998, pp. 10–11).

References

Burdekin, R. C. K. and P. Burkett (1996) *Distributional Conflict and Inflation: Theoretical and Historical Perspectives*, London: Macmillan.

Clarida, R., J. Galí and M. Gertler (1999) 'The Science of Monetary Policy: A New Keynesian Perspective,' *Journal of Economic Literature* 37: 1661–707.

Cornwall, J. (1990) *The Theory of Economic Breakdown*, Oxford, Basil Blackwell.

Dow, S. C. (2007) 'Endogenous Money: Structuralist,' in P. Arestis and M. Sawyer (eds), *A Handbook of Alternative Monetary Economics*, Cheltenham: Edward Elgar.

Fazzari, S. M., G. R. Hubbard and B. Peterson (1988) 'Financing Constraints and Corporate Investment,' *Brookings Papers on Economic Activity* 1: 141–95.

Flaschel, P., R. Franke and W. Semmler (1997) *Dynamic Macroeconomics: Instability, Fluctuations and Growth in Monetary Economies*, Cambridge, MA: MIT Press.

Keynes, J. M. (1936) *The General Theory of Employment, Interest and Money*, London: Macmillan.

Lavoie, M. (1992) *Foundations of Post-Keynesian Economic Analysis*, Aldershot: Edward Elgar.

Lavoie, M. and M. Seccareccia (1999) 'Interest Rate: Fair', in P. O'Hara (ed.), *Encyclopedia of Political Economy*, vol. 1, London: Routledge: 543–5.

Mishkin, F. S. (2002) 'Inflation Targeting,' in B. Snowdon and H. R. Vane (eds), *An Encyclopedia of Macroeconomics*, Cheltenham: Edward Elgar: 361–5.

Moore, B. J. (1988) *Horizontalists and Verticalists: The Macroeconomics of Credit Money*, Cambridge: Cambridge University Press.

Mosler, W. and M. Forstater (2004) 'The Natural Rate of Interest is Zero', working paper 37, University of Missouri, Kansas City.

Palacio-Vera, A. (2005) 'The "Modern" View of Macroeconomics: Some Critical Reflections,' *Cambridge Journal of Economics* 29: 747–67.

Palley, T. I. (1996) 'Accommodationism versus Structuralism: Time for an Accommodation,' *Journal of Post Keynesian Economics* 18: 585–94.

Palley, T. I. (1998) *Plenty of Nothing: The Downsizing of the American Dream and the Case for Structural Keynesianism*, Princeton, NJ: Princeton University Press.

Rochon, L.-P. and M. Setterfield (2007) 'Interest Rates, Income Distribution and Monetary Policy Dominance: Post-Keynesians and the "Fair Rate" of Interest', *Journal of Post Keynesian Economics*, 30: 13–42.

Rowthorn, R. E. (1977) 'Conflict, Inflation and Money,' *Cambridge Journal of Economics* 1: 215–39.

Setterfield, M. (2005) 'Central Bank Behaviour and the Stability of Macroeconomic Equilibrium: A Critical Examination of the New Consensus,' in P. Arestis, M. Baddeley and J. S. L. McCombie (eds), *The New Monetary Policy: Implications and Relevance*, Cheltenham: Edward Elgar: 23–49.

Setterfield, M. (2006a) 'Is Inflation Targeting Compatible with Post Keynesian Economics?', *Journal of Post Keynesian Economics* 28: 653–71.

Setterfield, M. (2006b) 'Macroeconomics without the LM Curve: An Alternative View,' Trinity College, mimeo, available at http://emp.trincoll.edu/~setterfi/mark_setterfield.htm.

Setterfield, M. (2007a) 'The Rise, Decline and Rise of Incomes Policies in the US During the Post-war Era: An Institutional-Analytical Explanation of Inflation and the Functional Distribution of Income,' *Journal of Institutional Economics* 3: 127–46.

Setterfield, M. (2007b) 'Are Functional Relations always the *alter ego* of Humean Laws?', *Review of Political Economy* 19: 203–17.

Skott, P. (1999) 'Wage Formation and the (non-) Existence of the NAIRU,' *Economic Issues* 4: 77–92.

Smithin, J. (2004) 'Interest Rate Operating Procedures and Income Distribution,' in M. Lavoie and M. Seccareccia (eds), *Central Banking in the Modern World: Alternative Perspectives*, Cheltenham: Edward Elgar.

Woodford, M. (2001) 'The Taylor Rule and Optimal Monetary Policy,' *American Economic Review* 91: 232–7.

Wray, R. (2004) 'The Fed and the New Monetary Consensus: The Case for Rate Hikes, Part Two', *Public Policy Brief* 80, The Levy Economics Institute of Bard College.

Wray, R. (2007) 'A Post Keynesian View of Central Bank Independence, Policy Targets, and the Rules Versus Discretion Debate', *Journal of Post Keynesian Economics*, 30: 119–41.

10
Labour Market Search and Monetary Shocks: A Theoretical Consideration
Jagjit S. Chadha and Qi Sun

Introduction

The real business cycle revolution (see Finn Kydland and Ed Prescott's respective Nobel Prize Lectures, 2004) seems to have been most tangibly captured by monetary theoreticians and practitioners. It might reasonably be argued that this a remarkable, almost perverse, outcome because a real business cycle economy is one in which agents follow optimal decision rules at all times and in all states of nature and where output lies at the flex-price equilibrium through time. That is one in which there is typically no unemployment. In other words it is also one in which there is no obvious role for a monetary policy-maker, whose role might be defined as that of ensuring an optimal rate of convergence to the flex-price outcome following shocks, and where the costs of business cycle fluctuations are limited.[1] How such models became the workhorse for studying monetary policy problems, where sequences of short term interest rates are chosen to offset the impact of expected divergences of output from its flex-price optimum, is a question that will no doubt intrigue future historians of economic thought.

The bolting of price-setting rigidities onto a real business cycle model by Yun (1996) using the Calvo (1983) price setting mechanism – a form of price rigidity that means only an exogenously set fraction of firms can reset prices in every period – allowed the introduction of meaningful monetary policy. In the Calvo-Yun set-up, productivity (or marginal cost) shocks impact on the optimal, or the desired, price level in each period, but as only some firms are given the signal to reset, the overall price level is suboptimal. So following a positive productivity shock, overall prices are too high, which means that output is too low (relative to the flex-price outcome) and that some firms suffer a lower than optimal profit level as their prices do not have an appropriate mark-up. The policy problem is thus to set a rule such that, contingent on such shocks, the expected sequence of interest rates ensures that the deviation of output from its flex-price optimum is minimized subject to informational constraints (see Woodford, 2003, for an elaboration). This paradigm has been hugely influential.

And yet the popular New Keynesian Phillips curve (NKPC) framework has not been especially successful in matching several aspects of the business cycle.[2] The current generation of monetary research, which has concentrated on the implications of nominal rigidities in prices or wages, has perhaps not sufficiently emphasized the possibility, of real rigidities such as habit formation in preference or labour market matching. In fact the labour market has been a particularly sore point of contention. King and Rebelo (2000) in their overview of the real business cycle developments outline a number of problems with the standard business cycle model in terms of the labour market: it implies too high an elasticity of labour supply to wages; business cycle hours variation arises from changes in the hours-per-worker in the model (the so-called intensive margin), whereas it is movements in numbers of people employed (the so-called extensive margin) that actually seem to determine fluctuations in total labour input; and so the model suggests a counterfactual degree of correspondence between labour inputs and its average product.

In this chapter we will highlight two aspects that the standard business cycle model needs to address: (i) the observed persistence in the response of employment patterns, wage rates and monetary variables; and (ii) the hump-shaped impulse response of output following a monetary policy shock. Following Walsh (2003), in which a dynamic stochastic general equilibrium (DSGE) model with labour market matching is introduced and calibrated for the US economy, we will examine the issue of labour market search in a DSGE model calibrated on UK data. The main focus will be on labour market rigidities that prevent unemployed workers from finding new jobs and firms with job vacancies from filling them immediately. This feature generates both a persistence of response in the labour market to monetary shocks and adjusts the nature of the policy problem faced by the authorities. Dynamic simulations are used to investigate the role the job matching process plays in affecting the economy's dynamic adjustment to shocks. Employing a degree of nominal rigidity as well, we will investigate the implications for monetary policy. We point to ways in which this work can be used to understand the role of the labour market in explaining the UK business cycle over the past 20 years.

As mentioned, there are two reasons why we pay attention to the labour market specification in a DSGE model. Firstly, most of the existing Real Business Cycle and DSGE literature use total hours as the labour input and consider the intensive margin of labour supply. In such a set-up unemployment is ignored in the analysis. Consequently, the model-generated dynamics imply highly procyclical real wages and smooth employment, as opposed to nearly acyclical real wages and volatile employment numbers in reality.[3] Therefore a more realistic model for labour supply, such as indivisible labour (Hansen, 1985), may be required. Secondly, nominal rigidities in price and wage setting are not sufficient to account for the inertia of macroeconomic variables versus the RBC models. In respect of the wage bargain, it might be argued that plans for long-term service may outweigh the incentive to renegotiate wages, and to some extent this undermines the microfoundations of Walrasian wage setting. Given these problems, the investigation of the implications of some sort of real rigidities, such as job-matching frictions, seems highly appropriate and may reconcile the debate of a frictionless labour market and match the persistence in the data.

Walsh (2003), Walsh (2005) and Ravenna and Walsh (2007) use a labour market search and matching model to incorporate this type of real rigidity. In Walsh (2005), this model predicts a hump-shaped response of output to a policy rate shock. The key to this result is the delay in production caused by the time required to fill job vacancies, which is a costly process for firms and workers. The job-matching feature also permits a considerably richer dynamic in inflation than the NKPC model.[4] This motivates us to repeat the empirical investigation on UK data, especially in relation to the past two decades, when the UK labour market became more flexible. For example, during this period, days lost in strikes have fallen markedly as a fraction of UK total hours, as a result, in part, to more rigorous legislation on union actions.[5]

In the next section we will outline the response of key UK variables to a monetary shock. We give the full set of linear equation for the Walsh model and in Tables 10.1, 10.2 and 10.3, the full set of calibration parameters we adopt. We will use these estimates to understand the extent to which output and unemployment respond in a persistent manner to monetary policy shocks. We then outline the key implications of the Walsh matching model for the Phillips curve, before going on to illustrate the resulting dynamics from a baseline simulation of the model and indicating the implications for monetary policy, in terms of the weight given to inflation rather than output in the policy rule. In the Appendix we give the full set of linear equations for the model and the set of calibration parameters.

UK data responses

To explore some of the ideas about persistence and speed of adjustment to shocks, we will estimate a simple model of the UK macroeconomy. We use quarterly data from 1978 to 2006 for UK bank rate (i), the real effective exchange rate based on relative CPI (er), the constant price GDP by the expenditure approach (y), the all-items RPI (π) and the unemployment rate (u) measured by the claimant count. We estimate a VAR of order 2 to understand the dynamics. Base rate and unemployment enter the VAR in levels, but the real exchange rate, real output and the price level are differenced. To identify the system, we use a Cholesky ordering restriction and examine the response of these variables to a monetary policy shock, where $i \to er \to y \to \pi \to u$.

Figure 10.1 shows the responses of the key macroeconomic variables to a 100Bp shock to the base rate. The abscissa shows the length of response in quarters and the y-axis the amplitude of the response in percentage point deviations from the mean of the series. Note first that the half-life of a 100Bp shock to interest rates is in the region of 12 quarters and represents the typical magnitude of a policy shock. The exchange rate responds earliest, and by the second quarter of the shock has undergone an appreciation in the region of 0.75 per cent, which decays back to nearly baseline after a year or so. For the UK, which is a relatively open economy with imports and exports each equal to nearly 30 per cent of

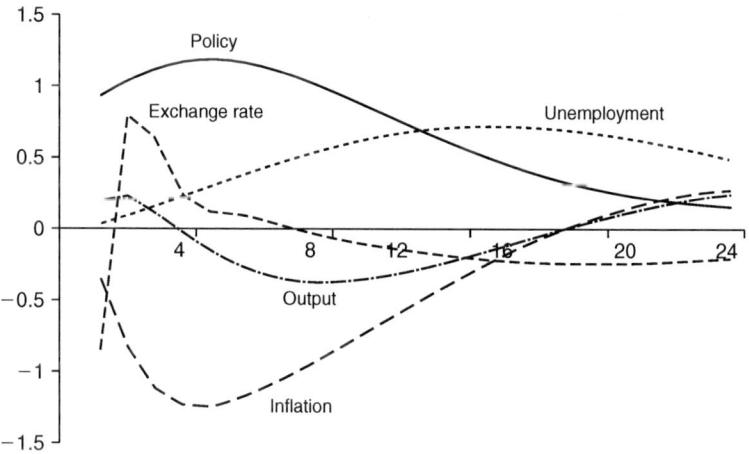

Figure 10.1 Responses to policy shock: UK

GDP, inflation mirrors the jump in the exchange rate and we observe a hump-backed response from inflation which falls most around a year after the initial policy shock, by around 1.25 per cent, and it is after about four years that it returns to base.

But the key message is that output adjusts slowly, with its initial response somewhat less than its largest response, with a 0.5 per cent fall in output around two years after the initial monetary policy shock. The impact of the shock decays to baseline in around year four. We note also that labour unemployment – that is, movements along the extensive margin – are perturbed for quite some time following a typical monetary policy shock, with the peak response in unemployment coming at about three to four years. And in fact on these estimates unemployment still seems to be adjusting some six years after the initial interest rate shock.

The gradual build-up of momentum on the real-side of the economy from a monetary shock, with output and unemployment responding persistently, has a number of implications. First, that even though inflation, which is likely to have a strong forward-looking element, may be stabilized from a given monetary policy shock, the real economy may still be some way from equilibrium and still imposing some losses on the representative household, which may be better off from stable inflation, but still likely to suffer from losses from some degree of unemployment. Secondly, this implies that monetary policy, which places any weight on output fluctuations, will be somewhat more cautious when stabilizing inflationary shocks. We shall explore below the implications of building more labour market persistence into the basic New Keynesian (NK) framework, in particular for the design of monetary policy.

Walsh matching model

In a standard NK model, the labour market is modelled as follows. Positive productivity shocks lower marginal costs and the Walrasian labour market continues to ensure that labour is paid at its higher rental rate. Higher real wages bid for the marginal leisure hours of workers, and output, which is Cobb-Douglas, increases. The main additional feature of this labour search and match model is the endogenous and exogenous job destruction in the labour market. Endogenous job destruction results from productivity entering the margin between maintaining a contract of employment or ending it. Such a margin may generate acyclical real wages as it is argued that low productivity (paid) workers are fired in downturns. There is also a possibility of exogenous job destruction. Shocks may impact on those who left positions to join the job seeker

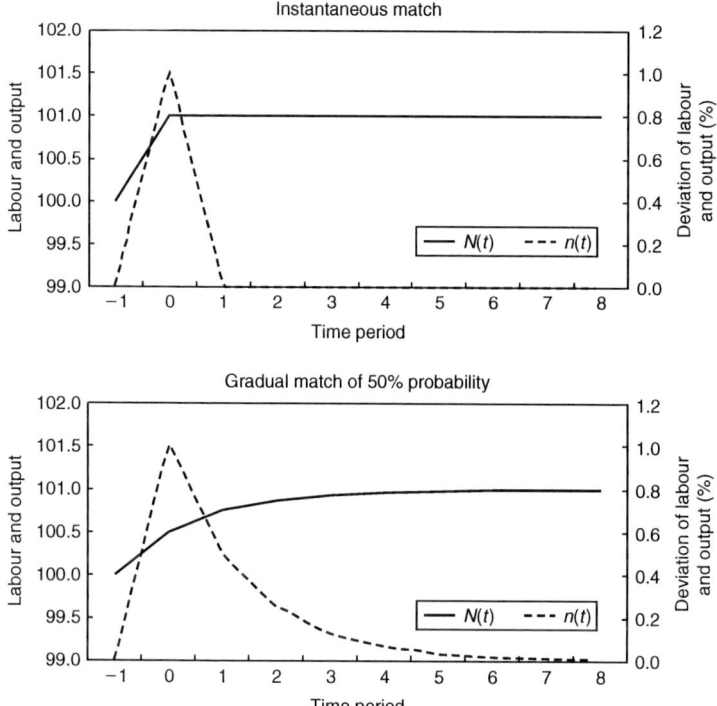

Figure 10.2 Job matching and persistence

pool and go through a matching process via job applications to posted vacancies. The difficulty in the matching of job seekers and vacancies decreases the instantaneous response of output to aggregate shocks. This structure creates inertia in the dynamics of key variables.

Figure 10.2 shows a very simple case of matching time and its implication on persistence in macroeconomic dynamics. In a world with only labour as production input and fixed productivity, at time 0 there is a 1 per cent permanent shock to labour input. With instantaneous matching (upper panel), output and labour adjust immediately – this is analogous to the NK model case. However, with a matching probability at, say, 50 per cent per period, the matching in the labour market will continue gradually until the new steady state is reached, thus generating significant persistence in the dynamics – with the overall time period for adjustment in the region of three to four periods.

Let us start from a typical Calvo-Yun economy where the production does not include capital accumulation $Y_t = Z_t N_t$, where Z_t denotes the exogenous technology variable, N_t is total labour hours and Y_t is output. With monopolistic competition in the final goods sector and sticky prices, we have:

$$w_t = \frac{Z_t}{\mu_t}, \tag{10.1}$$

$$\pi_t = \beta E_t \pi_{t+1} + \kappa mc_t, \tag{10.2}$$

$$mc_t = w_t - z_t, \tag{10.3}$$

where μ_t denotes mark-up of market prices to wholesale prices, $\kappa \equiv (((1-\omega)(1-\omega\beta))/\omega)$, which is the slope of the Phillips curve, ω is the probability that a firm receives a signal to reprice, β is the subjective discount factor, mc_t is the marginal cost and w_t is wages.

The Walsh model considers a form of job separation and a prolonged matching process. The probability of job matching $q(\theta_t)$ is a function of labour market tightness, θ_t, which is the vacancy–search ratio. The adoption of a matching technology complicates a firm's decisions on whether to post a vacancy and makes both labour market tightness and the cost of posting a vacancy determinants of the equilibrium wage. Real wages now take this form:

$$w_t = \frac{Z_t}{\mu_t} - \frac{\hat{\kappa}}{q(\theta_t)} + \beta(1-\rho)E_t\left(\frac{\lambda_{t+1}}{\lambda_t}\right)\frac{\hat{\kappa}}{q(\theta_{t+1})} \tag{10.4}$$

In equation (10.4), the real wage is determined by both the marginal product and the two terms from job matching. The real wage adjusts downwards in the current period and, when vacancies are posted, is adjusted upwards for any delay in posting a vacancy until the next period. If we substitute this key equation into the Phillips curve, augmented by matching in the labour market and by a term for impacting on the cost of search, i.e. in terms of the interest rate, we arrive at a considerably more complicated dynamic:

$$\pi_t = \beta E_t \pi_{t+1} + \kappa mc_t, \tag{10.5}$$

$$-mc_t = \mu_t = z_t - A(1-\xi)\hat{\theta}_t$$
$$\quad - A\beta(1-\rho)1 - \eta\theta q(\theta)](i_t - E_t\pi_{t+1})$$
$$\quad + A\beta(1-\rho)[1-\xi-\eta\theta q(\theta)]E_t\hat{\theta}_{t+1} \tag{10.6}$$

where (for both equations) A, given by $\mu\left(\frac{1}{1-\eta}\right)\frac{\kappa}{q(\theta)}$, $mc_t\left(=\frac{1}{\mu_t}\right)$, is the marginal cost, the steady-state mark-up for the retail sector is μ, $\hat{\kappa}$ is the cost of posting a vacancy, $q(\theta)$ is the steady-state probability of job matching, η is the worker's share in the wage bargain, ρ is the probability of job separation, ξ is the elasticity of vacancies with respect to matches, and $i_t - E_t\pi_{t+1}$ is the real interest rate. The expression of the mark-up, μ_t, implies that a tighter labour market today increases marginal costs and creates an incentive for inflation, though the likelihood of a tighter labour market tomorrow reduces current marginal costs and tends to lower inflation, and higher interest rates impact directly on marginal costs and so on inflationary pressure.

So the mark-up, as the inverse of marginal cost, is affected by the unit labour cost (z_t), adjusted by a cost-push channel (real interest) and labour market tightness terms (second and fourth term). A tighter labour market (higher θ_t) increases, to some extent, inflation instantaneously as the marginal cost rises in the cost of posting vacancies. Expectation of an increase in the level of future labour market tightness is also priced in current inflation but with a reverse effect. The reason is that an expectation of future labour market tightness motivates firms to post vacancies *ex ante*, pushing up current labour market tightness even further. But precautionary job matching and an increase in labour supplied ensures some pressure for wages is cut in the next period, inducing a fall in marginal costs. These two channels of job matching, as inflation drivers, are parallel to those of real wage determination in equation (10.4). These two terms decrease in vacancy posting cost and in matching efficiency.

In a comparison with Calvo-Yun, we see that the job matching terms simply disappear from the Calvo-Yun framework. With a frictionless labour market, the production adjusts simply to an exogenous shock (for instance a cost-push shock to the Phillips curve) and labour is bid into place with no further adjustment and thus the key variables do not show sufficient persistence. In contrast, a matching model implies an important role for sluggish adjustment in the labour market. The production is effected by labour market tightness across periods so that higher inertia is built into this model.

In the study of a calibrated model, we are particularly interested in impulse response to nominal rate shock and aggregate productivity shock and sensitivity analysis on deep parameters in the labour market, that is: (i) the probability of job separation via exogenous and endogenous job destruction; (ii) the probability of matching between firms and job seekers; and (iii) the cost of posting a vacancy. We will relate these parameters to UK labour market policy during the last two decades in the following section. And in the subsequent section we will explore the implications for stability from this type of Phillips curve.

UK calibration

We will now illustrate the relationship between UK business cycles, policy and the labour market within the context of a search and matching model. We are mostly interested in the model behaviour over the period from the late 1980s to 2007. The stylized facts of the UK labour market (see, Millard, 2000, for example) are as follows. Within the context of a more flexible labour market and weakening union power (or membership) over the past two decades, several aspects of labour market performance over the UK business cycle are noticeable: (i) employment and unemployment are more volatile after the 1980s reform; but (ii) hours (average and total) became less volatile; (iii) average hours worked rose in the early years after flexible labour market reform; and (iv) unemployment duration has remained quite stable since the early 1980s. Our calibration allows for these changes in labour market behaviour and so allows us to examine whether important degrees of persistence still remain in the real-side of the economy.

Labour market issues

We rely on a careful calibration against current UK data to evaluate this model. Tables 10.1 to 10.3 give the basic calibration parameters.[6] The model is solved for impulse response analysis. We wish to match the calibrated UK model to replicate major UK business cycle quantities, including output, inflation, unemployment, total hours, wages, vacancies and job separation. We need to try to understand the consequences of several major moves in labour market policy-making, including union legislation, immigration and reform, such as the 'New Deal'.

Table 10.1 Calibration of key labour market parameters

Coefficient	Walsh	Description	UK source
ρ	0.10	Total prob. of job separation	0.05 (ONS)
ξ	0.4	Vacancy elasticity of match	ONS
k^f	0.7	Prob. of filling a vacancy	ONS
k^w	0.6	Prob. of finding a job	0.42 (ONS)
N	0.95	Steady-state labour force	0.95
κ	0.6	Recruiting cost	0.33 (Millard)
η	0.5	Worker's share in wage bargaining	0.3 (Millard)

Note: The vacancy elasticity is estimated vía Cobb-Douglas type function relating matched jobs to vacancies posted and searchers in the labour market.
Sources: ONS Labour Market Review 2006, ONS Labour Market Statistics; Millard (2000).

Table 10.2 Key Variables

Variable	Definition
R_t	Nominal rate
y_t	Output
π_t	Inflation
n_t	Employment
φ_t	Survival rate
V_t	Vacancies
k_t^f	Probability of filling a vacancy (firms)
q_t	Expected excess value of match
a_t	Destruction margin (threshold productivity for continuing job contract)
u_t	Unemployed workers (searchers)
k_t^w	Probability of finding a job (workers)
μ_t	Mark-up
ρ_t	Endogenous job destruction
χ_t	Matched jobs (job creation)

Power of the trade unions

In the 1980s there were considerable changes in the UK labour market, in particular: (i) the power of trade unions in calling and sustaining a strike became more restricted; (2) collective wage bargaining became more decentralized. We wish to evaluate the matching model under a certain degree of union power in wage bargaining, and we find the dynamics are sensitive to this parameter. In the wage determination equations (10.4) and (10.7), the higher the power of the union, the higher the wage. The model shows explicitly how union legislation affects the macroeconomy via the wage bargaining channel.

Unemployment benefits

In the last two decades or so, the UK has seen some decreases in unemployment benefit. In this model we specify a household production channel for those who do not find a match in the matching process and leave the labour force. We can evaluate the role of unemployment benefit as one type of income source other than a paid job. In the search model this 'outsider' productivity has an impact on real wages. The vacancies posted by firms are also affected. We could answer the following questions: Does an increase in unemployment benefits lead to a slower or faster adjustment in a labour market hit by an exogenous shock? How does a decrease in UK unemployment benefit contribute to observed macroeconomic data quantitatively?

Table 10.3 Other key calibration parameters

Coefficient	Walsh	Description	Other source
ρ	0.10	Total prob. of job separation	
ρ^x	0.063	Steady state: exogenous unemployment	
$F(\bar{a})$	0.0343	S.S.: endogenous job destruction	
$\bar{a}$		S.S.: job destruction margin (threshold productivity)	0.77: from log normal distribution of a
$H(\bar{a})$	1	Expected mean productivity	
e_a^F	15	Elasticity of $F(a)$ to a	Approximation from log normal distribution of individual productivity a
e_a^H	1	Elasticity of $H(a)$ to a	
ξ	0.6	Vacancy share in generating a match	
k^f	0.7	Prob. of filling a vacancy	
k^w	0.6	Prob. of finding a job	
N	0.95	Steady-state labour force	
γ	0.6	Recruiting cost	0.33 (our estimate)
η	0.6	Worker's share in wage bargaining	0.3 (our estimate)
κ	0.05	Coefficient of marginal cost in NKPC	
θ	11	Demand elasticity of differentiated goods	
h	0	Utility of home production if unemployed	
δ	2	CRRA[7]	
Θ	1.01	S.S.: money growth	
β	0.989	Discount factor	

In this model, wages are determined both from wholesale producers' profit maximization (equation (10.4)) and workers' trade-off in entering or exiting the job market. The level of unemployment income (w^u, either home production or benefits) enters workers' wage bids and thus will tend to increase the reservations wage:

$$w_t = w^u + \frac{\eta}{1-\eta}\frac{\hat{\kappa}}{q(\theta)_t}$$
$$- \frac{\eta}{1-\eta}\beta(1-\rho)E_t\left(\frac{\lambda_{t+1}}{\lambda_t}\right)[1 - \theta_{t+1}q(\theta_{t+1})]\frac{\hat{\kappa}}{q(\theta_{t+1})} \quad (10.7)$$

Minimum wages

The National Minimum Wage Act of 1998 and the establishment of the Low Pay Commission have led to several increases in minimum wages

(NMW) since 1999. Although only a small fraction of around 6 to 8 percent of the labour force is affected by changes in the NMW, and more than one half of them are in part-time jobs, the estimated impact on total household nominal income is notable (a 0.2 to 0.5 per cent increase approximately with a 10 per cent increase in NMW). Although the real wage is endogenous in most DSGE literature, we can specify a minimum nominal wage and explore in this matching model the extent to which the NMW increase impacts on inflationary pressure. Does flexible labour market adjustment account for a muted response in aggregate economy to an NMW adjustment?

Let us look into the possibility of designing a labour-specific wage determination mechanism which is compatible with firm aggregate wage equation. Wage determination for individuals is required to surpass a threshold and is related to idiosyncratic productivity $Z_{i,t}$. It will take the following form:[8]

$$w_{i,t} = \underline{w} + \int_{\overline{Z}}^{Z_{i,t}} \left[\frac{Z_{i,t}}{\mu_t} - \frac{\hat{\kappa}}{q(\theta_t)} + \beta(1-\rho)E_t\left(\frac{\lambda_{t+1}}{\lambda_t}\right) \frac{\hat{\kappa}}{q(\theta_{t+1})} \right] f(Z)\,dZ. \quad (10.8)$$

Immigration policy

Economists and policy-makers are interested in the consequences of increased immigrants on the output-inflation trade-off. Job market slack caused by loosening immigration policy will ease inflation pressure but will increase unemployment. We are interested in the dynamics of interest rate adjustment accompanying the immigrants' infusion under a matching model and measuring the duration of assimilation.

The labour evolves in a job-destruction and matching process. An easing in the immigration law can be thought of as a shock to the predetermined labour count:

$$N_t = (1-\rho)N_{t-1} + v_t q(\theta_t), \quad (10.9)$$

where v_t denotes vacancies posted in time period t. In addition we wish to quantify the new steady state and the periods it takes to achieve it.

Other issues

There are more policy issues that might be incorporated in the discussion, such as the New Deal – introduced by New Labour in 1998, which can be seen as an effort to increase the steady-state probability of finding a job.

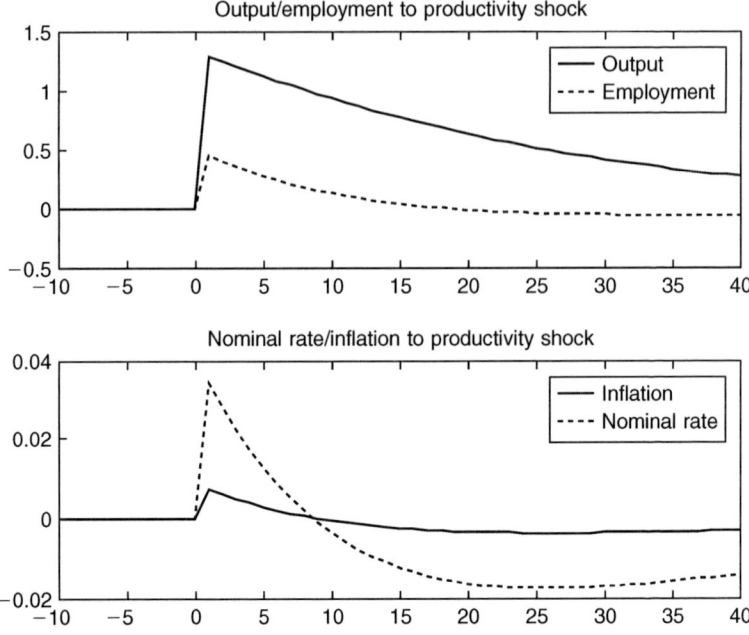

Figure 10.3 Responses of NK models to productivity shocks

Impulse responses

Figures 10.3 and 10.4 outline the output, employment (top panel), nominal interest rate and inflation responses to each of productivity and then of a monetary shock in a canonical NK model. In Figure 10.3, in response to a persistent productivity shock, output jumps immediately and employment jumps in a similar manner but with considerably less amplitude as hours take more of the strain. Interest rates and inflation jump in the same direction and inflation returns to base in around eight quarters. In the longer run the increase in productivity means that there is some overshoot, and inflation will tend to fall unless offset by cuts in interest rates. A key observation is that output follows closely the expected path of productivity and that interest rates work hard to stabilize inflation but that employment just mimics output.

Figure 10.4 shows the response of the economy to an unanticipated monetary shock. That is, an increase in the money supply over and above that suggested by the expected increase in nominal demand. The upper panel shows that output and employment have a temporary boom that

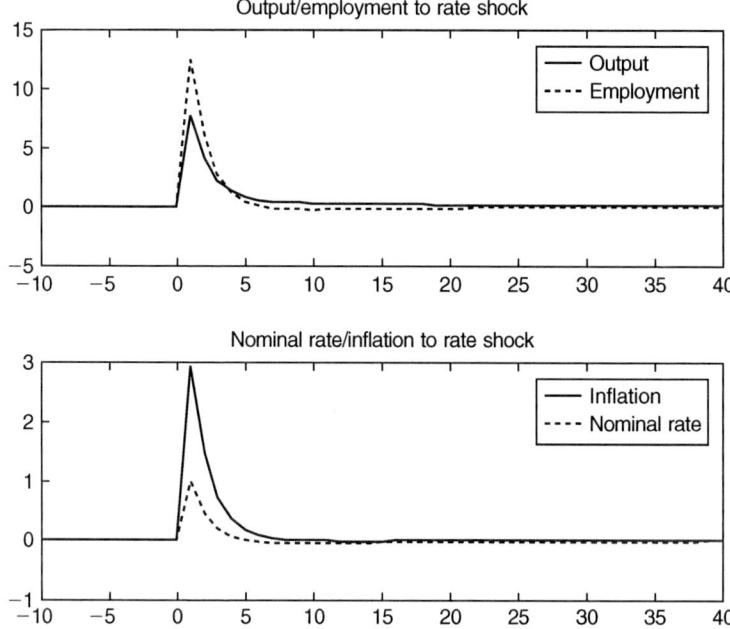

Figure 10.4 Responses of NK models to monetary shocks

lasts around four quarters. In the lower panel we note that there is a parallel temporary increase in inflation that drags up interest rates temporarily. But as this is a one-off money shock the economy stabilizes quickly. Again, the inflation is temporary and so is the problem for the economy.

In the DSGE model with labour market search the key is that the employment match does not happen in a Walrasian manner. In such a set-up, for example in Calvo-Yun, workers, operating on the full employment frontier, do not simply vary their hours in response to changes in the real wage, which is interpreted as the relative price of work to leisure. But now the margin of job destruction becomes revealed, which impacts on the search and vacancy dynamics of the labour market and inversely on the rate of job destruction. And the value of finding a match is found to be closely related to the probability of finding a match. A number of calibrations are possible. But what we illustrate here is with a baseline from our estimates on ONS data and based on the parameterizations in the literature and the issues discussed in the previous section.

Figure 10.5 shows how in the model with labour market search we can end up with greater amplitude in employment following a productivity shock. Overall there is twice the amplitude of employment to a productivity shock (see top left-hand panel). In this model productivity reduces the marginal incentive for job destruction (bottom right-hand panel) and accordingly this reduces job destruction alongside a persistent reduction in vacancies. The need for search falls as the probability of worker matching is persistently raised and firms find it more difficult to locate appropriate staff.

Figure 10.6 shows the considerably less amplitude in output and employment from a monetary shock. But clearly that employment drives output fluctuations. With a monetary shock both the survival rate increases and the destruction rate falls temporarily, which acts to reduce vacancies and the need to search. The probability of workers finding a match increases and so employment rises. As there is no increase in productivity, output is simply bid up in the extent of additional employment.

Compared with the Calvo-Yun model, inflation behaves in a relatively similar manner when we analyse the responses in a search model. The forward-looking behaviour of inflation setting seems to take care of that. But we find that the underlying output dynamics – even when we allow for considerably more labour market flexibility over time – appear considerably more persistent, where the endogenous probability of finding a match creates an ongoing perturbation to the labour market. We consider the implications of these calibrations for monetary policy in the next section.

The implications for monetary policy

The Taylor principle results most simply from an analysis of the stability conditions for the simple form of a forward-looking spending and Phillips curve equation in deterministic form:

$$y_t = E_t y_{t+1} - (i_t - E\pi_{t+1}), \tag{10.10}$$

$$\pi_t = \beta E_t \pi_{t+1} + \varkappa y_t, \tag{10.11}$$

$$i_t = \phi_\pi \pi_t + \phi_y y_t \tag{10.12}$$

which comprises the forward-looking spending (IS) equation in terms of output, y_t, the New Keynesian Phillips curve setting the intertemporal trade-off for inflation, π_t, in proportion to the current level of output

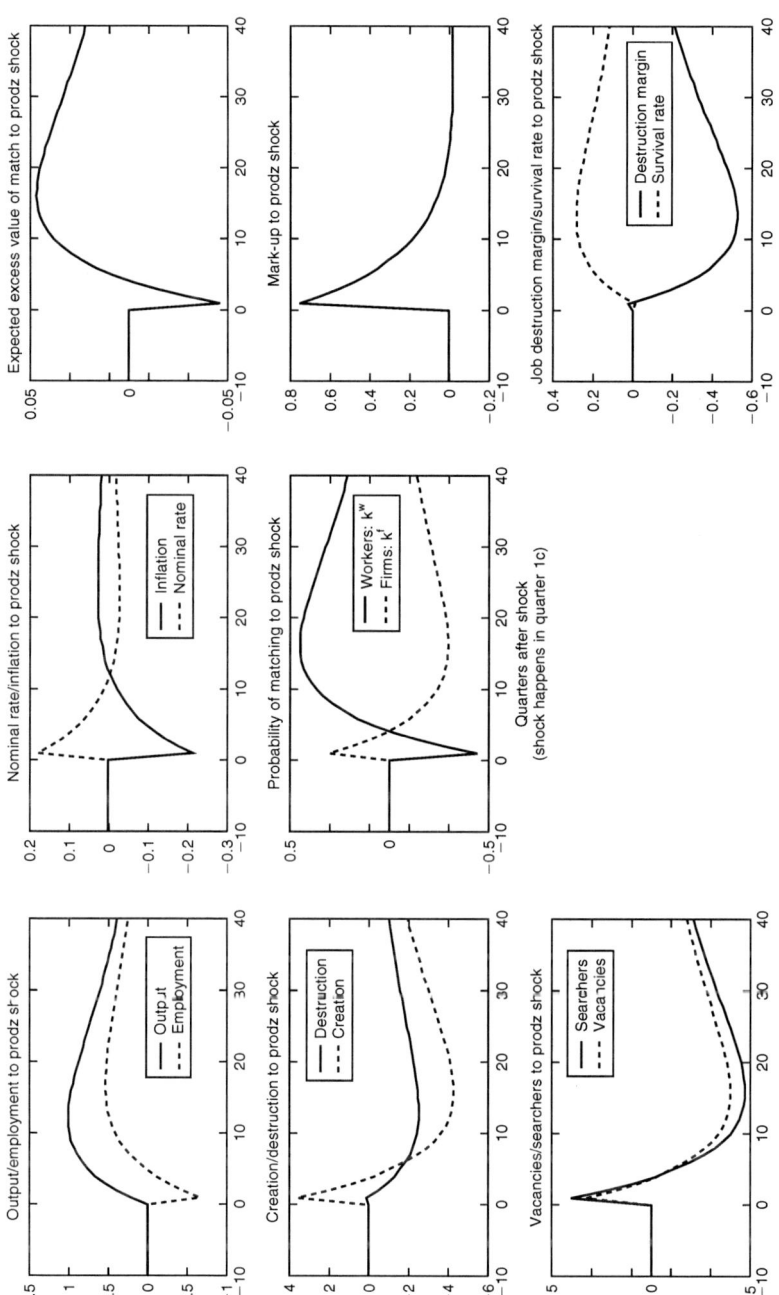

Figure 10.5 Responses of labour market models to productivity shock

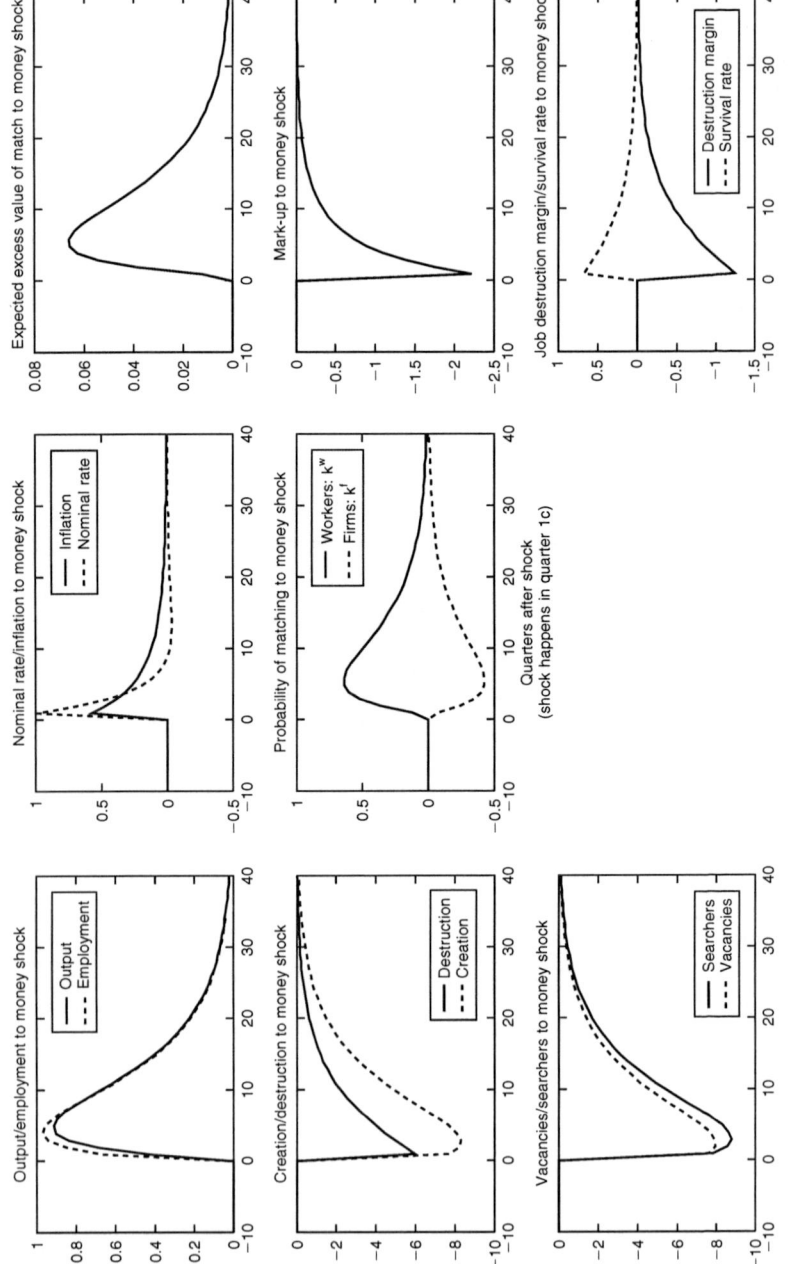

Figure 10.6 Responses of labour market models to monetary shock

and the policy rule for the interest rate in terms of output and inflation. It is well known (see Chadha, 2009, for an overview) that the stability of this simple Calvo-Yun system is given by the choice of policy parameters for the weight of inflation and output in the policy rule:

$$\frac{(1-\beta)}{\kappa}\phi_y + \phi_\pi > 1. \tag{10.13}$$

Note that independent of any choices for the parameter κ, the slope of the Phillips curve, or the rate of time preference, β, by choosing a sufficiently high weight on inflation, i.e. $\phi_\pi > 1$, the determinacy of this system can be assured and provides some rationale for a rather simplistic form of inflation targeting.

We can examine the Phillips curve resulting from the use of a search model to see what happens to these determinacy conditions. They become somewhat more complicated but show that when there are speed limit effects and a cost channel for monetary policy, the importance of targeting inflation alone is diminished. The IS equation and policy rule remain the same but the Phillips curve takes the following form:

$$\pi_t = \beta\pi_{t+1} + \kappa A y_t - \kappa B y_{t+1} + \kappa\lambda(i_t - \pi_{t+1}), \tag{10.14}$$

where kappa, A and B are parameters. Where current inflation, π_t, reflects future inflation, π_{t+1}, the current output gap, y_t, is reduced if slack is expected in the next period, y_{t+1}, and where current real rates, $(i_t - \pi_{t+1})$, impact on the cost base.[9] The extra terms in future output and on the cost channel of monetary policy result from the explicit modelling of the labour market. The output gap determines the level of slack in the labour market, and as we would expect when current output is high there is little labour market slack and so wages and costs are bid up. But note that there is a forward-looking element to the wage bargain. Insofar as if there is expected to be a similarly tight market in the next period some wage bargains will be brought forward to this period and there will be more vacancies in the next period. The consideration of optimal monetary policy cannot thus simply ignore the likely period of unemployment endured by the representative household. In fact what we end up with here is rather than inflation tilted by the paths of future output gaps, we see in this set-up that the change in inflation is proportional to the change in output plus an intercept term in the cost channel (assuming $A = B$ and $\beta = 1$):

$$\frac{1}{\kappa}(\pi_{t+1} - \pi_t) \approx (y_{t+1} - y_t) - \lambda(i_t - \pi_{t+1}). \tag{10.15}$$

To solve for the equivalent determinacy conditions we place the first order system $[\pi_t, y_t]$ in compact form and examine the roots of the Jacobian. The full derivation is available on request but for the determinacy a key condition is that:

$$\frac{(\phi_y + \varkappa\phi_\pi(A-\lambda)+1)}{\beta + \varkappa(A-\lambda)} > 1 \tag{10.16}$$

which we can compare directly with (10.13) above. Equation (10.16) clearly implies a greater efficacy from stabilizing output than inflation as each of $\varkappa$ and $(A-\lambda)$ are less than 1. Note that the term, λ, on the cost channel detracts from the stabilizing properties after strict inflation targeting.

Let us illustrate with a simple calculation taking 10.13 as our starting point. First let us set the weight on inflation in the policy rule to zero and then solve for the required weight on output:

$$\phi_y > \frac{\varkappa}{(1-\beta)} \tag{10.17}$$

For $\varkappa = 0.2$ and $\beta = 0.989$, $\phi_\pi = 0$, then $\phi_y > 18.2$ is required to ensure determinacy in the Calvo-Yun case. Now if we solve (10.11) in the same manner:

$$\phi_y > \beta + \varkappa(A-\lambda) - 1 \tag{10.18}$$

We find that for the Walsh set-up the threshold hardly bites if $(A-\lambda) = 0.8$ as $\phi_y > 0.15$. This result implies that the concentration on output alone can relatively easily stabilize a system with real labour market rigidities. Or at the very least that the efficacy of inflation targeting alone may be questioned when one allows for meaningful delays in job matching.

The intuition for the result follows from a simple manipulation of the Phillips curve in (10.9), where we note that the acceleration in inflation is closely pinned down by the growth rate of output. So ensuring an absence of large peaks or recessions in output may be the best way to prevent a deleterious inflation dynamic from developing.

Concluding remarks

How can we use this type of model to learn about the nexus between the labour market and overall macroeconomic fluctuations? Monetary policy-makers are mostly interested in issues that are related to inflationary pressures and the dynamics of inflation and output gap over business cycles (Chadha and Nolan, 2002). A calibrated DSGE model with labour market search has illustrated the extent of an interaction between the labour market and inflation-output dynamics. It turns out that the labour market is a crucial part of a prolonged adjustment mechanism for an aggregate economy. The extent to which the labour market is flexible or not will determine, to a considerable degree, the household level utility losses from economic shocks. But we have shown that even if the labour market has been reformed, as in the UK, issues connected with labour market search will still be likely to generate considerable persistence into the adjustment of the real economy to shocks. The consideration of optimal monetary policy cannot thus simply ignore the likely endured by the representative household. We have illustrated with empirical evidence, the impulse responses from a calibrated DSGE model and a simple analytical model how the persistence of the labour market adjustment ought perhaps to be a key consideration in the setting of monetary policy.

Appendix: Walsh (2003) labour matching DSGE model

Key equations:

- The policy rule for nominal money growth:

$$\hat{\Theta}_t = \rho_m \hat{\Theta}_{t-1} + \hat{\phi}_t; \qquad (10.19)$$

- The cash-in-advance constraint (in first difference form):

$$\hat{\Theta}_t = \hat{y}_t - \hat{y}_{t-1} + \hat{\pi}_t; \qquad (10.20)$$

- The evolution of the number of matches:

$$\hat{n}_{t+1} = \varphi \hat{\varphi}_t + \varphi \hat{n}_t + \left(\frac{vk^f}{N}\right)\hat{v}_t + \left(\frac{uk^f}{N}\right)\hat{k}_t^f; \qquad (10.21)$$

- The endogenous job destruction margin:

$$\hat{a}_t = \hat{r}_t + \hat{\mu}_t - \left(\frac{\mu Rq}{\tilde{a}}\right)\hat{q}_t - \hat{z}_t; \qquad (10.22)$$

- The survival rate $\varphi_t = 1 - \rho_t$:

$$\hat{\varphi}_t = -\left(\frac{\rho^n}{1-\rho^n}\right) e_{F,a} \hat{a}_t; \tag{10.23}$$

- The number of unemployed job seekers:

$$\hat{u}_t = -\left(\frac{\varphi N}{u}\right) \hat{n}_t - \left(\frac{\varphi N}{u}\right) \hat{\varphi}_t; \tag{10.24}$$

- The probability that a vacancy is filled:

$$\hat{k}_t^f = a\hat{u}_t - (1-\xi)\hat{v}_t; \tag{10.25}$$

- The equality of firms filling vacancies and workers finding matches:

$$\hat{v}_t + \hat{k}_t^f = \hat{u}_t + \hat{k}_t^w; \tag{10.26}$$

- The job posting condition:

$$\hat{k}_t^f = -\left(\frac{\eta k^w}{1 - \eta k^w}\right) \hat{k}_t^w - \left(\frac{q}{q+h}\right) \hat{q}_t; \tag{10.27}$$

- The output equation:

$$\hat{y}_t = \left(\frac{Q}{Y}\right)(e_{H,a}\hat{a}_t + \hat{n}_t + z_t) - \left(\frac{\gamma V}{Y}\right)\hat{v}_t; \tag{10.28}$$

- The Euler condition from the household's optimization problem:

$$0 = E_t \hat{y}_{t+1} - \hat{y}_t - \left(\frac{1}{\sigma}\right)\hat{r}_t + \left(\frac{1}{\sigma}\right) E_t \hat{\pi}_{t+1}; \tag{10.29}$$

- The inflation equation from the retail firms' pricing decisions:

$$0 = \beta E_t \hat{\pi}_{t+1} - \hat{\pi}_t - \kappa \hat{\mu}_t; \tag{10.30}$$

- The present value condition for matches:

$$\hat{q}_t = AB(e_{H,a}E_t\hat{a}_{t+1} - E_t\hat{\mu}_{t+1} - E_t\hat{r}_{t+1} + E_tz_{t+1})$$

$$+ \left[\frac{(1-\eta k^w)\beta\varphi(q-A)}{q}\right]E_t\hat{\varphi}_{t+1} - \left(\frac{q+h}{q}\right)(\hat{r}_t - E_t\hat{\pi}_{t+1})$$

$$- \left(\frac{\eta k^w}{1-\eta k^w}\right)\left(\frac{q+h}{q}\right)\hat{k}_t^w + (1-\eta k^w)\beta\varphi E_t\hat{q}_{t+1} \quad (10.31)$$

Notes

1. In fact in a famous thought experiment, Lucas (1987) showed that in a representative agent economy the actual costs from expected fluctuations were a small fraction of average consumption because the actual variance of per capita consumption and likely extent of risk aversion is limited.
2. We shall use the terms New Keynesian and Calvo-Yun interchangeably in this paper.
3. According to King and Rebelo's (2000) calibration, US data of output-real-wage correlation is 0.12 versus 0.98 in the RBC model; US relative volatility of employment to output is 0.99 versus 0.48 in the RBC model.
4. In Generalized Method of Moments (GMM) estimation, the Ravenna-Walsh model is not rejected for US post-war data, as opposed to its NKPC counterpart.
5. *Financial Times*, 12 June 2007.
6. According to den Haan *et al.* (2000), we need to know how many 'jobs counted as destroyed in a quarter fail to reappear in the following quarter' (72.3 per cent in the US) and what is the 'ratio of creation to employment' (i.e. the job-creation rate, 5.2 per cent in the US). Further explanation of variables and parameters are given in Tables 10.2 and 10.3. The Appendix lays out the key equations of the model, which boil down to the Phillips curve.
7. Constant Relative Risk Aversion, 'work days lost to strikes soar'.
8. This functional form aims to illustrate the intuition of modelling labour-specific wage. In a model where the *NWM* is enforced, the competitive wholesale sector requires that the retail market installs a lower mark-up, as the marginal cost is inflated by *NMW*. So the *NMW* might be thought of as a change in the steady-state mark-up.
9. Note that if $B = \lambda = 0$, we recover the NK standard Phillips curve.

References

Calvo, Gulliermo A. (1983) 'Staggered Prices in a Utility-Maximising Framework', *Journal of Monetary Economics* 12 (3): 983–98.

Chadha, Jagjit S. (2009) 'Policy Rules under Monetary and the Fiscal Theories of the Price Level', forthcoming in *Cambridge Handbooks in Applied Economics*.

Chadha, Jagjit S. and Charles Nolan (2002) 'Supply Shocks and the Natural Rate of Interest: An Exploration', in Lavan Mahadeva and Peter Sinclair (eds), *Monetary Transmission in Diverse Economies*, Cambridge University Press.

Haan, Wouter J. den, Gary Ramey and Joel Watson (2000) 'Job Destruction and Propagation of Shocks', *American Economic Review* 90 (3): 482–98.

Hansen, Gary (1985) 'Indivisible Labour and the Business Cycle', *Journal of Monetary Economics* 16: 309–27.

King, Robert G. and Sergio T. Rebelo (2000) 'Resuscitating Real Business Cycles', in Michael Woodford and John Taylor (eds), *Handbook of Macroeconomics*, North Holland.

Kydland, Finn E. (2004) 'Quantitative Aggregate Theory', Nobel Prize Lecture.

Lucas, Robert E. (1987) *Models of Business Cycles*, Oxford and Cambridge, MA, USA: John Wiley.

Millard, Stephen P. (2000) 'The Effects of Increased Labour Market Flexibility in the United Kingdom: Theory and Practice', Bank of England working papers 109.

Prescott, Edward C. (2004) 'The Transformation of Macroeconomic Policy and Research', Nobel Prize Lecture.

Ravenna, Frederico and Carl E. Walsh (2007) 'Vacancies, Unemployment, and the Phillips Curve,' Kiel working papers 1362, Kiel Institute for the World Economy.

Walsh, Carl E. (2003) 'Labor Market Search and Monetary Shocks', in Sumru Altug, Jagjit S. Chadha and Charles Nolan (eds), *Elements of Dynamic Macroeconomic Analysis*, Cambridge University Press.

Walsh, Carl E. (2005) 'Labor Market Search, Sticky Prices, and Interest Rate Policies', *Review of Economic Dynamics* 8 (4): 829–49.

Woodford, Michael (2003) *Interest and Prices*, Princeton, NJ: Princeton University Press.

Yun, Tack (1996) 'Nominal Price Rigidity, Money Supply Endogeneity and the Business Cycle', *Journal of Monetary Economics* 37 (2): 345–70.

Index

Key: **bold** = extended discussion; f = figure; n = note; t = table.

Advanced Macroeconomics (Romer)   57
aggregate consumption   186–7
aggregate demand (*AD*)   **8–14**, 76–9
   'a determinant of real wage rate'   76
   alterations   62
   changes   146(n2)
   components   31
   goods   184
   labour   65–6
   miscellaneous   4, 7, 15, 36, 38, 47, 54(n6), 58, 60f, 60, 63, 69–71, 72–3, 75, 80, 104, 131, 133–4, 136–8, 141, 144–5, 146(n3), 157–8, 185–7, 195
   shortfall   143
   'simplistic model'   78
aggregate demand (expected receipts)   40
aggregate real activity   153
aggregate supply (*AS*)   40, 58, 68f, 68, 80, 133
   full employment level   60
   labour   65–6
aggregate supply (necessary receipts)   40
aggregate supply and demand (equilibrium)   154
aggregate supply function   40
aggregate supply in New Consensus (chapter four)   2–3, **57–82**
   aggregate demand schedule   76–9
   assumptions   59, 60, 62, 68, 69, 70, 71, 73, 74, 76, 77, 81(n3)
   chapter purpose   57, 59, 62, 76
   compare and contrast (Mankiw and Keynes)   73–6, 81(n3)
   concluding remarks   79–81, 82(n4)
   empiricism   73
   equations   61, 64, 76
   framework of analysis (AS/AD structure)   58
   introduction   57–8
   involuntary unemployment (Keynes)   64–73, 81(n2)
   literature   66, 79
   theory versus reality   79
   three approaches to aggregate supply   59–64, 81(n1)
   two simple approaches to aggregate supply in New Consensus   58–9
agriculture   47, 50
Allsopp, C.   134
Amato, J. D.   178(n7)
Anglo-Saxon countries   26
anti-deflationary strategy   141, 142
applied labour economists   41
Arestis, P.   xi, **4–5**, 13, 15, 27(n2), 27, 105, 106, 124, 126(n4), 127(n15), 127–8(n18), 132, 134, 149, 153–4, 178(n12)
   publications   ii, **128**
Artis, M. J.   161
'aspiration gap'   191
'aspirational hysteresis'   196(n7)
asset prices   5, 162
assets (capital values)   13
Atesoglu, H. S.   105
Australia   23t
Austria   xii, 23t, 42t, 44f
Austrian theory of capital   177(n2)

'backward countries' (Kalecki)   16, 26
Baddeley, M.   ii
balanced budget   9, 10, 12, 17, 158, 171
balanced budget multiplier   158
Balassa, B.   99(n14), 102
Ball, L.   105, 126(n2)
Bank of England   45, 132
Bank of England: Monetary Policy Committee   147(n5)
bank rate (UK)   205
bank reserves   152
banks/banking   50, 107, 122, 127(n9, n13), 188
   role in savings/investment process   160
bargained rate of real product wage inflation (BRWI)   86–7, 90, 98–9(n8–9)

225

Index

Batool, T. 6
Beckerman, W. 99(n14), 102
Belgium 23t, 42t, 43, 43–4f
Bernanke, B. S. 135
Blanchard, O. J. 41, 54, 96, 101–2(n29, n31–2), 105, 126(n2), 128
Blanchflower, D. G. 147(n5)
Blinder, A. 134
Boltho, A. 21
bonds 50, 128(n18)
'boom and bust' policy strategy 145
booms 141–4, 146
Bowles, S. 17, 21
British Association for Advancement of Science 31–2
budget deficits 1, 7, **8–14**, 42, 44
  structural versus cyclical 45
  sustainability **12–13**
budget surpluses 10, 10
business confidence 165, 167
business cycle 8, 12, 13, 146(n3), 175, 203, 210, 220
  general equilibrium model 5
  see also real business cycle

Calvo, G. 160
Calvo price-setting mechanism 202
Calvo-Yun paradigm 202–3, 207–8, 209, 215, 216, 220
  'interchangeable with New Keynesian' 223(n2)
Cambridge Centre for Economic and Public Policy 1, 6
'Cambridge equation' 184, 185
Cambridge Journal of Economics 147(n4)
Cambridge University x–xii, 1, 2, 6, 57
Cambridge University: King's College (Keynes versus Pigou) 66
Campbell, D. A. 14
Canada 23t
capacity 8, 23, 26, 159
  effective 26
  and inflation **14–17**
capacity utilization 14, 24, 117–18, 184
  equilibrium rate 112
  stable inflation rate 111
capital 4, 50–1, 113–14, 122, 149, 174, 178(n9)
  new 152

return on 150, 160, 178(n10)
supply price 152
capital: ratios
  capital–labour ratio 48, 198(n11)
  capital–output ratio 9, 26–7(n1), 48–9, 52, 184
  capital–potential output ratio 106
capital accumulation 2, 34, 47–8, 52–3, 156, 158–9, 207
  government role 49
capital equipment 8, 14, 15, 16
capital goods 152
capital stock 4, 8, 15, 21–2, 105–7, 111, 127(n13), 177(n2), 178(n10), 197(n9)
  growth 127(n10)
  growth rate 175
  size 1–2
capital stock–labour force ratio 185
capitalism 8, 14
  conceptions 181
  'real exchange economy' 5
capitalist economy 7, 17
  demand deficiency and plentiful capacity 22
capitalists 7, 105
Carlin, W. 98(n3), 99(n9), 126(n1), 132
cash flow 186
cash-in-advance constraint (equation) 221
central bankers 136
central banks
  absence of intervention (NAIRU as strong short-run attractor) **113–17**, 127(n7–8)
  'activist' position versus 'parking-it' approach **120–2**, 127(n14)
  capacity to adjust unemployment towards NAIRU 'asymmetric' 118, 127(n9)
  changes in short-run nominal interest rate 133
  credibility 141, 153
  'deliberate' or 'conventional' strategy **136–9**, 140–6
  different circumstances, different weights attached to policy objectives 143
  'direct control of inflation' 149
  evolutionary perspective 141
  feedback rule 163, 165
  independence 199(n18)
  inflation target 158, 165

inflation-targeting 105, 112, 196(n1)
inflation-targeting (NAIRU as short-run attractor) 117–19, 127(n9)
  limitations (on effectiveness) 145
  miscellaneous 4, 81, 107, 124, 126, 128(n18), 132, 138, 166–7, 169–71, 188–91, 193, 198(n12), 199(n22)
  modern conundrum 134
  monetary policy 160–1
  neo-Wicksellian models 154
  'nominal' versus 'real' variables 145
  'opportunistic' strategy 131, 136–7, **139–45**, 146
  overnight interest rate 198(n14)
  reactions towards financial market instabilities 122
  setting of interest rates 154
  target rate of inflation 161
  willingness to create negative output gap 160
Chadha, J. S. xi, **5–6**, 219, 223
Chick, V. ii
China 178(n10)
Cholesky ordering restriction 205
circular and cumulative causation 3, 83, 85
  'cumulative causation mechanism' (extended Kaldorian model) 91
  'cumulative process' (Wicksell) 150, 152
Clarida, R., *et al.* (1998, 2000) 161, 179
  Galí, J. 179
  Gertler, M. 179
Clarida, R., *et al.* (1999) 126(n1), 128, 133, 147, 199(n22), 199
  Galí, J. 128, 147, 199
  Gertler, M. 128, 147, 199
class consciousness 17
classical economics 2, 3, 30–1, 39–40, 46, 57, 67
  divergence between theory and reality 38
  theory of labour-market adjustment 57
classical economists 34, 36, 58, 64, 80
  Keynes' criticisms 37, 66–7, 69–71
Clinton administration 46

closed economy 106, 120
Cobb-Douglas production function 100(n22), 174, 206, 210n
codetermination 21
commodities 16, 106
  'bidding wars' 151
companies *see* firms
'competing claims equilibrium' (Carlin and Soskice) 99(n9)
competition 75
  goods market 182
  imperfect 133, 153
  perfect 34, 69, 72
competition policy 199(n17)
competitiveness
  non-price 92, 97, 98
  price 89
  relative price 93, 98–9(n8)
competitor economies 87, 98(n6)
conditional closure 198(n13)
confidence intervals 176
consumer confidence 160, 165, 167
consumer expenditure 1, 7
consumer goods 16, 22, 26
consumer price index (CPI) 139, 205
consumer prices 152
consumption 10–13, 31, 39, 52, 133, 175, 223(n1)
  inter-temporal optimization 158
  interest-rate-sensitive expenditures 77
  present versus future 38, 158–9, 176
  subsidies 8–9
consumption goods 10–11
  inelastic supply 15
Cornwall, J. 54(n6), 199(n17)
corporate debt
  ratio to capital stock 184
cost channel 219–20
cost-of-job-loss approach 20–1
cost-push shocks 209
costs 219
counter-cyclicality 10
  real wage rate 155
credit 29, 50, 107, 122, 127(n13), 188
credit-money economy 152
CRRA (Constant Relative Risk Aversion) 212t
Cuaresma, C. J., *et al.* (2004) 178(n7), 179
  Gnan, E. 179
  Ritzberger-Grünwald, D. 179

'cumulative process' (Wicksell) 150
Czech Republic 23t

Daveri, F. 102(n33)
Davidson, P. 31, 106, 127(n15)
De Benedictis, L. 100(n22)
'Death of Keynesian/Economics' (Lucas, 1980) 33–4, 55
debt
  public 10
  real 105
debt to capital ratio 108, 111
debt to GDP ratio 13, 42
debt stock 107–8, 192
decision-makers 183
deficit financing 2, 34, 50, 111, 124, 127–8(n18)
deflation 42, 52, 53, 118, 141, 189
  balanced 67, 186, 187
  'debt-deflation effects' 186, 198(n12)
deflationary gap 14
deindustrialization 155, 162, 169
demand
  centre of economy 158
  deficit-financed by government 111
  deflationary shock 50
  domestic 167
  excess 113
  endogenous 154
  falls 167
  increases 15
  for labour 30
  miscellaneous 1, 2, 8, 16, 18, 24, 26, 30, 31, 61–2, 151, 163, 165, 181
  see also aggregate demand
demand conditions 98(n3)
demand deficiency 31–2, 42, 50, 87
demand deflation 33
demand effects 114
demand elasticity of differentiated goods 212t100(n19)
demand expansion policies 41
demand function for labour 34
demand for goods and services 158
demand for labour
  marginal productivity theory 67
demand management 5, 45, 52, 53, 123, 125
demand shocks 138–9, 144, 146, 150, 165–6
  long-lasting 156
  negative **169–73**
demand side 4, 133, 185
  feedback to supply side 83, 85, 88, 90
  source of inflation (NCV assumption) 137
demand-determined real outcomes 195
Denmark 23t, 42t, 43, 43–4f
depreciation 175
developed countries 30, 48
developing countries 14, 22, 29, 30
direct price effect 93
'discipline in factories' (Kalecki) 17, 18, 26
discount factor 212t
discount rate 176, 177(n2)
  inverse 158–9
disinflation 140–2
  unexpected 113–14, 118
disinflation strategy 137
dismissal threat 17, 18
distribution **106–12**
distribution theory 155
distributional conflict 3–4
Dixit, A. K. 176
Dixon, R. 30, 99(n15)
Dixon and Thirlwall model 83, **84–5**, 98(n1–3) , 99(n15), 102
Domar, E. D. 9, 13
Douglas, Major 37
Dow, J. C. R. 22–3
Dow, S. C. ii, 198(n14)
Dubber, A. 6
Dublin Summit (1996) 44–5
Duménil, G. 14
Dunlop, J. 37
'Dutch disease' 162
Dutt, A. K. 14
dynamic stochastic general equilibrium (DSGE) model 203, 215
  calibrated 220–1
  labour market specification 203–4

early retirement 99(n13)
Eastern Economic Association x
Eatwell, J. ii
econometrics 41–2
  structural models 178(n7)
economic activity 7, 11, 15, 17, 26
  capitalist versus socialist 14

Index   229

demand-constrained versus supply-constrained   14
full employment level   127–8(n18)
economic growth   43, 53, 106, 135
  circular and cumulative   83, 85
  export-led   84
  extended Kaldorian model (Roberts)   3
  'natural' versus 'warranted' rates   48–9, 49f
  not influenced by monetary policy   154
  possibility of unemployment trade-off   92–7, 100–2(n22–33)
  secular   178(n9)
  Solow–Swan model   2–3
  warranted versus natural rate   52
economic growth rate   155–6
  'determined in long run by supply considerations'   154
  regional or national (joint determinants)   83
economic growth and unemployment in extended Kaldorian model (chapter five)   3, **83–103**
  assumptions   83–4, 85, 86, 88, 93, 96, 97, 98(n2–3, n6–7), 99(n9), 100–1(n23), 101(n25), 102(n32)
  chapter purpose   83, 97
  chapter structure   83–4
  equations   84–8, 91, 92, 98–9(n7–9), 99(n11), 99–100(n14–16)
  literature   83, 91, 92, 97, 100(n22), 101(n29), 102(n32)
  policy implications   97
  standard Kaldorian model and worker passivity   84–5, 86, 97–8, 98(n1–3, n7), 99(n14–15)
  summary and conclusions   97–8
  see also 'Kaldorian model: extended'
economic history   30
Economic and Monetary Union (EMU, 1999–)   41, 42, 53
  Stability and Growth Pact (EU)   10, 12, 44
economic policy   41
  'can offset long-lasting shocks'   150
economic theory
  'missing chapter'   40
economics of happiness   147(n5)
economists   8, 53, 65, 79, 140, 213
  anti-Keynesian   33

classical and neoclassical   34, 36, 64
  Keynesian, New Keynesian, New Classical   59
  'laugh at Keynesian theorising'   38
  younger generation   30, 54(n2)
economy
  fine-tuning   122, 126
  full employment equilibrium level   124
  interest-rate policies   122
  intrinsic workings   192, 194
  long-run equilibrium   161–2
  modern   61
  slow-growing versus fast-growing   99(n14)
  social construction   195
  stagnationist   187, 194–5
Edgeworth, F. Y.   37
education   10
effective demand   1, 10, 11, 14, 15, 17, 31, 38–40, 60, 69, 72, 80, 104–5, 111, 116, 127(n6), 185
  high employment levels   125
  Kalecki   26
  Malthus   37
  stabilization   124
efficiency   48
efficiency wages   19
elasticity of investment   114, 116
elasticity of labour supply to wages   203
elasticity of labour-force growth   95
elasticity of substitution
  current versus future consumption   159
elasticity of vacancies with respect to matches   209
elections   17, 94
employers   62, 73, 81, 86
employers' organizations   90, 124
employment   **108–11**
  actual level (determinants)   35
  equilibrium rate   185, 188–190, 192–4
  equilibrium rate (new)   195
  ex ante goods market equilibrium rate   112
  ex post goods market equilibrium rate   115
  ex post rate   114
  goods market equilibrium rate   112–15
  goods-market determined   117

employment – *continued*
  improvement without increasing inflation 4
  versus inflation-targeting 181–201
  inimicality of inflation-targeting (depending on conduct of macroeconomic policy) 181, 187–95, 198–9(n13–21)
  market-clearing level 63
  miscellaneous 59, 62, 104, 106, 126, 144–5, 146(n3), 211t
  movements in numbers of people employed 203
  'natural' rate 41
  part-time 213
  PK alternative to NCMs 3
  price relative to leisure 215
  response of labour market models to monetary shocks 216, 218f
  response of labour market models to productivity shocks 217f
  response to monetary shocks (NK models) 214–15, 215f
  response to productivity shocks (NK models) 214f, 214
  stable-inflation level 109, 112–15, 117–18, 120, 123–4
  supply-determined rate 5
  sustainable 135
  volatility 210
  volume 40, 66
  see also vacancies
employment contracts 206, 211t
employment creation 29, 34, 51, 53, 223(n6)
employment exchange system (UK) 33
employment function 187, 189f, 189–92, 193f, 195
employment growth 49, 93, 95
  constrained by output growth 87
  rate 87, 99(n10–11)
  relative 101(n26)
employment level 65, 99(n10), 178(n10), 184–7, 197–8(n9–12)
  neo-Kaleckian model (modified) 184
employment match/job matching 203, 206–7
  'does not happen in Walrasian manner' 215
  frictions 204
  probability of finding 210t, 212t, 215
  steady-state probability 209, 213

employment opportunities 87
employment patterns 203
employment policy
  planned 37
employment protection 42
employment rate 108–9, 111–13, 123, 182–3, 187, 193–5, 196(n6)
  high and stable medium-run 120
  paradox of thrift 185–6
  supply-determined equilibrium 190
employment target 124–5
employment theory
  classical 2, 34–6, 54(n4)
employment-output ratio 185
entrepreneurs 70, 76, 150, 160
equation of exchange (Fisher) 76
equilibrating mechanisms 174
equilibrium models 178(n7)
equipment 150
'Essay in Dynamic Theory' (Harrod, 1939) 48
Essays in Persuasion (Keynes, 1931) 29, 52, 55
Eugenics Society 48
Euler condition 222
euro exchange rate 45
Europe
  'Common Market regional policy' 31–2
  demand stimulus required in high-unemployment regions 31–2
  Keynesian counter-revolution 53
European Central Bank 37, 41, 53
  'compromise interest rates that suit no country' 45
  'ECB President' 45
  'needs to remove classical blinkers' 46
  setting of interest rates 45
European Commission 45
European Union 1, 2, 10, 30, 33, 147(n5)
  inflation 42t
  smaller countries 43, 44
  unemployment 34, 41–6, 54(n6–7)
eurozone 10, 12, 34, 41–5
  'not an optimal currency area' 45
'excess employment' 118, 119f
exchange agreements/conducted in nominal terms 183

exchange rate   22, 205f, 206
  nominal   98(n1)
  real effective   205
expectations effect   93
expected excess value of match
    211t
  response of labour market to shocks
    217–18f
expenditure   205
  interest-rate-sensitive   77
export markets   85
  real income growth rate   84
exports   8, 11, 127–8(n18), 205–6
  cross-price elasticity of demand   85
  demand   167
  income elasticity of demand   92
  non-price competitiveness   97
  price competitiveness   89
  real growth rate   84, 88, 93, 98(n1)
  relative price competitiveness
    98–9(n8)
'extensive margin'   203

factors of production   31, 159
'fair rate of interest' (Pasinetti)   122,
    192–3, 199(n19–20)
'farmers' (Mankiw)   61
Fazzari, S. M., *et al.* (1988), 197(n9),
    200
  Hubbard, G. R.   200
  Peterson, B.   200
Federal Open Market Committee
    (FOMC)   4, 131, 139–40, 146
  'deliberate' (conventional) strategy
    versus 'opportunistic' strategy
    136–7
Federal Reserve Board (author)   136,
    147–8
Federal Reserve System   4, 46, 131–2,
    135, 139–40, 146
Federal Reserve System: Board of
    Governors   136, 145
Ferreiro, J.   ii
filtering approaches (univariate)
    178(n7)
final consumption goods   86
'final finance'   107, 127(n13)
finance   **106–12**
financial bubbles   162
financial markets   135
financial sector   153
Financial Times   223(n5)
Finland   23t, 42t, 43, 43–4f

firms
  claims on total income   108, 191,
    199(n17)
  costs   120
  debt-servicing   184–5, 197(n9)
  decisions on whether to post a
    vacancy   208
  domestic   85, 98(n3, n7), 99(n9)
  elasticity of investment   114, 116
  excess capacity   14
  failure to fill employment vacancies
    203
  incomplete bargaining power   182,
    183
  interest payments to rentiers   108
  investment decisions   158, 175–6
  mark-up pricing   108, 160,
    196(n6)
  miscellaneous   3, 8, 12, 18, 21–2,
    62, 74, 86–7, 89, 102(n32), 107,
    111, 117, 122–3, 126, 174, 183,
    194, 197(n8), 202–4, 216, 217–18f
  'monopolistic competition'   160
  price-setting as mark-up on unit
    labour costs   93
  pricing behaviour   20
  pricing decisions (implications for
    real wages)   83, 97
  pricing power   156
  production shifted abroad
    178(n10)
  profit aspirations   109
  real debt   186
  retained earnings   108
  target gross profit share   108
  target rate of return on assets
    199(n17)
  target share of total income   182
first-order difference equations
    100(n19)
fiscal policy
  'can offset long-lasting shocks'
    150
  combined monetary-fiscal strategy
    135
  deflationary   44
  discretionary (neglected in NCM)
    124, 127(n17)
  expansionary   124
  flexibility required   53
  'ineffective within NCM analysis'
    178(n8)
  long-run development of economy
    124

fiscal policy – *continued*
  miscellaneous 1, 5, 7, 10, 14, 26, 27(n2), 27, 104, 106, 134, 149, 158
  PK view: means of real stabilization 124
  role in modern macroeconomics 135, 147(n4)
  role in offsetting long-lasting shocks 156
  'should complement monetary policy' (Fontana) 145
  stabilization: real 4, 124–5
  stabilization tool 126, 135
  stabilization tool: replaced by monetary policy 131
  see also monetary policy
fiscal stimulus
  'only policy that can offset demand shock' 171, 172f, 174
Fischer, S. 81, 82
Fisher, I. 151, 177(n2)
  equation of exchange 76
fixed wage model 73
Flaschel, P., *et al.* (1997) 197(n7), 200
  Franke, R. 200
  Semmler, W. 200
flex price 5, 202, 203
Fontana, G. xi, **4**, 105, 133, 146(n3), 148, 160
Forstater, M. 190
forward-looking spending (IS) equation 216
France 1, 23t, 41–5
Franke, R. 200
'free market'
  'inevitabilities' 195
Friedman, M. 46, 79, 81, 82, 177(n5)
Frowen, S. F. 150, 177(n4), 179, 180
full capacity output 108
full employment (FE) 1–2, 58, 60, 68f, 68, 75, 80, 124, 128(n18), 142, 144, 146, 150, 215
  policies to achieve **7–28**
  political obstacles 8
  wartime 30
full-employment (natural) level of real income ('Y') 61–4, 67–73, 75
'functional finance' 9, 28, 124, 127–8(n14), 129
'fundamental reforms' 21, 26
future generations 12

Galí, J. 128, 147, 179, 199
Galbraith, J. K. 79
General Theory of Employment, Interest and Money (Keynes, 1936) 30, 35, 41, 55, 60, 62, 64, 80
  'Changes in Money-Wages' (chapter 19) 59, 69, 73, 77
  connection between money wages and employment 66
  'contains only one diagram' 81(n2)
  determinants of real wage rate **71–3**
  first eighteen chapters 59, 69
  'gets off to dreadful start' **64–6**
  'relied on assumption of given money wages' 81(n3)
  versus Mankiw, *Macroeconomics* 73–6, 81(n3)
generalized method of moment (GMM) 223(n4)
geometric Brownian motion 175, 176
George, E. 45
Germany xi, 1, 23t, 41–5
Gertler, M. 128, 147, 179, 199
Gessell, S. 37
Glick, M. 14
globalization 150, 155, 162, 169, 178(n10)
Glyn, A. 21
Gnan, E. 179
Gnos, C. 106
gold standard 151
'Golden Rule' of growth theory 177(n4)
Goodhart, C. A. E. 160
goods
  'bidding war' (Fisher) 151
  fixed supply 154
  home-produced 86
goods market 138, 158, 183–4, 197(n8), 208
  competition 182
  supply and demand 155
goods market disequilibrium
  spill-over from money market 151–2
  transmission 154
goods market equilibrium 111, 127(n6), 152
  ex ante 112
  ex ante employment rate 113
  ex post 114–15

ex post temporary 113
ex post unemployment curve 118
long-run 163–4, 164f, 178(n11)
government borrowing 11
Government Economic Service (UK) 30
government expenditure 1, 7, 8, 11, 50, 171
  multiplier effect 50
  'productive' 10
  social priorities 10
  on training 100(n22)
government policy 47, 91
government role 52–3
  'inflationary' finance 49
  rate of capital accumulation 2, 49
governments 9, 94, 124
  chances of re-election 17
  deficit-financed demand 106
  deficit spending 15
  normative priorities 52
Greece 23t, 24, 25f
gross capital income 106
gross domestic product (GDP) 12, 13, 42, 45, 171, 205–6
gross investment: definition 175
'guest workers' 87

Haan, W. J., *et al.* (2000) 223(n6), 223
  Ramey, G. 223
  Watson, J. 223
Hahn, F. 34
Hansen, G. 204
Harris, C. P. 30
Harrod, R. 48, 81(n2)
Hayek, F. A. von 81(n1)
health 10
Hein, E. ii, xi, 3–4, 105, 106, 120, 126(n3–4, n6), 127(n7, n10–11, n16), **129**
historical sequence 141
History of Economic Thought (course) 30
Holy Inquisition 37, 53
homogeneity 160, 178(n10)
Hooper, P. 99(n15)
horizontalists 190, 200
households
  consumption/saving decisions 158–9, 175, 176
  nominal income 213

optimization problem (equation) 222
  representative 206
housing 162
Hubbard, G. R. 200
human capital accumulation 92, 100(n22)
Hungary 23t
hysteresis effects 33, 144–5, 146
  artificial 159
  'strike at heart of macroeconomics' 145

IMF 53
immigration 210, **213**
imports 11, 24, 86, 123, 127–8(n18), 138, 205–6
impulse responses 209, 210, **214–16**, 217–18f
income 39, 176
  conflicting claims **108–11**, 191
  future (expected rate of growth) 159
  nominal 198(n12)
  real 61
income distribution 11, 12, 112, 182, 196, 199(n17)
  stable 126
  wages versus profits 18
income elasticity of demand 47
  exports 85, 92, 97–8
income redistribution 14, 54(n11), 87, 99(n9), 104–5, 113–14, 116
  demand effects 117–18
  from firms to rentiers 186–7
  macroeconomic effects 114
  rich to poor 9
  towards wages 10
  wages to profits 161
income-expenditure model 69
income-generation process 105, 111–12(n26–7(n6))
incomes policies 106, 191, 193–5, 199(n21)
  cooperative versus conflictual 199(n17)
  stabilization role 123, 127(n15)
incomplete indexation 183–4, 197(n7–8)
individuals 12, 133
inflation
  accelerating/decelerating 105, 117–18
  actual versus expected 182

234 Index

inflation – *continued*
  actual versus target rate 161, 188, 189–90
  adjustment to permanent drop in demand 169f, 170
  aggregate-supply-induced 141
  capacity and **14–17**
  'conflicting-claims process' 182, 196(n3, n6)
  cost-push 160
  current and future 219
  current rate 141–4, 153
  demand-driven 138
  demand-induced acceleration 139
  desired rate 133
  downward pressure 145–6, 167, 168f
  equilibrium rate 183, 192–3, 196(n6)
  fiscal stimulus 172f
  high 51
  home-produced goods 88, 89
  hump-backed response 205f, 206
  initial equilibrium rate 193, 194
  inter-temporal trade-off 216
  'less costly than unemployment' 147(n5)
  low 144, 145, 199(n18)
  miscellaneous 4, 6, 8, 22, 24, 26, 33, 42–3, 46, 53, 87, 99(n14), 104, 124, 150, 154, 156, 166f, 166, 171f, 173–4, 204, 210, 211t, 214f, 214
  'monetary phenomenon' 79
  PK alternative to NCMs 3
  PK conflicting-claims models 108, 126(n4)
  politics and **17–21**
  rate of change 133
  response of labour market to monetary shocks 216, 218f
  response of labour market to productivity shocks 217f
  response to monetary shocks 215f, 215
  response to productivity shocks 214f, 214
  response to transient drop in demand 167, 168f
  rising 155, 166
  short-run barrier 3
  short-run trade-off with unemployment 146(n2)
  stable 120–1, 142, 144–5, 152, 155, 173
  sustained 151
  trade-off with output 213
  under direct control of central bank 149
  unexpected 99(n9), 101(n25), 107–8, **108–11**, 112–18, 122–3, 125, 126(n5)
  unexpected: distribution effects 127(n6)
inflation barrier 20, 21, 105, 106
  short-run 109
inflation cure 132
inflation determination 153
inflation and employment: determination **182–7, 196–8**
inflation equation 222
inflation expectations 107, 110, 112–13, 117–18, 120, 138, 153, 159, 161, 163, 182, 197(n7–8)
  by workers 86, 89, 98(n8), 99(n9)
  see also 'inflation/unexpected'
inflation level 140, 142f, 142
inflation process 105, **182–4**, **196–7(n3–8)**
inflation rate
  changes (effect on employment rate) 113
  constant 146(n1)
  current 137–8
  influenced by monetary policy 154
  low 141, 146
  miscellaneous 3, 43–4f, 44, 51, 98(n6), 139, 158, 190, 192
  stable 123, 125–6, 146
  steady state 191
  see also price inflation rate
inflation shocks 137, 142
  demand-induced versus supply-induced 144, 146
inflation target/s 105, 121, 123, 134, 137–8, 141, 143–4, 146, 146(n1), 161, 163, 165
  two per cent 45
  see also inflation-targeting
inflation tax 2, **50–2**, 54(n9–11)
inflation-generating process **106–12**
inflation-targeting 5, 219, 220
  adverse employment effects 189f, 189
  beneficial for equilibrium rate of employment 194

Index   235

by central bank **117–19**,
127(n10–12)
definitions 196(n1)
'neutral with respect to
employment' 192, 199(n18)
Pasinetti rule 193f, 193
inflation-targeting: degree of
inimicality to employment
(chapter nine) 5, **181–201**
assumptions 182, 184, 185, 186,
188, 190, 197(n8), 198(n10, n12),
199(n19)
chapter purpose 181, 195
chapter structure 181
conclusion 181, 195–6
conduct of macroeconomic policy
181, 187–95, 198–9(n13–21)
empiricism 197–8(n9)
employment level 184–7,
197–8(n9–12)
equations 182–92, 194,
196–8
inflation process 182–4,
196–7(n3–8)
interaction 196(n6)
Keynesian features 183–4, 185–6,
187–8
literature 195
model closures 'conditional rather
than absolute' 198(n13)
parameters 185
policy interventions: impact on
macroeconomic outcomes
187–95, 198–9(n13–21),
steady-state equilibrium 182
workings of economy:
determination of inflation and
employment 182–7, 196-
inflation-targeting interest rate rule
117, 120, 121f
inflationary pressure 41, 49, 138,
142, 209, 220
impact of NMW 213
inflationary shocks 206
information asymmetry 133
informational constraints 203
'initial finance' 107, 127(n13)
inputs (imported) 138
institutions 32, 41–2
non-labour-market 98
'intensive margin' 203
interest payments 12–13, 107, 111,
120
'real' 108

interest rate/s
base rates versus market rates
127(n9)
commercial 198(n14)
effect on income distribution 120,
127(n12)
equilibrium 189, 190, 192–3,
198(n10)
equilibrium real 117, 153
ex ante real 107
ex post real 107
expected 153
falling 77
fiscal stimulus 172f
fixed nominal (inflation-targeting)
191f
impact on capital stock 160,
178(n10)
lagged 161
long-term 13–14
long-term stabilization 122
low 124, 126
lower bound problem 135
natural **149–80**
natural ('exogenous to
neo-Wicksellian models') 149
miscellaneous 9, 31, 42, 80, 142–3,
194, 198(n10), 203, 208, 219
raising/lowering 118
real 4, 122, 124, 126, 127(n11),
144–5, 154–5, 158, 183, 199(n22),
209
real (*ex ante* changes) 120, 121f
real (short-term) 133, 153
response to transient drop in
demand 167, 168f, 178(n13)
setting (ECB) 45
short-term 135, 202
'smoothing' 161
zero 122, 127(n13)
see also nominal interest rate
interest rate adjustment
immigration impact 213
to permanent drop in demand
169f, 170
interest rate changes 4, 127(n6),149,
154
destabilizing distribution effects
126
interest rate gap 149–52, 154,
173–4
interest rate inverse IS-curve 105
interest rate mechanism 40

236 *Index*

interest rate operating procedure (IROP)   190, 192, 199(n22)
  'activist' (Rochon and Setterfield)   188
interest rate policies   106
interest rate shocks   205–6
interest rate tool   104
  activist' position versus 'parking-it' approach   **120–2**, 127(n14)
  counter-cyclical stabilization   121
interest rate variations
  distribution effects   105
  medium- to long-run effects   112
International Labour Organization (ILO)   29, 46, 47
intertemporal optimization   153
investment
  aggregate   186
  determinants   4
  entrepreneurs' decisions   107
  equals savings in equilibrium   159
  expenditure   11–12
  expenditure (interest-rate-sensitive)   77
  government   50
  labour-intensive projects   2
  made independent of savings (Wicksell)   152
  miscellaneous   1, 7, 13, 14, 16, 18, 31, 38, 49–51, 53, 111, 133, 155, 158, 161, 175–6, 177(n2)
  planned   127–8(n18)
  private   9–11
  productivity growth effects   105
  profitability   12
  public   10–11, 12, 47
  rate of new   40
  real yield from inflation tax   51
  sensitive to variations in profit   184
  volume   41
investment ability   186
investment decisions   160
  real debt effects   4
investment function
  canonical neo-Kaleckian   184, 197(n9)
investment subsidies   9
investors   45
involuntary unemployment   2, 30–1, 34, 35, 52–3, **64–73**, 75–6, 81(n2), 87
  definitions   36, **64–6**
  Keynes   **36–41**, 54(n5)

Ireland   23t, 42t, 43–4
Is There a New Consensus in Macroeconomics? (Arestis and Ross, 2007)   132
'Is Unemployment More Costly than Inflation?' (Blanchflower, 2007)   147(n5)
IS-LM model   77, 132, 133
  IS curve   105, 133, 154, 158, 219
  LM curve ('redundant')   154
Italy   xi, 23t, 41, 42t, 43–5

Jackman, R.   103, 129
'Jacobian'   220
Japan   23t
'Jevons's well-known formula' (Wicksell)   177(n4)
Job Centres   33
job creation-destruction
  response of labour market to shocks   217–18f
job destruction   215, 219
  endogenous   206, 209, 211t
  exogenous   206, 209
  marginal incentive   216
  quarterly   223(n6)
job destruction margin
  endogenous (equation)   221
job destruction margin/survival rate
  response of labour market to shocks   216, 217–18f
job posting condition (equation)   222
job seekers   206–7
  effectiveness   90
job separation   210
  probability   209, 210t
  total probability   212t
Johnson, H. G.   32, 54(n3)
Jorgensonian user cost of capital   176
Journal of Economic Issues   147(n4)
Journal of Post Keynesian Economics   147(n4), 198(n15)

Kaldor, N.   84, 100(n21), 103, 127(n12), **129**
  'horizontalist' monetary view   107
Kaldorian model: extended   **83–103**
  assumptions   85, 86, 88, 93, 96, 98(n6–7), 99(n9), 100–1(n23), 101(n25), 102(n32)
  cumulative causation mechanism   91

Index 237

empiricism 88, 96, 100(n22), 100–1(n23)
equations 84–7, 91, 92, 98–9(n7–9), 99(n11), 99–100(n14–16)
equilibrium solution 89
exogenous variables 88, 98(n2), 101(n25)
explicit equilibrium solution 91–2, 100(n19)
growth and unemployment 85–97, 98–102(n4–33)
growth 'exogenous' 91
lags 87, 88, 93, 99(n15), 101(n26)
linear dependence 86, 98(n5)
literature 91, 92, 97, 100(n22), 101(n29), 102(n32)
parameters 86, 88, 90, 92, 100(n22)
policy implications 97
possibility of growth–unemployment trade-off 92–7, 100–2(n22–33)
set-up of model 85–8, 98–100(n4–16)
solution of model 88–92, 100(n17–21)
transitional dynamics 88, 99–100(n15–16)
wedge 86, 98–9(n8)
see also 'economic growth and unemployment'
Kaldorian model: standard 83, **84–5**, 86, 97–8, 98(n1–3, n7), 99(n14–15)
exogenously determined variables 85
versus 'extended' version 3
Kalecki, M. **1–2**, 111
aspects of work 'little recognised' 8, 15
comparison between capitalism and socialism 14
writings 7–8, **27–8**
Kalecki on causes of unemployment and policies to achieve full employment (chapter two) **1–2**, **7–28**
aggregate demand and budget deficits 7, 8–14, 26–7(n1–2)
assumptions 9, 19
capacity and inflation 14–17
chapter purpose 7
conclusions 26

deficits: sustainability 12–13
equations 11, 19
implications for current situations 7, 21–6
inflation, capacity, and politics 8, 14–21
monetary policy 13–14
policy regimes 18
politics and inflation 17–21
terminology 17–18
unemployment rate and output gap (various countries, 2005) 23t, 23–4, 25f
Kaleckian approach 105
Kaleckian distribution and growth models 127(n7)
Kaleckian investment function 4
'Kaleckian' models 14
Karakitsos, E. ii, xi, **4–5**, 161, 178(n12), 179
Katz, L. F. 96, 101(n29), 102(n32), 126(n2)
Keynes, J. M.
attack on classical theory of employment **34–6**, 54(n4)
aversion to diagrams 81(n2)
critics 81(n3)
definition of full employment output 60
determinants of real wage rate **71–3**
failure to deal with lags in adjustment 82(n4)
involuntary unemployment **64–73**, 81(n2)
labour market adjustment: rejection of classical theory 3
marginal productivity theory of demand for labour 62, 67, 71
miscellaneous 7, 17, 58, 67, 70, 77, 79, 177(n2)
monetary contributions 132
'one equation short' 72
on Pigou's *Theory of Unemployment* 35
publications 55
quantity theory of money 80
reaction (1939) to Dunlop and Tarshis 37
real wage 184
theory of prices (overlooked aspect) 72
versus Mankiw, *Macroeconomics*, **73–6**, 81(n3)

238 Index

Keynes, J. M. – *continued*
  views on money wage rigidity 73, 81(n3)
  see also General Theory
Keynes: relevance today *re* unemployment (chapter three) 2, 29–56
  assumptions 31, 35, 37, 41
  chapter purpose 34, 52
  classical employment theory 34–6, 54(n4)
  empiricism 33, 41, 51, 53
  inflation tax 50–2, 54(n9–11)
  involuntary unemployment 36–41, 54(n5)
  literature 37, 41
  personal reminiscences 29–34, 54(n1–3)
  policy implication 53
  policy options 49–50
  'price worth paying' 45–6
  summary and conclusions 52–3
  unemployment in EU 41–6, 54(n6–7)
  unemployment in poor countries 46–50, 54(n8)
Keynes effect 73, **77**, 78f, 198(n12)
Keynes–Harrod model (rates of growth) 48
Keynes' General Theory (Pigou, 1950), 81(n1)
Keynesian counter-revolution 53
Keynesian economics 73, 135
  with sticky prices 57
Keynesian economists 9, 46, 59, 131, 134
  French 80
  neo-classical synthesis 132
Keynesian 'Golden Age' (1960s) 131, 132
Keynesian models 153
Keynesian revolution 30, 38, 45
King, M. 143, 153
King, R. G. 203, 223(n3)
knowledge (perfect versus imperfect) 61–2
knowledge spillovers 92, 100(n22)
Kohn, D. L. 136–7, 140, 145
Kriesler, P. 106, 127(n16)
Krugman, P. 88
Kydland, F. E. 202

labour 16, 113, 114, 122, 156, 159, 192, 207f, 207
  chronic demand deficiency 44
  diminishing returns 35, 36, 37
  increasing returns 36
  indivisible 204
  marginal disutility 35
  marginal physical product 35
  organized 76
  perfect mobility 34
  supply and demand 33, 49
labour demand 72–3, 74
labour force
  growth 87–9, 99(n10–11), 101(n26)
  growth rate 48, 154
  growth rate (exogenous) 87, 91, 95–6, 99(n12), 101(n29)
  growth rate (ignored) 156, 178(n9)
  miscellaneous 22, 175
  participation 87, 96, 99(n13)
  size 99(n10), 185
  steady state 210, 212t
labour function 61
  'labour-force supply function' 99(n14)
labour immobility 30, 45
  labour mobility: barriers 42
labour input 204
  determination of fluctuations 203
labour market/s
  domestic 87
  'equilibrium' 87, 90
  excess supply 69, 70, 77
  expectations 209
  friction-less 204, 209
  frictions 35
  functioning 33
  hysteresis 4, 138, 144
  impure hysteresis 83, 84, 90–1, 98
  level of slack 219
  miscellaneous 6, 36, 75, 136, 138, 145, 197(n7), 203, 210
  non-competitive behaviour 75
  organized 124
  standard NK model 206
  structural characteristics 104
  structural or institutional changes 41–2
  structural reforms 122
  stylized facts (UK) 210
  tightness 83, 208, 209
  truly competitive 66
  Walrasian 206

Index 239

labour market adjustment
  classic theory 57
  classical versus Keynesian theory 3
labour market analysis 67
labour market characteristics 45
labour market conflict 86, 99(n9)
labour market flexibility 154, 210, 213, 221
labour market institutions 92, 97–8
labour market issues (UK) **210–13**, 223(n6)
labour market models
  responses to shocks 216, 217–18f
labour market persistence 206, 207f
  mechanisms 127(n10)
labour market reform 97, 221
labour market 'rigidities' 5, 53, 203, 220
labour market search and monetary shocks: theoretical consideration (chapter ten) **5–6, 202–24**
  calibrated model 209
  Calvo–Yun paradigm 202–3, 207–9, 215–16, 220, 223(n2)
  chapter purpose 203
  chapter structure 204
  dynamic stochastic general equilibrium (DSGE) model: labour market specification (UK) 203–4, 220–1
  empiricism 204
  equations 208, 212–13, 216, 219–22
  hump-shaped impulse response of output following monetary policy shock 203
  'key message' 206
  'key observation' 214
  labour matching DSGE model 221–2
  literature 203–4, 213
  parameters 204, 209, 210t, 211, 212t, 215, 219, 223(n6)
  policy implications 216, 219–20, 221, 223(n8)
  problems with standard business cycle model 203
  productivity shocks/responses (NK models) 214f
  Ravenna–Walsh model 204
  response of employment patterns and wages rates and monetary variables 203
  terminology 223(n2)

UK calibration 210–16, 217–18f, 223(n6–7)
UK data responses 205–6
variables 211t
Walsh matching model 206–10
labour power 29–30
labour productivity 17, 47–9, 96, 106, 156, 182, 196(n4–5)
  medium-run growth 123
  rate of growth 199(n19)
labour productivity growth 46, 87, 185
  changes **96–7**, 102(n33)
labour productivity growth rate 84, 91, 96, 101(n28–9)
  equilibrium rate 96–7
  exogenous rate 84–5, 92–3, 95–7, 100(n22)
  long-run rate 97
labour supply 35, 36, 53, 74, 100(n22), 209
  more realistic model required 204
labour supply function 61, 63f, 63–4
labour–output ratio 106
labour-productivity growth 88
labour-specific wage 223(n7)
  determination mechanism 213
lags 87, 88, 93, 99–100(n15–16), 101(n26)
Laidler, D. 153
laissez-faire capitalism 17, 18, 21
land 47
Landesmann, M. 88, 92
Laski, K. 9
Lavoie, M. 105–6, 122, 126(n4), 127(n7, n14, n16), **129**, 196(n3), 197(n9), 199(n20)
  horizontalist' monetary view 107
Layard, R., *et al.* (1991) 86, 91, 96, 101(n29), 103, 126(n2), 129
  Nickell, S. J. 103, 129
  Jackman, R. 103, 129
'laziness' 32
Le Heron, E. ii
Leijonhufvud, A. 67, 82
leisure 32, 75, 215
Lemke, W. 180
'lender of last resort' 122
León-Ledesma, M. 87, 103, 101(n27)
Lerner, A. 9, 127(n18), 177(n2)
Lévy, D. 14
Lewis, A. 51–2, 55
Lindahl, E. 153
Lindsey, D. E. 138

'liquidity preference' (Keynes) 54(n2)
living standards   10, 32, 48, 49
loan rate of interest   152, 155, 160
'loans create deposits' multiplier   152
long-run aggregate supply schedule ('*LRAS*')   59, 60f, 68f, 68, 69f
Lovejoy, T.   105
Low Pay Commission (UK)   212–13
Lucas, R. E.   33–4, 38, 55, 79, 223(n1), 223
Luddite effect   93, 95–6
Luxembourg   23t, 42t, 43–4f

Maastricht Treaty (1992), 2, 34, 41, 43
  convergence criteria   42
macroeconomic
  conditions   190
  fluctuations   220
  models   17
  objectives   135, 199(n18)
  performance   5, 181
macroeconomic policy   194
  coordination   126
  design   195
  'inflation-targeting' versus 'employment'   181, **187–95**, 198–9(n13–21)
macroeconomic policy authorities   199(n18)
macroeconomic policy mix (Post Keynesian versus NCMs)   **104–30**
macroeconomic variables   205
  inertia   204
macroeconomics   30, 155, 173
  hysteresis effects   145
  inflation-targeting   187
  mainstream models   5
  modern   145
  New Consensus view   4, **132–5**, 146–7(n1–4)
  New Wicksellian tradition   169
  'no place for long-run aggregate demand'   145
  'pre-eminent position of monetary policy'   134–5
  short-term versus long-term framework   2–3, 57
  'unemployment bias' (New Consensus view)   **131–48**
Macroeconomics (Mankiw)   57–8, 62, 82
  'deeply flawed' (Trevithick)   2–3

versus Keynes, *General Theory*   **73–6**
Malinvaud, E.   80, 82
Malthus, T. R.
  concept of 'effective demand'   37
Mankiw, N. G.   **2–3**, 30, 57, 61, 81, 82, 126(n2)
  approach to aggregate supply   **58–9**
  fixed money wages   73
  'pioneer of New Keynesianism'   78
  'sticky-prices' model   62
  sticky-wages model   58, 62, 63–4, 73–6, 81
  versus Keynes, *General Theory*   **73–6**
manufacturing   22, 33
  'industrial sector'   48
marginal (labour) cost for output ('*MC*')   67–72
marginal costs   206, 208, 209, 223(n7)
  shocks   202
marginal disutility
  employment/labour   31, 40, 70–1
marginal efficiency of capital (Keynes)   158, 177(n2)
marginal efficiency of investment (MEI) (Lerner)   152, 176, 177(n2)
marginal physical product of labour (MPPL), 67, 68f, 69f, 71, 72, 74
marginal product
  capital   152, 177(n4)
  labour   155
  new capital   **150**
marginal productivity   40, 62, 67, 71, 75, 155
marginal-cost pricing   67
mark-up   211t
  response to shocks   217–18f
  steady-state   223(n7)
mark-up growth rate   84, 85, 91
mark-up pricing   89, 108, 123, 203, 208
  inverse of marginal cost 209
market clearance   61–2
market-clearing imperfect information model   81
market failures   133
market forces   64, 124
market power   18
market prices   61
market structure
  perfectly competitive versus monopolistic   156

Index 241

markets
  competitive 31
  incomplete 133
Marshall, A. 30, 37, 67, 69
  aversion to diagrams 81(n2)
Marx, K. H. 37
mathematics/mathematicians 81(n2), 177(n8)
McCombie, J. S. L. ii, x, xi, 87, 92, 99(n12), 103
menu costs 160
Meyer, L. H. 139, 142, 143
microeconomic turbulence 99(n11)
microeconomics 155, 173, 178(n7)
migrant workers 143
migration 87
  rural-urban 47
Millard, S. P. 210t, 223
minimum wage 30, 212–13, 223(n7)
Mishkin, F. S.
  definition of 'inflation-targeting' 196(n1)
monetarism/monetarists 33, 78–9, 131
  conspicuous failure (UK, 1980s) 79
  rejected 132
monetary authorities 134
  price stability 'only appropriate policy aim' 137
monetary base 188
monetary foundations
  horizontalist 198(n12)
monetary policy 13–14
  associated real and nominal stabilization 124, 127(n17)
  convergence of theory and practice 131, 145
  credible 161
  deflationary 44
  expansionary 160
  flexibility required 53
  'hydraulic' view 145
  implications of labour-matching DSGE model 216, 219–20, 223(n8)
  'inappropriate as stabilizer' 126
  inflation-targeting 105, 118
  inflation-targeting (NCM) 126
  inflation-targeting (main NCM stabilization tool) 119
  limitations 118
  mechanism affecting profits 160
  medium-run endogeneity of NAIRU 119–20, 127(n10–12)
  miscellaneous 5, 6, 46, 60, 81, 104, 106, 109, 117, 124–5, 174, 188, 191
  natural interest rate 'plays crucial role' 154
  neutral 154–5
  neutral, tight, easy 149
  PK alternative to NCMs 3
  'pre-eminent position in modern macroeconomics', 134–5
  primary goal 196(n1)
  response to shocks 161–2
  restrictive strategies 140
  'should be complemented with fiscal policy' (Fontana) 145
  'simple feedback rule' 161
  stabilization tool 4, 131
  theory and practice 153
  tight 154
  'unemployment bias' in NCV 136–9
  see also fiscal policy
monetary policy design 206
monetary policy instrument 195
monetary policy problems 202–3
monetary policy rule 122, 133
monetary policy strategy 143–4
  combined with fiscal strategy 135
'monetary production' economy (capitalism) 127(n13), 181, 183, 188, 195–6, 197(n7), 199(n18)
monetary shocks
  labour market search and 5–6, 202–24
  NK models 214–15, 215f
  response of nominal interest rate/inflation 215f, 215
  response of output/employment 214–15, 215f
  responses of labour market models 216, 218f
  unanticipated 214–15, 215f
monetary targeting rule 132
monetary theory (PK) 188
monetary unions
  country-specific shocks 135
monetary variables 203
money 5, 38
  cost of borrowing 150, 160
  endogeneity 154, 173
  excess demand 152
  exogeneity (neoclassical economics) 153

money – *continued*
 income velocity of circulation ('V') 76, 78
 'neutral in long run' 153, 154, 173, 181
 non-neutral 195
 opportunity cost of holding 51
 'peculiar properties' (Keynes) 31
 purchasing power 51
 'residual' 154, 178(n6)
 supply and demand 151, 154
 'zero elasticity' (Keynes)
money in circulation 188, 198(n12)
'money illusion' 54(n4), 183
money interest rate 152
money market disequilibrium 151–2
 transmission 154
money market interest rate 152
money stock 132
money supply 46, 50–1, 61, 67, 79–81, 128(n18), 152, 214
 endogenous (Wicksell) 151–3
 excess 151
 exogenous 151
 nominal ('M'), 76, 78
 real 51, 76, 77
 unexpected increase 63, 75
money unit of account 183
money wage/s 3, 31, 35–6, 39f, 40–1, 57–60, 64, 76, 81
 allowed to fall 69
 changes 66–7
 current 65
 falling 77
 fixed (Mankiw) 73
 level ('essential standard of value', Keynes) 79
 'only price capable of revision either upwards or downwards' (Keynes) 70–1
 ratio to income 51
 rigidity (Keynes' views) 73, 81(n3)
 rigidly downwards 73
 sticky 69
money wage rate ('W') 62, 63f, 65–75, 80
Monopolistic Competition (Chamberlin) 30
monopolistic competition 160, 208
Montreal x
Moore, B. J. 107, 190
Mosler, W. 6, 190
multifactor productivity 154, 156, 164f, 174
exogenous variable 159
rate of growth 158, 165
multiplier effect 50, 77, 152, 158
Mundell, R. 45
Myrdal, G. 153, 177(n3)

National Bureau of Economic Research (NBER, USA) 147(n5)
national debt 12
 post-tax rate of interest 13
national economy 87, 98(n1)
national income 12, 51
 real 58f, 58, 76–8
National Minimum Wage Act (UK, 1998) **212–13**
natural interest rate 4–5, **149–80**
 adjustment to permanent drop in demand 169f, 170
 definitions 152, 153, 154, 173
 endogenization 150, 160, 174
 fiscal stimulus 172f
 neo-Wicksellian definition 154
 original insight 'lost in modern models' 154–5
 'plays crucial role in modern monetary policy' 154
 terminology 177(n2)
 Wicksell 150–3, 173, 177(n2–4)
natural rate hypothesis 136
'natural rate of growth' (Harrod, 1939) 48–9, 49f, 101(n27)
'natural rate of unemployment' (Friedman) 177(n5)
natural resources 162
necessary and expected receipts 38–40
negative feedback mechanism 3
neo-classical economics 32, 67
 exogeneity of money 153
 'monetary' versus 'real' sectors 153
neo-classical economists 34, 36, 64
neo-liberalism 21
neo-Ricardians 127(n12)
neo-Wicksellian model (reformulated) **4–5, 156–66,** 178(n9–11)
 steady state and stability of system 163–6, 178(n11)
neo-Wicksellian models **153–6,** 177–8(n5–8)
 internal inconsistency 149, 155, 174
 natural interest rate 'exogenous' 149
 pure versus reformulated 150

role of banks in savings/investment process 'completely missing' 160
steady states 149, 150, 155–6
terminology 177(n1)
unemployment and natural interest rate 149–80
net investment
definition 175
ratio to output 26–7(n1)
Netherlands 23t, 42t, 43, 43–4f, 162
new classical economics 59, 61–2
New Consensus Macroeconomic (NCM) models
aggregate demand-aggregate supply curve 163–4, 164f, 165, 166
deficiencies and problems 105
'dominate mainstream economics' 104
general equilibrium 153
literature 195
macroeconomic policy mix **104–30**
miscellaneous 126(n1), 149, 160, 162, 174, 177(n1)
monetary policies 105
PK critique **3–5**
see also neo-Wicksellian models
New Consensus View (NCV)
aggregate supply **57–82**
'downplays role of fiscal policy' 136, 145
'no role for aggregate demand' 136
monetary policy 146(n3)
'no long-run trade-off between inflation and unemployment' 137
PK critique **133–5**, 146(n3–4)
'unemployment bias' 4, **131–48**
New Deal (UK, 1998-) 210, 213
New Keynesian economics 5, 30, 59, 61, 78, 206
New Keynesian (NK) models 207, 214f, 214
'interchangeable with Calvo-Yun' 223(n2)
responses to monetary shocks 214–15, 215f
New Keynesian Phillips Curve (NKPC) 203, 204, 216, 223(n4, n8)
coefficient of marginal cost 212t
New Labour 213
New York x
New Zealand 23t

Nickell, S. *et al.* (2005) 41, 55
Nunziata, L. 55
Ochel, W. 55
Nickell, S. J. 103, 129
Nobel Prize 34, 54(n1)
Nobel Prize Lectures (2004) 202
nominal interest rate
determination 188
equilibrium value 188, 198(n13)
miscellaneous 107, 111, 117–18, 122, 137–8, 141, 184, 190, 193, 198(n12), 211t
response to shocks 214–15, 214–15f, 217f, 218f
short term 132–3, 153, 157, 160, 161, 163, 164f, 165
versus real 151
nominal wage/s 18, 122–3, 182, 183, 184, 197(n8)
growth 183, 190
rate of growth (w) 182, 196(n4, n6)
rigidities 153, 203
nominal wage demands 88
inflationary macroeconomic effects 109
nominal wage inflation
negotiated 93, 96
nominal wage inflation rate ('w') 84, 85–6, 89, 90, 96, 98(n5, n7–8)
Non-Accelerating Inflation Rate of Unemployment (NAIRU)
adjustment towards 122, 124
'always below actual unemployment rate' 142
as attractor/non-attractor 115–16f
concepts 126(n2)
deviation of actual unemployment from 105, 113, 118, 122–3
endogeneity (medium- to long-run) 106
endogenous convergence towards 112
equal to actual unemployment 165, 173
exact meaning 137
higher than actual unemployment 139
'hysteric' 197(n7)
'invariant to aggregate demand and monetary policy alike' 138
long-run endogeneity 105

Non-Accelerating Inflation Rate of Unemployment (NAIRU) – *continued*
  lower than actual unemployment 2, 118, 131, 136–8, 142, 144, 146, 167–70
  medium- to long-run endogeneity channels 127(n10)
  medium-run endogeneity (associated effects) 119, 127(n11)
  medium-run endogeneity through monetary policy 119–20, 121f, 127(n10–12)
  miscellaneous 4, 5, 96, 101(n29), 109–10, 143, 149–50, 154, 158–60, 183–4
  'not a strong attractor for actual unemployment' (Sawyer) 104
  'not self–stabilizing' 117
  persistent shocks 166–7
  stability (or otherwise) 104–5
  stability requirement 116
  stabilization 118
  stabilized by inflation-targeting central bank 118, 119f
  strong attractor 117
  strong attractor in short run versus exogenous in long run 112–20, 127(n7–12)
  strong short-run attractor (without central bank interventions) 113–17, 127(n7–8)
  tendency of unemployment rate to exceed 136–7
non-quantity theoretic framework 132
non-wage goods 35
North America 2, 57
Norway 23t
Nunziata, L. 55

Ochel, W. 55
OECD countries 23t, 101(n27)
  cyclical unemployment 54(n6)
  response of wage inflation to unemployment 98(n5)
  unemployment 97–8, 101–2(n31–2)
  unemployment rates (disparities) 83, 84, 91–2, 99(n20)
Office for National Statistics (ONS, UK) 210t, 215
oil discovery 162

oil prices 16
  increases 160, 162
  rate of change 155
oil shocks 22, 33, 137–8
Okun's Law 159
ontology 198(n13)
open economy 11, 123
open market operations 128(n18)
'opportunistic' approach (monetary policy without 'unemployment bias') 4, **139–45**, 147(n5–6)
  limitations 144
  main features **140–3**
  strengths and weaknesses 140
opportunity cost 176
Oswald, A. 41
outcomes
  demand-determined versus supply-determined 181
output
  adjustment to permanent drop in demand 170f, 170
  affects level of demand faster than supply 159
  aggregate 151
  aggregate demand price versus aggregate supply price 40
  aggregate supply-driven or potential level 146(n2)
  Cobb–Douglas 206
  current 153, 146(n2), 176
  current (rate of growth) 157
  current, past, future 158
  demand-determined 158, 159
  demand-determined in short run 174
  endogenous supply 156
  equilibrium level 163
  fiscal stimulus 172f
  growth rate 220
  hump-shaped impulse response following monetary policy shocks 203
  hump-shaped response of output to policy rate shock 204
  long-run supply 159, 164f, 164–5, 166, 178(n11)
  long-run supply function 158
  lost 140
  miscellaneous 5, 18, 48, 59–60, 62, 70, 72, 76, 81, 104, 110, 133, 137, 141, 144–5, 149–50, 155–6, 167, 173, 202, 205f, 207–8, 210, 211t, 214–15, 220

natural level 58
not influenced by monetary policy 154
'not necessarily self-financing' 38
potential 106, 146(n3), 159, 164f, 164–5, 166, 174, 178(n11)
potential (long-run supply) 163
potential (long-term determinants) 174–5
potential (rate of growth) 157, 159
rate of growth 157, 163, 177(n4), 178(n10)
rate of growth in long run 174
real 50, 198(n12), 205
real (actual rate of growth) 101(n27)
response of labour market to monetary shocks 216, 218f
response of labour market to productivity shocks 217f
response to monetary shock 214–15, 215f
response to productivity shock 214f, 214
theories 153
trade-off with inflation 213
output costs 138
output deviations 6
output dynamics 5
output equation 222
output gap 133–4, 146(n1–2), 154, 157, 159–63, 166–9, 219–20
  changes 146(n3)
  persistent shocks 166–7
  'simply a constant' 163
  various countries (2005) 23t, 23–4, 25f
  zero 163, 165
output growth 167, 168f, 171f, 171
  equilibrium rate 165
  see also real output growth
output level 165, 178(n10)
output loss 140
output price 156, 160
  excess over ULC 160
output stabilization 138, 143
'outside' (fiat) money 198(n12)
'outsider' productivity 211
overheating 142
over-investment 14
own-price elasticity of demand for exports, 85
Oxford University Institute of Statistics 7

Palacio-Vera, A. 105, 133, 146(n3), 195
Palgrave Macmillan x, 6
Palley, T. I. 105, 127(n14), 130, 187, 199(n16, n23), 200
paradox of thrift 185–6
Pasinetti, L. 127(n12)
Pasinetti rule ('fair' interest rate) 122, 192, 199(n19)
  distributional effects 199(n20)
  inflation-targeting 193f, 193
path dependency 4, 131–1, **141**, 143–4, 146, 146(n3)
Paula, L. F. de ii
perception 99(n13)
perpetual call option 176
persistence (in macroeconomic dynamics) 207f, 207, 209
Peterson, B. 200
Petit, P. 92
petty service sector 46
Phillips curve
  expectations-augmented 46, 132, 136
  expectations-augmented (simple three-equations model) 133
  inertia 132, 136
  long-run 104, 183
  miscellaneous 6, 82, 99(n14), 123, 125f, 146(n2), 162, 187, 189f, 189–94, 208–9, 216, 219–20, 223(n6)
  negatively sloped 183, 197(n7)
  shifting outwards 33
  short-run 104, 109, 115, 116f, 116, 118
  vertical 154, 165, 171, 183
Pigou, A. C. 2, 34–5, 37, 57, 64, 76, 58, 81(n1), 82
  connection between money wages and employment 66
  labour market analysis 81
  'savage treatment' by Keynes 66
Pigou effect 73, **77**, 78f, 195, 198(n12)
Pindyck, R. S. 176
Pivetti, M. 127(n12)
planning restrictions 92
policy instruments 53
policy interventions
  combination 199(n18)
policy interventions: impact on macroeconomic outcomes **187–95**, 198–9(n13–21)

policy rule for nominal money growth (equation) 221
policy shocks 206
policy-makers 41, 52, 53, 135, 140, 181, 191–4, 213
  dilemma 93–4
  monetary 202, 220
policy-making 34
'Polish plumber' effect 143
'Political Aspects of Full Employment' (Kalecki, 1943) 1, 7, 27
'political business cycle' (Kalecki) 17
political economy 94
'political stability' 17
politics and inflation 17–21
poor countries 2
  unemployment 46–50, 54(n8)
  unemployment–inflation coexistence 'not a paradox' 49
population 48–9
Portugal 23t, 42t, 43, 43–4f, 44
positive feedback mechanism (Kaldorian) 3
Post Keynesian (PK) economics 3–5, 37, 181, 187
  critique of 'unemployment bias' of NCV **138–9**
  monetary economics 121
  monetary theory (first principles) 188
  monetary theory ('structuralist' tradition) 198(n14)
  open-systems ontology 198(n13)
  'opportunistic approach' 143–4
  research agenda ('zone of discretion') notion 141
Post Keynesian economists (PKs) 127(n12), 135, 190, 198(n15)
  conflicting claims models of inflation 108, 126(n4)
  critique of NCMs 104
  horizontalist' monetary view 107
Post Keynesian macroeconomic policy mix (alternative to NCM approach) (chapter six) **3–4, 104–30**
  adaptive expectations 109, 111, 114
  assumptions 104–9, 111, 117
  basic model 106–12
  chapter purpose 106, 126
  conflicting income claims, employment, unexpected inflation, distribution 108–11, 126(n4–5)
  counter-cyclical stabilization 121
  economic policy 105–6
  empiricism 124
  endogeneity channels 106, 126(n3)
  equations 107–14, 116–18, 120, 122–4
  income generation process 111–12, 126–7(n6)
  literature gap 106
  literature review 104–6, 126(n1–3), 127(n16)
  NAIRU: medium-run endogeneity through monetary policy 119–20, 121f, 127(n10–12)
  NAIRU: short-run attractor (with inflation-targeting central bank) 117–19, 127(n9)
  NAIRU: strong attractor in short run, exogenous in long run 112–20, 127(n7–12)
  NAIRU: strong short-run attractor (without central bank interventions) 113–17, 127(n7–8)
  parameters 119, 122–3, 126
  PK macroeconomic policy assignment 120–6, 127–8(n13–18)
  policy implications 126
  policy mix 125f
  production, finance and rentiers' income 106–8
  production, finance, distribution, and inflation-generation process 106–11, 126(n4–5)
  'puzzling case' versus 'normal case' 114, 117–18, 127(n7)
  questions 112
  simpler model 127(n11)
  theory 124
post-Malthusians 38
post-war era (1945-) 22, 92
pound sterling 22
poverty 47
  means of escape 29
  one dollar per day 47
Prescott, E. 202
present value condition for matches (equation) 222
price curve 18–19, 19f, 21
price deflation ('balanced') 70

price determination 184
price expectations 154
price inflation 183, 190
  home country 93
price inflation rate
  competitor economy exports 84, 91, 98(n8), 99(n9), 101(n29)
  home-produced goods 84, 93, 98(n7–8)
price level 60, 65–6, 76, 153, 178(n10), 198(n12), 205
  absolute 3, 57, 58f, 58, 61–3
  aggregate 151
  rate of growth 178(n10)
  unexpected change' 62
price rigidity 202
price stability 45, 53, 104, 131, 135–7, 140, 143–5, 146(n1)
  long-run 140–1
  permanent benefits 138
price-determined rate of real product wage inflation (PDWI) 85, 86–7, 90, 98(n3), 99(n9), 102(n32)
prices
  downward pressure 143
  falling 31, 77, 138
  general rise 151
  market versus wholesale 208
  miscellaneous 2–3, 8, 15, 26, 35–6, 58–9, 132, 152, 197(n8)
  nominal 60, 73, 79, 80–1, 182
  nominal rigidities 153, 203, 204
  'plastic' 64
  'plastic' or 'elastic' (Pigou) 57
  relative 60, 186
  relative movements 88
  stable 4
  sticky 2, 5, 57, 62, 81, 133, 153, 208
pricing/price-setting
  domestic firms 85
  interaction with wage determination (Sawyer) 18
  supply of output and factors of production 159
Principles of Economics (Marshall, 1890), 30
private sector 45, 51, 54(n11), 188
  expectations 153
probability of matching
  between firms and job seekers 209
  response of labour market to monetary shocks 216, 218f

response of labour market to productivity shocks 217f
probability that vacancy is filled (equation) 222
Prodi, R. 45
producer price index (PPI) 139
product markets 98(n3), 136, 146
  hysteresis effects 144
production 106–12, 127(n13), 204, 207
  average costs 14
  capital-intensive 48
  current 178(n10)
  home 212
  labour-intensive 34, 47, 48, 49–50, 53
  shifted abroad 169–70
  variable cost 156
production bottlenecks 50
production function 156, 178(n9)
  short-run 72–3
production input 207
production techniques 48
productive capacity 109, 156, 158
productivity 18, 22, 159, 165, 178(n10), 206, 207, 216
  exogenous 160
  expected mean 212t
  individual 212t
  slowdown 83, 98
  unforeseen increase 143
productivity growth 48–9, 102(n32), 122
  shocks 96
  slowdown 102(n32)
Productivity Growth and Economic Performance (McCombie, Pugno, & Soro, 2002) ii, x
productivity shocks 6, 202, 206, 209, 216
  response of inflation (NK models) 214f, 214
  response of nominal interest rate (NK models) 214f, 214
  response of output/employment (NK models) 214f, 214
  responses of labour market models 216, 217f
profit aspirations 4, 127(n10)
profit margin 156, 160
  rate of growth 178(n10)
profit rate
  definition 177(n2)
  endogenous 155

profit rate – *continued*
  history   159
  increase   164f, 164, 165
  miscellaneous   9, 14, 106–7, 151, 165, 171f, 171, 177(n2), 184
  'rate of enterprise profits'   184, 197(n9)
  real   4, 149, 150, 152, 154–7, 160, 173–4
  real (endogenization)   156
  reduced form equation   162
  response to transient drop in demand   167, 168f, 178(n13)
  treated as constant in NCM models   163
  Wicksell's definition   177(n2)
  see also natural interest rate
profit squeeze   21, 27
profitability   14
  expected average rate of growth   158
  past and current   156
  rate of growth   159
profits
  adaptive aspirations   105
  expected future   176
  gross   114, 184, 187
  medium-run interest-rate effect   120
  miscellaneous   17, 52, 54(n11), 104, 113, 127(n12), 160–1, 175–6, 197(n9)
  rate of growth   178(n10)
  realized share   108
  retained   111, 112, 186–7
  target rate   120, 198(n10)
propensity to:
  consume   40, 114
  invest   11–12
  save   4, 11–12, 111, 116, 184
property   29–30
public finances   134
public sector   50
Public Sector Borrowing Requirement (PSBR)   45
public works   47
  labour-intensive   52, 53
Pugno, M.   ii, x, 98(n4), 103
purchasing power   16
pure labour-constrained economy   100(n21)

Qi Sun   5–6
quantity theory of money   67, 72, 80, 151, 153
  transmission mechanism (Wicksell)   150
quantity-theoretic framework   132

Ramey, G.   223
randomly distributed disturbance term   61
'rate of return over cost' (Fisher)   177(n2)
rate of trading revenue   177(n2)
rational expectations   132, 161
Ravenna, F.   5–6, 204, 224
Ravenna–Walsh model   204
raw materials   8, 16, 22, 26
Reagan, R. W.
  'greatest Keynesian'   46
real balance effects   51, 124
real balances   198(n12)
real business cycle   132, 153, 202, 203
  'RBC'   204, 223(n3)
'real cash flow rate'   197(n9)
real consumption wage/s   85
  growth rate (expected)   86, 99(n8)
real economy   135, 137, 145, 195, 206, 210, 221
'real exchange' economy (capitalism)   181, 195, 197(n7)
real output growth   89, 93, 99(n8)
  rate   84, 87–97, 100(n17), 100–1(n23), 101(n28, n30)
real product wage   18, 20, 85, 86, 99(n8)
  growth rate   86, 102(n32)
real sector   153
real wage/s
  determining factors   71–3, 76
  changes   66–7, 215
  endogeneity   196(n7)
  endogenous in most DSGE literature   213
  market-clearing level   63, 66, 76
  miscellaneous   3, 8, 17–20, 22, 31–2, 34–7, 39f, 40, 54(n4), 61–2, 65, 69–76, 81, 83, 87, 122, 183, 196–7(n6–8), 206, 208, 211
  pro-cyclical   204
  'target'   63, 73–5, 123, 182, 184, 196(n7), 197(n8), 199(n17)
  'target' versus 'initial'   63f, 63–4

real wage growth 102(n32)
  excess growth 102(n32)
  flexibility versus rigidity 90,
    100(n18)
real world 174, 178(n14)
Rebelo, S. T. 203, 223(n3)
recession risk 135
recessions 16, 22–3, 27, 45, 127(n9),
    141–4, 146, 165–6, 170, 220
  abroad 167
  'downturns' 206
  'secular stagnation' 48
  'slowdowns' 10
  unforeseen 143
redistribution 9
regional economy 87, 92
regulations 92
relative price competitiveness 93
rent [economic] 186
rentiers 3, 29, 52, 105, 107, 111,
    114, 122, 126, 127(n13), 187,
    192, 197(n9)
  conflicting income claims 108
rentiers' income 17, **106–8**, 112,
    114, 116, 117
representative agent economy
    223(n1)
research and development 100(n22)
  government-sponsored 92
'reserves constraint' 152
retail firms' pricing decisions 222
retail market 223(n7)
retail price index (RPI) 205
retail sector
  steady-state mark-up 208
returns to scale
  constant 174
  dynamic increasing 84, 85, 88, 92
Review of Political Economy 147(n4)
reward of capital 152, 154, 155, 173
Ricardian equivalence theorem 124
Ricardo, D. 37
rich countries 2, 52
rich and poor countries
  unemployment **29–56**
risk assessments 127(n9)
risk aversion 223(n1)
Ritzberger-Grünwald, D. 179
Roberts, M. xi, 3, 96, 100(n17, n19),
    101–2(n23–4)
Robertson, D. H. 82(n4)
Rochon, L.-P. 105, 106, 120,
    126(n6), 130, 199(n20) , 200
  'activist' IROPs 188

Rodríguez González, C. ii
Romer, D. 57
Ross, A. 132
Rottemberg, J. J. 153, 161
Rowthorn, R. E. 86, 101(n29),
    102(n33), 105, 126(n4), 130,
    196(n3)
rural areas 46, 48, 53
Rustem, B. 161

Saad-Filho, A. ii
sales (expected) 111
saving/s 4, 9–10, 11, 38, 50, 107,
    111, 152, 155, 158–9, 161, 175–6,
    177(n2), 186
  growth rate 184, 185
  savings decisions 160
  savings ratio 48–9
Sawyer, M. ii, x, xi, **1–2**, 13, 15, 18,
    27(n2), 27, 104–6, 124, 126(n4),
    127–8(n18), **128**, 133–4
Say, J. B. 151
Say's Law of Markets ('supply creates
    its own demand') 37–40
  'buried once and for all' 38
  'incompatible with quantity theory
    of money' (Wicksell) 151
  rejected 152, 153, 154, 156, 158,
    173
  short-run versus long-run 152,
    153, 154, 156, 158, 173
  Wicksell's interpretation 152
scarcities 16, 22, 26
Seccareccia, M. 199(n20)
self-employment 61
Semmler, W. 200
sensitivity analysis 209
Serrano, F. ii
Setterfield, M. x, xi, 5, 105–6, 120,
    122, 126(n6), 127(n15, n17), 130,
    195, 196(n1–2), 197(n8–9),
    199(n17, n20), **200**
  'activist' IROPs 188
  definition of 'inflation-targeting'
    196(n1)
Shackle, G. L. S. 150, 177(n2–4),
    179, 180
Shapiro, C. 17, 20, 21
'shirking' 17–18, 21
shocks
  country-specific 135
  dynamic adjustment of economy
    166–73, 178(n12–14)

250 *Index*

shocks – *continued*
  exogenous 126(n5), 209, 211
  labour input 207
  long-lasting 150, 155–6, 161–2,
    169–73, 174
  miscellaneous 5, 16, 22, 47, 50,
    90, 96, 101–2(n32), 108–9, 134,
    137–40, 178(n13–14), 202–3,
    205–6, 213, 214f, 221
  negative demand 165–6
  persistent (auto-correlated)
    161–2
  persistent 166
  random 161
  transient 150, 155, 161–2, **167–9**,
    170, 174, 178(n13–14)
  transient versus long-lasting 149,
    150, 159
Singh, A. ii
Skott, P. 196(n7)
small countries/economies 84,
  99(n14)
Smith, A. 29–30
Smithin, J. 105, 106, 122, 195
Snell, A. 88, 92
social attitudes 32
'social bargain' 199(n17)
social benefit system 104
socialism 14
Solow/Swan model 2–3, 57
'Some Economic Consequences of
  Declining Population' (Keynes,
  1937) 48
Soro, B. ii, x
Soskice, D. 98(n3), 99(n9), 126(n1),
  132
Spain 1, 23t, 37, 42t, 43–4, 53,
  99(n20)
spatial interdependence 100(n22)
Sraffa, P. 127(n12)
stabilization 105–6, 134, 135
'stable growth' mechanism 22
'stagnationist bonus' 195
state economic activity 106
state employment 106
state role (developing countries) 47
stationarity 161
steady state (long-run equilibrium)
  163–6
  endogenous job destruction
    212t
  exogenous unemployment 212t
  initial 169, 171–4
  initial versus new 150

job destruction margin (threshold
  productivity) 212t
new 170, 207
sticky money-wage contracts 81
sticky-prices model 62, 81
sticky-wages model 58, 62, 63–4,
  73–6, 81
Stiglitz, J. 17, 20, 21
Stockhammer, E. xii, **3–4**, 104–5,
  126(n3–4, n6), 127(n10), 129, 130
stop-go policies
  avoidance 161
strikes 17, 204, 211, 223(n5)
structural adjustment 53
structural reform/s 92, 93, 95–7
'structuralist' tradition 198(n14)
subsidies to mass consumption 8–9
subsidy 32
Summers, L. H. 105
suppliers 61, 88
supply 15, 16, 35, 36, 50, 159, 165,
  181
supply constraint 106–7
supply curve 31
supply and demand 3, 22, 32, 47,
  151, 155, 159, 169, 178(n11), 184
  endogenous versus exogenous 154
  goods 154
  goods market 155
  increase 165
  labour 33, 40, 65
  long-lasting shocks 156
  money 151, 154
  output 151
  see also Say's Law
supply function
  long-run output 158
supply of goods (exogenous) 154
supply of labour schedule 74–5
supply of output 157, 174
supply shocks 134, 138–41, 143–4,
  146, 147(n6), 156
supply side 8, 26, 104, 156, 185,
  197(n7)
  short-run aggregate 133
survival rate 211t, 221
Sutcliffe, R. 21
Svensson, L. E. O. 161, 180
Sweden 23t, 42t, 43, 43–4f
Switzerland 23t, 99(n20)

Tabellini, G. 102(n33)
Tarshis, L. 37
tax base 51

tax revenue   11–12, 50
tax system (progressive)   12
tax theory   51
taxation/taxes   1, 7, 106, 127–8(n18), 171
  annual capital tax (Kalecki)   12
  labour taxes   42
  payroll taxes   99(n8)
  taxes on income and profits   9
Taylor, J. B.   161
Taylor principle   195, 199(n22), 216
Taylor Rule   137, 154, 188
Tebbit, N.   32
technological progress   91, 101(n29)
technology   72, 79–80, 156
  'a determinant of real wage rate'   76
  constant coefficient   106
  exogenous   207–8
textbooks   37, 79, 132
Thatcher, M. H.   32, 79
Thatcher Government
  monetarism   22
  PSBR (1979-)   45
Theory of Unemployment (Pigou, 1933)   34–5, 66
Third Biennial Canada/US Eastern Border Post Keynesian Workshop (Montreal 2007)   x
Thirlwall, A. P.   ii, xii, 2, 30, 54, **55–6**, 87, 99(n12), 101(n27), 102–3
  cyclical component of unemployment   31
  Dixon-Thirlwall model   83, **84–5**, 98(n1–3), 102
  doctoral thesis   31
  inflation tax   54(n9), 55, 56
  on 'natural rate of unemployment'   46, 56
  optimal inflation rate (for growth and employment)   54(n7)
  personal reminiscences   **30–4**
  policy-making to reduce unemployment   32–3
  publications   **55–6**
  techniques of production in developing countries   48, 54(n8), 56
time, 10, 13–14, 22, 24, 25f, 41, 46, 50, 62, 81(n3), 85–6, 88, 90, 93–6, 98(n2), 99(n9–10), 101(n32), 109, 143, 147(n6), 158, 160–1, 166, 175–6, 192, 202, 204, 207f, 207, 213, 216

Tinbergen, J.   53, 56
total factor productivity   101(n32)
Tract on Monetary Reform (Keynes, 1923)   50, 55
trade   43
  'foreign trade'   9, 11–12
  'trade-dependence'   99(n14)
trade unions (labour unions)   30, 33, 64, 90, 100(n22), 109, 124, 162, 199(n17)
  legislation   210
  power   41, 75, 100(n22), 204, 210, **211**, 223(n5)
  training   100(n22)
transversality condition   161
Treatise on Money (Keynes, 1930)   52, 54(n11), 55
Trevithick, J. A.   xii, **2–3**, 73, 81(n3), 82
'true inflation' (Keynes)   60, 80

uncertainty   127(n9), 198(n13)
underemployment   22, 29, 46, 52, 62
  demand side   48
  rural   47
unemployed people
  job-seekers 211t, 221
  'reserve army of labour'   8, 21
  'surplus labour'   29
  training   100(n22)
  utility of home production   212t
unemployment
  actual   46, 105
  actual (adjustment to NAIRU)   124
  adjustment to permanent drop in demand   170f, 170
  causes   1, **7–28**
  causes (and non-causes), 30–1
  convergence to exogenously-given NAIRU   154
  current versus NAIRU levels   139
  cyclical   54(n6)
  cyclical component identified by Thirlwall   31
  demand-deficiency   87
  demand-side   47–8
  deviation from NAIRU   105, 113, 118, 122–3
  duration   90, 210
  during 1930s   1
  equal to NAIRU   165, 173
  equilibrium rate   101–2(n32–3)
  EU   **41–6**, 54(n6–7)

unemployment – *continued*
  exceeding NAIRU 2, 118, 131, 136–8, 142, 144, 146, 167–70
  extended Kaldorian model (Roberts) 3
  fiscal stimulus 172f
  frictional 33
  'frictional' versus 'voluntary' 35, 36
  general (origin) 64
  Keynesian 64
  Keynesian demand-deficient 50
  Keynesian features 47
  lower than NAIRU 139
  miscellaneous 58, 104, 108, 110–11, 127(n10), 133–4, 149–50, 155–6, 159–60, 174, 202–6, 213
  'more costly than inflation' 147(n5)
  'natural' rate 2, 33–4, 41, 46, 53
  'not influenced by monetary policy in long run' 154
  policy-making 32–3
  possibility of trade-off with economic growth 92–7, 100–2(n22–33)
  quantity theory of money 80
  regional differences 30, 31
  relevance of Keynes **29–56**
  rich and poor countries 2, **29–56**
  short-run trade-off with inflation 146(n2)
  structural 33, 46, 47
  structural (non-demand deficient) 43
  volatility 210
  see also involuntary unemployment; NAIRU
unemployment benefits **211–12**
  length of entitlement 90
  level 212
  'overgenerous' 41–2
  'unemployment compensation payments' 30, 42
'unemployment bias' of New Consensus View of macroeconomics (chapter seven) **4, 131–48**
  assumptions 133, 137–8, 144, 146(n2)
  chapter purpose 131, 133, 145–6
  chapter structure 131–2
  clarification and caution 144–5
  concluding remarks 145–6
  'deliberate' strategy 136–46
  empiricism 146(n3)
  equations 133
  further research required 144, 146
  lags 134
  literature 136
  monetary policy without 'unemployment bias' ('opportunistic' approach) 139–45, 146, 147(n5–6)
  NCV in macroeconomics 132–5, 146–7(n1–4)
  'opportunistic' strategy: limitations 144
  PK perspective 138–9
  policy implications 144
  practical and theoretical arguments 132–3, 145
  theory 134, 136, 144, 146(n3)
  transmission mechanism (monetary policy in NCV) 133f, 145
  'unemployment bias' in NCV of monetary policy 136–9
  vicious circle 138–9
unemployment and natural interest rate: neo-Wicksellian model (chapter eight) **4–5, 149–80**
  amplitude of cycles (increasing with time) 166f, 166
  appendix 174–6
  assumptions 149, 150, 152–3, 154, 156, 159, 160, 167,169, 173, 174, 175, 176
  chapter contribution to literature 174
  chapter purpose 149–50, 155, 156, 173
  chapter structure 150
  cumulative process 150, 152
  dynamic adjustment of economy 166–73, 178(n12–14)
  empiricsm 173, 178(n7)
  endogenous variables 163
  equations 151, 156–7, 162–3, 174–6
  hypothesis 156
  'interim equilibrium' 169
  lags 161
  literature 161, 178(n7)
  natural interest rate 150–3, 177(n2–4)
  neo-Wicksellian model (reformulated) 156–66, 178(n9–11)

Index 253

neo-Wicksellian models 153–6, 177–8(n5–8)
numerical model 166, 167t
policy implications 149, 155, 171, 173, 174
recursive versus post-recursive variables 177(n6)
shocks: long-lasting 169–73, 174
shocks: negative demand 169–73
shocks: transient 167–9, 174, 178(n13–14)
standard deviation 161, 176
steady state: new 170
steady-state and stability of system 163–6
stochastic processes 161
terminology 177(n1)
theory 149, 173
unstable model 166f
'Unemployment: Past and Present' (conference, Cambridge, 2007) x, 1, 6
Unemployment: Past and Present (this volume)
assumptions 3
structure and contents 1–6
theory 5
unemployment rate 85–97, 98(n5), 99(n9–10), 100(n17), 101(n24, n29–30), 205
competitor-economy 87, 95
equilibrium 91
lowering 88
percentage of labour force 158
various countries (2005) 23t
unit costs 8, 15, 16, 22
unit labour costs (ULC) 84–5, 88, 93, 108, 123, 156, 160, 167, 168f, 197(n8), 209
adjustment to permanent drop in demand 170f, 170
fiscal stimulus 172f
mark up in firms' pricing 120
nominal 123
rate of growth 158, 160, 178(n10), 182, 196(n4)
unit profit 178(n10)
United Kingdom
business cycle 203
calibration (labour market search and monetary shocks) 210–16, 217–18f, 223(n6–7)
'conspicuous failure of monetarism' 79
data 203
data responses 205–6
'England' 45
'Great Britain' 36
immigration policy 213
impulse responses 214–16, 217–18f
inter-war era 73, 76
labour market (stylized facts) 210
labour market flexibility 204
labour market issues 210–13, 223(n6–7)
labour market policy 209
labour market reform 221
minimum wages 212–13, 223(n7)
miscellaneous xi-xii, 22–3, 23t, 27, 31–2, 42t, 43–4, 90, 100(n21)
'more active manpower policies' 33
'relatively open economy' 206
responses to policy shock 205f
time-series on unemployment and output gap 24, 25f
trade union power 211
unemployment (nature and types) 30
unemployment benefits 211–12
United Kingdom: Department of Employment and Productivity (Research and Planning Unit) 33
United Kingdom: Treasury 12
United States of America
economy 41, 135
Keynesian counter-revolution (1960s-) 53
low unemployment, low inflation (mid-1990s) 139
miscellaneous xi, 23t, 30, 33, 42t, 43, 46, 178(n10), 223(n6)
output-real wage correlation 223(n3)
post-war data (Ravenna–Walsh model) 223(n4)
relative volatility of employment to output 223(n3)
see also Federal Reserve System
universities xi-xii, 57
University of Kent xi-xii
University of Leeds xi
University of Ottawa 197(n9)
urban areas
majority of world's population (2007-) 47

254 *Index*

vacancies   207, 210, 211, 213, 216
  cost of posting   209
  probability of filling   210–12t
  recruiting cost   210t, 212t
  response of labour market to shocks   216, 217–18f
  time required to fill   204
  see also   labour market search
vacancy elasticity of match   210t
vacancy share in generating a match   212t
vacancy–search ratio   208
Value, Capital, and Rent (Wicksell)   177(n4)
vector auto-regression (VAR)   205
Verdoorn coefficient   85, 90
Verdoorn's Law   ii, x, 85, 87, 91, 100(n22), 101(n28)
  Kaldor's reformulation   99(n11)
'vicious spiral' (prices and wages)   15
Vines, D.   134
voodoo economics   45, 46

wage aspirations   4, 127(n10)
wage bargain   204, 209
  forward-looking element   219
wage bargaining   4, 69–70, 74–6, 81(n3), 90, 91, 182, 183, 197(n7)
  centralization   199(n17)
  conflict theory   3, 83, 88, 97
  coordinated   18, 124, 127(n16)
  decentralization   122, 211
  nominal stabilization role   124
  PK alternative to NCMs   3
  workers' share   210t, 212t
wage bargaining institutions   97, 104
wage bargaining parties   125, 126
wage curve   19f, 19–20, 20f, 21
wage demands   *see* nominal wage demands
wage determination   19, 42, 184
  interaction with price-setting (Sawyer)   18
wage formation   122
wage goods   36, 40, 65
wage inflation   17, 159, 160, 183
  adjustment to permanent drop in demand   170f, 170
  fiscal stimulus   172f
  nominal (endogenization)   85, 87, 98(n4)
wage policies   106, 125, 126
  stabilization role   123, 127(n15)
wage rate   20–3, 178(n10)

  nominal (rate of growth)   157–8
  real   15, 155
wage relativities   36
wage rigidity   30, 204
wage-led economies   123
wage–price ratio   22
wage-push factors   86, 91
wage-setting (Walrasian)   204
wages
  actual versus targeted   182
  acyclical   206
  adaptive aspirations   105
  downward pressure/cuts   31, 138, 143, 167, 168f
  equilibrium (determinants)   208
  equilibrium real   183, 184, 186, 197(n8)
  equilibrium share   194
  flexibility   122–3
  flexibility (destabilizing effects)   123
  increases   162
  'inflexibilities'   41
  miscellaneous   10, 54(n11), 80, 99(n14), 104, 112–13, 116, 127(n12), 159, 161, 165, 195, 210–12
  rigid   45
  sticky   58, 62, 63–4, 73–6, 81, 133, 153
  see also   money wage/s; nominal wage/s; real wage/s
Walras's Law   151
Walsh, C. E.   5–6, 203, 204, 210t, 212t, 220, 224
Walsh matching model   206–10
war debt   10
'warranted rate of growth' (Harrod 1939)   48, 49f
wartime conditions   16
Watson, J.   223
Wealth of Nations (Smith, 1776)   29–30
Weber, A., *et al.* (2007)   153, 173, 177(n1), 178(n7), 180
  Lemke, W.   180
  Worms, A.   180
Western Europe   21
White Paper on Employment Policy (Ministry of Reconstruction, UK, 1944)   10, 12
wholesale producers' profit maximization   208, 212
wholesale sector   223(n7)

Wicksell, K.   177(n1–3), 150, 152,
      160, 180
   definitions of natural interest rate
      152–3
   did not distinguish between
      nominal and real rates of interest
      151
   distribution theory   155
   influence on Friedman   177(n5)
   makes investment independent of
      savings   152
   monetary contributions   132
   natural interest rate versus marginal
      product of capital   177(n4)
   'true spirit'   160
   see also   natural interest rate;
      neo-Wicksellian models
'Wicksellian muddle' (Laidler)   153,
   155, 173, 177(n3)
Wiener process   175
Williamson, J.   45
Wolfers, J.   41, 101–2(n29, n31–2)
women   87
Woodford, M.   153, 161, 199(n22),
   203
work intensity   17
work organization   21
worker dissatisfaction   93
worker passivity   83, **84–5**
workers
   bargaining power   184, 189,
      196(n6)
   claims on total income   191,
      199(n17)
   conflicting income claims   108
   consumption expenditure   86
   incomplete bargaining power   182,
      183
   incomplete indexation   183–4,
      197(n7–8)
   'labourers'   111, 122, 126

marginal leisure hours   206
militancy   88
miscellaneous   3, 62, 73, 81, 90,
   102(n32), 123, 204, 215, 217–18f
'myopic perfect foresight' (Flaschel
   et al., 1997)   197(n7)
perfect knowledge 99(n9)
rational expectations   86–7, 88, 93,
   99(n9)
realized wage share   109, 110f, 110
'repressed rather than liberated'   26
reservation wage   96
'responsible for own misery'   64,
   81(n1)
target share of total income   182
target wage   120, 199(n17)
target wage share   108, 110f, 110
trade-off in entering or exiting job
   market   212
unionization   211
wage aspirations   108
working class   52
   economic and political power   7
   power in periods of high
      employment   21
   self-assurance   17–18
working hours/hours worked   61,
   203–4, 208, 210, 215
working-age people   96
World Bank   47, 53
Worms, A.   180
Wray, R.   106, 127(n13), 190

Young, A.   84, 103
Yun, T.   202
Yunus Mohammad   29, 54(n1)

Zezza, G.   ii
zone of discretion   4, 131–2, **141–3**,
   143–4, 146